The Macroeconomic Dimensions of Arms Reduction

Pew Studies in Economics and Security

Series Editors
Craufurd D. Goodwin
and Jim Leitzel, Duke University

*The Macroeconomic Dimensions
of Arms Reduction,*
edited by F. Gerard Adams

*Power, Economics, and Security:
The United States and Japan in Focus,*
edited by Henry Bienen

FORTHCOMING

Incentives in Procurement Contracting,
edited by Jim Leitzel and Jean Tirole

Economics and National Security,
edited by Jim Leitzel

*Coping with Complexity in the
International System,*
edited by Jack Snyder and Robert Jervis

Funded by
The Pew Charitable Trusts
Through the Program for
Integrating Economics and National Security

The Macroeconomic Dimensions of Arms Reduction

EDITED BY

F. Gerard Adams

Westview Press

BOULDER • SAN FRANCISCO • OXFORD

Pew Studies in Economics and Security

Copyright © 1992 by Westview Press, Inc.

Published in 1992 in the United States of America by Westview Press, Inc., 5500 Central Avenue, Boulder, Colorado 80301-2877, and in the United Kingdom by Westview Press, 36 Lonsdale Road, Summertown, Oxford OX2 7EW

Library of Congress Cataloging-in-Publication Data
The Macroeconomic dimensions of arms reduction / edited by F. Gerard Adams
 p. cm. — (Pew studies in economics and security)
 ISBN 0-8133-8552-0
 1. Arms Control—Economic aspects. 2. Macroeconomics. I. Adams, F. Gerard (Francis Gerard), 1929– . II. Series.
HC79.D4M33   1992
338.4'76234—dc20   92-9686
                                                                                           CIP

Printed and bound in the United States of America

The paper used in this publication meets the requirements
(∞) of the American National Standard for Permanence of Paper
for Printed Library Materials Z39.48-1984.

10   9   8   7   6   5   4   3   2   1

Contents

Introduction

That defense buildups and arms reduction have powerful macro-economic effects is readily apparent from even the most cursory glance at economic statistics over the past half century. Booms and busts have been closely linked to the rise and fall of armaments spending. This relationship holds despite the expectation that civilian uses of resources would contribute more to economic welfare, productivity, and growth than military spending.

Interest in the macroeconomics of defense spending has been sporadic and has come largely when changes in military spending are in prospect. The chapters in this volume are no exception. They come at a time when resource allocations to national security are undergoing radical change. When we began the most recent phase of our work on macroeconomics and national defense in 1989, the question was oriented in the traditional way: What has been the effect of increased outlays for defense? Today, the discourse on national security has been refocused. The antagonistic relationship between East and West appears to be at an end. The arms race between the major powers of the East and West has taken a U-turn toward mutually coordinated arms reduction. But we cannot yet speak of full disarmament. Continued regional conflicts and the political uncertainties connected with the dissolution of the Soviet bloc may call for continued arms spending—for certain kinds of armaments even temporary buildups. The purpose of the chapters in this book is to evaluate the potentials of arms reduction. Can arms reduction yield a macroeconomic peace dividend? What are the challenges of transforming "swords" into "plowshares"? What are the macroeconomic policies necessary to accompany a transition from defense-led economies to a more peaceful focus for economic activity?

The macroeconomic dimensions of arms reduction extend widely in a qualitative as well as quantitative sense. When my colleagues on Project LINK and I first focused on this topic, we appreciated the difficulties of introducing arms reductions scenarios into the diverse models representing the countries participating in the world economy. But many of us did not fully take into account the diversity of the channels through which arms reduction and its correlated policy measures would have their effect, the differences between the economies—industrial market, centrally planned, and less developed (terms that are not always mutually exclusive)—the difficulties of measuring the various possibilities of arms reductions and transformation and of evaluating their impacts on output and welfare. After participating for several years in the Pew Charitable Trust's Economics and National Security (ENS) program we came to recognize the broader dimensions of the linkages between the macroeconomy and the defense effort. These linkages operate through supply as well as demand. They involve global international dimensions. They call for complex evaluation of the structure of the economies in which arms reduction takes place. They frequently involve technological and institutional transformations.

This volume reflects this experience. The concept of macroeconomics has been interpreted broadly and sometimes differently by the authors who have contributed to this book.

The macroeconomic issues of arms reduction and conversion are greatly different in various parts of the world: in the industrial market economies, the less developed economies, and in what used to be the centrally planned economies. This has governed the organization of this volume. After an introductory discussion of the issues of arms reduction and macroeconomics, we focus Part One on the impact of arms reduction in the industrial countries. Part Two is concerned with the questions of the impact of military spending and possibilities for conversion in the less developed countries. And Part Three focuses on the closely linked issues of arms reduction, conversion, and economic reform in the socialist countries.

We do not seek a single or even firm set of conclusions. The issues are so complex that we must be satisfied with an overview of the problems, the available techniques for analyzing them, the results that have been obtained so far, and an assessment of their implications for policy. The question of the impact of arms reduction is current and likely to be continuing. It will remain a central question influencing economic development policy in all parts of the world for it is reallocation of resources from military to civilian uses that offers the biggest available opportunity for improving consumer welfare, worldwide.

F. Gerard Adams

1

Modeling Arms Reduction

F. Gerard Adams

National security is a matter of economic as well as of military or political strength. Balances of power depend on countries' economic potential as well as on their stocks of armaments. Consumer welfare, in turn, has been greatly influenced in the last four decades as resources have been directed from consumption or investment to military preparedness.

The arms race between East and West has come to an end as a massive defense establishment became too costly for both the Socialist bloc and Western countries. The former Soviets have adopted initiatives to reduce the burden by disbanding armies and phasing out costly weapons systems in the hope that the resource saving will yield significant improvements in economic performance. Unfortunately, we have not yet achieved an age of general disarmament. Regional conflicts, of which the confrontation with Iraq is only the most recent example, continue. The most massive arms efforts, however—those related to the East-West conflict—are, at least, being scaled down or dismantled. In the optimal case, the total arms budget will be reduced or at least transformed to different types of expenditures, and the resources released from military use will improve growth and human welfare internally and permit transfers to poor countries. However, if the resources are not used properly or if they are misallocated, economic conditions may fail to improve or even deteriorate.

It is important to know how arms reduction and transformation might affect the world economy, but predictions are not simple. The economic impact of arms reduction depends on the amount and nature of the resources that become available and on how the resources are used—will they be reallocated to consumption or investment, for example? The economic setting and policies that accompany disarmament help to determine the economic impact of reduced military spending.

This chapter considers the macroeconomic effects of the new national security environment. After a brief summary of global studies of arms reduction, I consider the issues that apply to modeling the quantitative significance of reduced military spending: the size and nature of the "peace dividend," the method of reallocating resources, possible policy decisions and their impact, and the interaction between countries.

Global Studies

The impact of military expenditures on economies has been seen in different ways. On the one hand, there is the view exemplified in the studies of the United Nations that "the vast problems of accelerating the process of socio-economic development, particularly of the developing countries, continue to be subordinated to the expanding claim of the arms race on global resources, human and material" (United Nations 1983). The concern is with the damaging impact of military spending on growth and development. The implicit corollary of this view is optimistic; that arms reduction would release resources and yield a peace dividend.

On the other hand, there has also been support for a less optimistic view of arms reduction. It has been suggested that arms expenditures have a positive impact or at least little negative effect on economies. A reduction in arms expenditures, therefore, would provide little or no peace dividend. Fears have been expressed that in the industrial countries reductions in defense outlays may lead to demand deficiencies and depression. (But it has long been known that these effects can be offset by tax reductions, increases in government civilian spending, or reductions in interest rates.) In Socialist economies, arms reduction could have adverse economic effects (but need not) because of the close relationship between investment and military spending: the military sector is an engine of growth. And, finally, there is the long-lasting controversy following Benoit's finding (1978) that in the LDCs economic growth and defense spending appear to be positively related.[1]

The empirical outcomes of simulation studies of disarmament reflect a corresponding range from optimism to a less sanguine view. Studies that assume that resources released from military use are fully utilized in the civilian economy generally yield a substantial peace dividend. This occurs, for example, in the classic study of Leontief and Hoffenberg (1961) and in the more recent work of Leontief and Duchin

(1983). From the beginning, Leontief's input-output studies for the United States assumed that reduced military spending would be *compensated* for by increases in civilian final demand. Leontief's more recent work is based on a highly detailed (15 regions and 50 industries, including 11 military) world input-output model. Although the system provides enormous detail about the industrial impact of disarmament on a global scale, the model operates under the constraint of constant employment in the industrial countries and constant balance of payments in the LDCs. Reductions in military spending are more than compensated for by increases in civilian demand, which produces a favorable outcome for GDP performance, particularly in the poor countries where increased inflows of capital goods permit more rapid growth.

The computable general equilibrium (CGE) approach (for example, the work of Roland-Holst, Robinson, and Tyson [1988]) also yields optimistic results for somewhat similar reasons. The study by Roland-Holst et al. focuses on the United States only and assumes that allocation of resources from military to civilian uses will follow from the reestablishment of supply and demand equilibrium through the adjustment of relative prices in a Walrasian system. The results, again, hang on the implicit assumption of market equilibrium–based full resource reallocation and predict positive effects on economic growth.

More traditional econometric models often yield less optimistic results. The simulations of econometric models of the United States by the Congressional Budget Office (CBO 1988), the WEFA Group, and DRI McGraw-Hill show only relatively small gains from arms reduction. In work with Project LINK,[2] Klein and Pauly predict modest improvements in economic activity, as well as improvements in other important dimensions of economic performance like inflation and balance of payments.[3] Because the econometric models do not automatically guarantee complete reallocation of resources from defense to civilian purposes, the impact is less favorable, particularly during the recessionary period of adjustment. Similar phenomena are apparent in the simulations of Bremer and Hughes (1990) using the Globus model, a world system that combines elements of economics and political conflict positioning. According to the Globus simulations, the economic gains from reduced arms spending are positive overall, but small.

The results of arms reduction simulations depend on the structures of the models used, the assumptions about arms reduction scenarios and about the economic objectives, and the policy responses to arms reduction.

What Approach Is Best?

Supply and demand considerations interact in determining the impact of arms reduction.

From the supply side, the growth theory approach to arms reduction postulates a reallocation of resources from defense to other uses. Traditional arguments have held that defense spending is damaging to growth because of resources being diverted from investment. In the opposite case, if arms reduction allows increased investment—swords into plowshares—the positive impact on economic growth is readily apparent. If, on the other hand, the substitution of resources is toward consumption—guns versus butter—there may be no growth impact, although the short-term effect on consumer welfare will be greater.

An extension of the supply side view considers the linkages, positive or negative, between military expenditures and the civilian economy. One theory sees defense as an advanced sector, in contrast to traditional civilian activities. The military sector can supply technology, training, and advanced equipment to the civilian economy in the LDCs (Ram 1987, 1989; Adams, Behrman, and Boldin 1991).[4] Intersectoral effects also occur in more advanced countries; spillovers from the defense program have been of benefit in the development of commercial aircraft and communication satellites in the United States. On the other hand, a defense program diverts the best engineering and managerial talent from private sectors. The externalities and intersectoral effects are often difficult to measure and incorporate into econometric studies.

On the demand side, the Keynesian aggregate demand approach yields a straightforward channel by which, in an economy with spare capacity, defense spending can have a positive impact on economic activity. The demand-side effects often dominate, so that mobilization serves as the engine of economic expansion and, frequently, inflation. In turn, demobilization and arms reduction are accompanied by readjustment and recession.

In practice, modern econometric models encompass elements from both the supply and demand sides (Klein 1977), but the Keynesian paradigm dominates many of them, at least with respect to short-run adjustment. In many systems, arms reduction leads to reductions in demand and recession, effects that are not, or not quickly, compensated for by offsetting adjustments. Most macro models of market economies recognize the potential for such adjustments through interest rate or price reductions that will lead to alternative utilization of resources. In many models, as is probably true in the real world, offsets to arms reduction must be imposed through explicit policy changes.

What then is the appropriate model for evaluating global arms reduction? What factors should such a model take into account?

1. The model should consider the various dimensions of economic and social performance. Growth has a high priority in recent studies, but other dimensions of economic performance such as prices, balance of payments, and income distribution cannot be left out.

2. The model must be sufficiently structured and disaggregated to illustrate the principal relevant phenomena. It is sometimes effective to cut through some of the complexities of the economy by highlighting only a few of the principal relations or by using a "reduced form" approach. But a useful model should show structural relations of the major supply- and demand-side forces. It should include price determination and a monetary mechanism and be able to deal with trade and balance of payments.

3. The model should recognize interactions between countries. Arms reduction not only affects the countries reducing military spending, but also influences their trade partners. Hopefully, disarmament will release resources for the poor countries.

4. The model should be based on realistic behavioral parameters and should be able to provide up-to-date simulations of developments in the global economy. This implies the possibility of testing the model against real world situations.

5. Although the model should have long-run equilibrium properties, it must recognize that economic adjustments are often difficult. The dislocation resulting from arms reduction is likely to result in substantial economic disequilibrium. It may take many years for the new equilibrium, fully utilizing all available resources, to be achieved. The evaluation of arms policies must take into account the adjustment period as well as the ultimate equilibrium results.

6. Finally, the model should be able to accommodate explicit policy actions that may influence the ultimate effects of arms reduction programs.

These are demanding requirements, which are not likely to be met in full by any system.

Input-output methods have a significant advantage in describing the interaction between sectors of the economy. A switch of demand from defense to civilian activities results in broad shifts, direct and indirect, between the sectors. The input-output approach thus focuses on the sectoral impact of arms reduction. On the other hand, unless the model is extended to deal with the determinants of macroeconomic activity, the input-output system does not deal realistically with broader questions of aggregate resource use. It is typical to assume, as we have noted above, that resources will be fully reallocated. Moreover, the typical fixed coefficient input-output system does not recognize shifts in production methods that might be associated with arms reduction or transformation. In most applications, it is assumed that input-output coefficients are invariant regardless of the allocation of resources between military and civilian uses. This assumption is particularly a problem in the case of the centrally planned economies where it is hoped that economic restructuring will significantly affect production methods.

The computable general equilibrium (CGE) models extend the input-output paradigm to equilibrate demand and supply (subject to resource constraints.[5]) The models have varied in form and potential. Generally, they are static, based on coefficients derived from a social accounting matrix. They solve for a general Walrasian equilibrium, for the prices that will fully equilibrate demand and supply.

In theory, the CGE system seems to be highly suitable to study arms reduction. But many of the models are artificial, comparing static equilibria. They do not show the dislocations that occur as a result of arms reduction, dislocations that cannot simply be ignored. Furthermore, the underlying assumption that the economy before long reaches a "general equilibrium" may not be an acceptable one.

Simulation models, like Bremer's Globus, allow considerable flexibility to the theory and the nature of the relationships assumed. Whether based on theory, econometric estimation, or technical information, the parameters could reflect the changes that are anticipated as a result of arms reduction. On the other hand, the tradition of simulation modeling is far removed from conventional econometric thinking. Simulation models are seldom tested against historical experience. The results obtained are ultimately determined by the structure and parameters assumed in the model.

Econometric models, too, are based on a large number of choices with regard to structure and parameters that affect the evaluation of disarmament scenarios. But the econometric model systems do have advantages of using coefficients statistically estimated from real world data, being consistent with the national accounts and trade statistics, being based on a comprehensive theoretical framework, and presenting the structural relationships and dynamics of the economy. The models can incorporate all or some of the input-output relationships that are used in the Leontief approach. Their performance can readily be checked against historical experience.

Their principal handicap, of course, is the failure in some cases to maintain equilibrium adjustment even in the long run and in many cases to allow fully for changes in structural parameters, even those that may change as a result of the disarmament scenario. For these reasons econometric models must be used flexibly with appropriate adjustments. Although global econometric systems like Project LINK may not yet be the ideal device, they offer a serious instrument for measuring the worldwide impact of disarmament.

Will Disarmament Yield a Peace Dividend?

The notion of a peace dividend is understandably attractive. But some students of economic and social phenomena have argued that cutting back on armed forces will bring little economic improvement: disarmament might not yield a peace dividend.

There can be no question that reducing military expenditures releases resources, manpower, and investment potential, which can be used for alternative purposes. An important distinction must be made, however, between what can be called a *peace resource dividend* and a *peace product dividend* that reaches consumers. Arms reduction clearly yields a resource dividend, but we cannot be sure that the resources will be turned into a product dividend.

Whether the available resources are large or small is a matter of perception, depending on whether we see "a glass half empty or half full." Since military expenditures account for 6 percent of GNP in the United States and perhaps 20 percent of GNP in the former Soviet Union, even as large a reduction of armaments as 50 percent would account for an increase of available resources to the civilian economy of only 3 and 10 percent, respectively, for the United States and the Soviet Union.[6] Further, the amount might be reduced by the need to make sizeable expenditures during the process of readjustment to pay for bringing troops home or mothballing armaments, for example. On the other hand, these values seem large when compared to other parameters of the economy—compared, for example, to fixed investment in plant and equipment in the United States of about 10 percent of GNP or the budget deficit of around 5 percent of GNP. It might be argued that if all the released resources could be reassigned to fixed investment in plant and equipment—*a big "if"*—a 1 percent annual increase in the growth rate of GNP might be possible.[7] In the Soviet Union, if 10 percent of GNP could be transformed into investment *efficiently*, a 3 percent annual rise in the growth rate might be achieved. But such gains are beyond the limits of credibility. They would require massive economic restructuring, particularly in republics that made up the Soviet Union. The allocation of resources between countries and among uses is also important. The global potential is far from trivial, but it depends on the degree of arms reduction and on how the available resources are used.

The specifics of arms reduction policy can be crucial. Are the resources released from military use suitable for civilian purposes? Will the cuts reduce defense manpower, military or civilian? Will the reductions affect purchases of equipment, and, if so, purchases of rifles or of high technology aircraft? Will armaments factories be adaptable to producing civilian products?

Put this way, resource reallocation appears difficult. In fact, the problem may be a matter of timing rather than lack of substitutability. Guns cannot be turned into plowshares or butter in the short run. But over time, many years in cases, resources can be transferred from military to civilian purposes. If arms reduction occurs gradually or if it is accomplished by simply slowing the growth of military spending rather than by making reductions, resource transfers should pose less serious problems. In any case, a great deal of patience will be required.

In a market economy the transfers are effected through changes in relative prices, whereas in a command or planned economy they may call for manipulation. In either case, the transfers may involve significant dislocations: population movements, new investments in infrastructure and housing, and changes in trade patterns. Retraining of specialized workers and reorientation of scientific and educational systems may be necessary. Thus, if disarmament occurs suddenly, there may be significant short-run costs and few gains, but in the longer run, unless resources are misallocated or under-utilized, there is likely to be a gain in real output, a peace *product* dividend.

The Influence of Policy

The policies that accompany arms reduction also contribute to the economic outcome. In market economies, the macroeconomic issue is whether demand will be maintained in the face of a reduction of public expenditures on defense. If civilian expenditures are substituted dollar-for-dollar for military expenditures, there may be little or no direct impact on aggregate demand, although sectoral and regional effects may be important. If the reduction in military spending is absorbed by deficit reduction, however, simple aggregate demand theory suggests that significant declines in demand and recession would occur. More complex theorizing suggests that adjustments in interest rates and/or prices would occur, so that an increase in private demand might ultimately offset the decrease in public demand. Here macroeconomic policy can play an important role. A monetary stimulus timed to match arms reduction can go a long way toward easing the demand shortfall, for example. The impact of such a policy extends beyond the current level of inflation and prices; it affects growth and productivity, for macroeconomic policies influence the allocation of resources between consumption and investment and the terms of trade.

Policy also plays an important role on a more micro level. It matters, for example, whether a reduction in military manpower releases foot soldiers or computer scientists and engineers. Micro-economic policies can also alter significantly the impact of defense reductions. For example, expenditures on retraining or reallocation of workers can improve the results of arms reduction by facilitating the transition. Expansion of civilian scientific activities can absorb resources previously devoted to defense-related efforts, making the civilian sector less dependent on the spillover effects from military activities. Incentives for investment and manpower use also can influence the nature and pace of readjustment.

Finally, policies related to the diversion of resources from industrial nations to the LDCs through grants, debt reduction, and foreign investment contribute to the transition.

Centrally planned economies face particular challenges of industrial reallocation. The process of arms reduction comes at a time when most centrally planned economies are turning toward decentralized decision making and privatization. Arms reduction offers an opportunity to divert resources toward organizations that are independent of government control. It is difficult, however, to predict how these organizations will operate, what technology they will utilize, and how their capital needs will be met. In short, conversion in the centrally planned countries is difficult to model and predict.

Global Effects of Arms Reduction

Arms reduction, by its very nature, has impact beyond the limits of any particular country. To begin with, cuts in military spending are likely to occur in two or more countries at the same time, since it is not probable that one country will engage in unilateral arms reduction for long. In an interrelated world economy, the changes in economic conditions in the disarming countries may have important effects on global enterprise through linkages of trade, financial flows, and capital movements. This is the rationale for analyzing arms reduction scenarios in the framework of world models like LINK, Globus, or the Leontief model.

Since production of arms is concentrated in the major powers and in few developing economies like Brazil, Israel, and China, there is significant world trade in armaments. When armament purchasing is curtailed in favor of other resource allocations, there are, consequently, direct trade impacts. Indirect effects through reduced needs for strategic materials also affect world commodity markets and the earnings of the nonferrous metals producers, many of them LDCs. Finally, many proponents of arms reduction hope that it will increase the flow of money—in the form of aid and investment—from the industrial countries to the less developed world.

Predicting the specific global impact of arms reduction depends on the nature of the scenarios that are tested: which countries are included, how much reduction is allowed, what cuts are assumed, and so forth—the same factors that are improtant when studying individual countries. It is also necessary to evaluate trade and balance-of-payments policies as well as domestic macro- and microeconomic policies. The results of arms reduction are likely to be different in a world of free trade compared to one of protectionism, for example.

The availability of resources for foreign aid as a result of reduced expenditures for military purposes raises some challenging questions. It is not likely that released resources can be simply reallocated broadly as aid toward economic development. Numerous uses, among which foreign aid is only one, compete for the available resources. It should be noted, moreover, that much foreign aid is motivated by strategic objectives. These aims may disappear or change in a disarmed world without military threat, so that aid could be reduced or reallocated to different recipients. Assumptions about changes in distributions of international aid must be made carefully. Arbitrarily assuming that aid will be distributed evenly or that it will go to the poorest countries may not be realistic.

Simulating Arms Reduction

Scenario simulation is the typical approach to using global models to evaluate the impact of arms reduction (illustrated in Chapter 2, by Adams and Huang). The standard procedure is to establish a base simulation projecting developments assuming a continuation of current arms programs and policies. Alternate simulations making alternative assumptions about arms programs and policies are then prepared. The alternative simulations are compared to the base solution to establish the impact of arms reduction in a variety of scenarios. Because the range of possibilities is very large, it is important to run scenarios that reflect a reasonable and likely set of arms reduction policies. The assumptions about domestic and international policies are crucial and require intensive investigation of alternative possibilities. Each participating country, and others as well, will be seeking an outcome that makes the most of the available resources along various dimensions of economic performance. The industrial countries not only will seek to maximize GNP, but also may want also to assure full employment, current account balance, and price stability. The centrally planned economies will seek to advance the welfare of their civilian populations, perhaps in the context of a newly organized market economy, as quickly as possible. The developing countries will seek to draw on the available resources for their technical advancement, and so forth.

An alternative approach to simulation is through optimal control (Petersen 1988) seeking a set of policies that will optimize the results from a given set of arms reduction assumptions. With this approach, also, a realistic set of assumptions about arms reduction must be the starting point. Assumptions about the targets of economic policy must also be realistic. How important to policymakers is targeting employment relative to growth or to price stability, for example?

The discussion above suggests that it may not be useful to present one, and only one, simulation of arms reduction.[8] A matrix of policy choices can be examined systematically in a series of alternative simulations. Optimal control simulations avoid the choices since they derive the most effective policy set. But even optimal control simulations can test multiple alternatives by proposing various objectives and/or weighting them differently, or by recognizing the fact that optimization may be joint or involve separate optimal objectives for each participant.

Finally, I want to make a comment on the concept of balance in arms reductions. It has been customary to visualize arms reduction as equal on two sides: the Soviet Union and the United States remove an equal number of troops or missiles from Europe, for example.[9] Those who expect balanced reductions view only the immediate impact on troop strength or on the number of weapons. They lose sight of the fact that national security involves economic as well as military considerations. Economic gains associated with arms reduction may well offset any immediate loss in national security. The concept of balanced reductions must incorporate economic power as an important component of national security.

Notes

1. For a review of this controversy and alternative conclusions, see chapter 6.

2. The LINK econometric models are discussed in Ball (1973) and Sawyer (1979). Other world systems are summarized in Hickman (1983) and Bryant et al. (1988). An industrially disaggregated system is presented in Adams, Gangnes and Shishido (1992).

3. However, earlier work by Klein and Kosaka (1987) that introduces simulations from an arms race model into the world economy shows some positive stimulus to economic activity as a result of *increased* arms expenditures.

4. These studies take an approach similar to that of Feder (1982), who dealt with externalities from the export sector in LDCs.

5. For a good discussion, see Dervis, de Melo, and Robinson (1982). A recent application of a world trade CGE system to arms reduction is shown in Haveman, Deardorff, and Stern (1990), Chapter 4.

6. Many scholars have argued that in recent years the Soviet Union has directed a much larger share of its GNP, perhaps as much as 27 percent, to defense (Rowen and Wolf 1990).

7. I assume an incremental capital output ratio of 3:1.

8. It is obvious that different magnitudes of arms reduction have different impacts. But that is not the point here unless the economy is strongly non-linear or unless the range of alternatives considered is very large. If the effects are approximately linear, a reduction of $20 billion has approximately twice as much impact as one of $10 billion.

9. That is why the recent unbalanced agreement about Soviet troop reductions in Europe evoked such surprise.

References

Adams, F. G., J. R. Behrman, and M. Boldin (1991) "Government Defense Expenditures and Economic Growth on the LDCs: A Revised Perspective." *Conflict Management and Peace Science*, Volume 11, No. 2, Spring, pp. 19-35.

Adams, F. G., B. Gangnes and S. Shishido (1992) *Economic Activity, Trade, and Industry in the US-Japan-World Economy: A Macro Model Study of Economic Interactions* (forthcoming).

Ball, R. J. (1973) *The International Linkage of National Economic Models*, Amsterdam: North Holland.

Benoit, Emile (1978) *Defense and Economic Growth in Developing Countries*, Lexington, Mass.: D. C. Heath.

Bremer, Stuart A. (1987) *The Globus Model: Computer Simulation of Worldwide Political and Economic Developments*, Frankfurt am Main and Boulder, Colo.: Campus Verlag and Westview Press.

Bremer, S. A., and B. Hughes (1990) *Disarmament in Development: A Design for the Future?* Englewood Cliffs, N.J.: Prentice-Hall.

Bryant, R. C., D. W. Henderson, G. Holtham, P. Hooper, and S. A. Symansky

(1988) *Empirical Macroeconomics for Interdependent Economies,* Washington, D.C.: Brookings.

Congressional Budget Office (1988) "U.S. Ground Forces and the Conventional Balance in Europe." Washington, D.C.: GPO.

Dervis, K., J. de Melo, and S. Robinson (1982) *General Equilibrium Models for Development Policy,* Cambridge: Cambridge University Press.

Feder, Gershon (1982) "On Exports and Economic Growth," *Journal of Development Economics* 12 (1/2): 59-73.

Gronicki, M., and L. R. Klein (1988) "Impacts of Military Cuts on the Soviet Economy." Department of Economics, University of Pennsylvania. Photocopy.

Haveman, J. D., A. V. Deardorff, and R. M. Stern (1990) "The Economic Effects of Unilateral and Multilateral Reductions in Military Expenditures in the Major Industrialized and Developing Countries." Paper presented at meeting of the American Economic Association, Washington, D.C., December 1990.

Hickman, Bert G. (1983) *Global International Economic Models,* Amsterdam: North Holland.

Klein, Lawrence R. (1971) "The Role of War in the Maintenance of American Economic Prosperity." *Proceedings of the American Philosophical Society* 115 (6): 507-516.

Klein, Lawrence R. (1978) "The Supply Side." *American Economic Review,* Volume 68, No. 1, pp. 1-7.

Klein, L. R., and M. Gronicki (1990) "Conversion: The Tradeoff Between Military and Civilian Production in the Warsaw Pact Countries." *Conflict Management and Peace Science,* 2 (1): 45-56.

Klein, L. R., and H. Kosaka (1987) "The Arms Race and the Economy." Department of Economics, University of Pennsylvania. Photocopy.

Klein, L. R., and P. Pauly (1990) "International Macroeconomic Implications of Defense Spending: Cutbacks Among NATO Countries." Department of Economics, University of Pennsylvania. Photocopy.

Leontief, W., and F. Duchin (1983) *Military Spending,* New York: Oxford University Press.

Leontief, W., and M. Hoffenberg (1961) "The Economic Effect of Disarmament." *Scientific American.*

Petersen, Christian (1988) "Dynamic Bilateral Tariff Games, An Econometric Analysis." Ph.D. diss. University of Pennsylvania.

Ram, Rati (1987) "Government Size and Economic Growth: A New Framework and Some Evidence From Cross-Section and Time-Series Data." *American Economic Review,* 76 (1): 191-203.

Ram, Rati (1989) "Government Size and Economic Growth: A New Framework and Some Evidence From Cross-Sections and Time- Series Data; Reply." *American Economic Review* 79 (1): 281–284.

Roland-Holst, D. W., S. Robinson, and L. Tyson (1988) "The Opportunity Cost of Defense Spending: A General Equilibrium Analysis." Department of Economics, University of California, Berkeley. Working paper #8871.

Rowen, H. S. and C. Wolf, Jr., eds. (1990) *The Impoverished Superpower: The Defense Burden on the Soviet Economy*, San Francisco: ICS Press.

Sawyer, J. A. (1979) *Modelling the International Transmission Mechanism*, Amsterdam: North Holland.

United Nations, Department of Disarmament Affairs (1983). "Economic and Social Consequences of the Arms Race and of Military Expenditures." New York: United Nations.

PART ONE

Arms Reduction and the Industrial Market Economies

Arms reduction represents a varied challenge for the industrial market economies of North America, Western Europe, and Japan. The degree to which these economies have allocated resources toward defense efforts and their involvement with military related production differs greatly. In the United States military spending amounts to 6 percent of GNP, with more than 50 percent share of scientific spending in one way or another related to defense. In Japan the so-called "Self Defense Force" accounts for only about 1 percent of GNP. A reduction of armaments expenditure or a transformation toward a different type of military spending will have considerably greater impacts on those economies allocating a large fraction of their GNP to defense than on those where military spending accounts for a lesser part of total output. The quantitative dimensions of a disarmament scenario depend on the magnitude of the cutbacks, the nature of the cutback—manpower, armaments, or advanced scientific effort—the linkages of the military and armaments sectors to the rest of the economy, and on the policies—macroeconomic, fiscal, and monetary—which accompany arms reduction.

It has become almost traditional to study the issue of arms reduction using simulations of macroeconomic models. The large models, widely used to forecast and simulate the behavior of the industrial economies, are a good instrument for evaluating macroeconomic effects stemming from mobilization and demobilization and have been used for this purpose since World War II. Over the years these models have become more and more complex and, one hopes, also more realistic. Project LINK has extended the single country models to a global approach linking the models of 79 countries through their trade flows, trade prices, and exchange rates. The LINK approach demonstrated how arms reduction has the potential to affect the entire world economy. A version of LINK is used in Chapter 2 by Adams and Huang. It is important to see that the countries participating in arms reduction are clearly the most affected and have the greatest potential for alternative resource use, but the other countries of the world are also influenced by changes in international flows of trade and by modifications in international development assistance. Worldwide interactions are also considered in a computable general equilibrium model framework in Chapter 4 by Haveman, Deardorff, and Stern.

A more detailed sectoral perspective of arms reduction is provided by integrating the macro model and the input-output approaches as shown in Chapter 2 by Adams and Huang. Input-output emphasizes the linkages between the sectors of the economy and produces results on a sectorally disaggregated level as compared to the largely aggregate picture shown by the macro model approach. On the one hand, this view of the economy calls for more detailed breakdown of the arms reduction scenario. On the other hand, it provides a more carefully delineated picture of what happens in the economy on a sectoral basis. This is very important because the impact—positive, negative, and dislocational—of an arms reduction program is often more visible on the sectoral than on the aggregate level. Whether an arms reduction scenario contains reduction of conventional weapons, manpower, or high tech equipment may make only little difference in the aggregate. But it will affect particular sectors and/or particular regions much more than others. Even when adjustments in the economy or policy changes result in a full demand offset of the arms reduction at the aggregate level, there may be substantial differences for specific sectors, some worsening their position and others improving. Chapter 3 by Doggett illustrates the dimensions of the dislocations that occur at the sectoral level.

Other ways of looking at the macroeconomy are also helpful to evaluate the impact of arms reduction. In Chapter 5, Dekle and Makin see arms reduction in a longer term perspective. The growth accounting paradigm provides a simple but central mechanism for evaluating the effects of a changed pattern of government spending, away from military to alternative uses. It must be stressed, however, that, as in the more complex macro models, the results of such calculations are highly dependent on the nature of the arms reduction scenarios that have been assumed.

We should also note that Murrell's chapter, included in Part Three, on the (formerly) centrally planned economies is more philosophical and less readily quantitative—in keeping with his evolutionary view of the economy. A similar evolutionary view might be a useful approach to arms reduction and conversion in the industrial economies Such a perspective contributes ideas about economic development, which are not sufficiently emphasized in the more traditional and less flexible model-based perspectives.

2

Defense Expenditure Reductions and the U.S. Economy: Sectorally Disaggregated Macro Model Simulations

F. Gerard Adams and Gene Huang

The Gulf War has demonstrated once again the fragility of projections of defense expenditures. Now that the conflagration has been put out, we can again seriously project reductions in military spending. We summarize here some recent macro model simulations of the economic effects of cutbacks in U.S. defense expenditures.

The primary objectives of our work are to put some quantitative dimensions on the impact of defense cutbacks, particularly at the sectoral level, and to demonstrate the need to combine arms reduction with appropriate macro policy changes. The study makes use of a highly detailed model of the United States (the Wharton Long Term and Industry Model) linked to a similarly industrially disaggregated model of Japan, the IUJ/FAIS model. Both econometric models have been integrated into the LINK world model system, so that the simulations are consistent on a worldwide basis and allow us to show some of the effects of U.S. arms reduction on the rest of the world.

Another motivation of our work is to explore the contrast between macroeconomic simulation and computable general equilibrium (CGE) calculations, which are presented in Chapter 4 by Haverman, Deardorff, and Stern (hereafter, HDS). The two types of models are, of course, considerably different in structure and coefficients. For this reason we do not attempt an in-depth comparison. Our primary concern is somewhat broader: What effect do the differences in the two approaches have on the outcome of the calculations? In particular, we note that a disaggregated econometric model can deal simultaneously with impacts at the macroeconomic and the sectoral level, whereas the CGE model, at least as applied by HDS, assumes a constant macroeconomic environment and focuses only within it on the sectoral breakdowns.[1] Secondly, we note that the CGE application does not show the dynamic movement over time, which is described year by year by the macro model simulations. We recognize that the macro model neither attempts to maintain economic equilibria nor offers as detailed a structure of market price responses as the CGE system.[2]

After a brief description of the macro models, we present the simulation scenarios and results. We contrast the sectoral impacts with those obtained in the HDS study.

The Macro Model System

The models used for these simulations are classic macroeconomic models which have been widely used for forecasting and simulation studies. The U.S. and Japanese models are described in detail by Adams, Gangnes, and Shishido (1992). They combine the typical Keynesian demand formulation with supply-side modeling on the sectoral level, introducing flexible price–responsive input-output systems as the linkage between aggregate demand and sectoral output. As a consequence, the models consistently translate detailed final demand changes, associated with arms reduction, into changes in the macroeconomy and into economic activity and trade for more than 50 sectors (more than 20 manufacturing industries). The trade equations distinguish trade between the United States and Japan from trade with the rest of the world. U.S.-Japanese trade is directly linked from one country to the other at the sectoral level. But with respect to the rest of the world, trade retains the LINK four-sector breakdown (foods, raw materials, fuels, and manufactures), although macroeconomic feedbacks operate on a worldwide basis. In any case, although the system could deal with worldwide arms reduction in broad terms, we focus here only on sectoral effects of U.S. arms reduction.

Alternative Scenarios

The simulations are intended to contrast a baseline simulation with alternatives incorporating reductions in military spending in the decade of the 1990s. The baseline is a typical long-term forecast for the U.S. economy (see Table 2.1). The projection, which has been lined up approximately with the late 1990 forecasts of Project LINK and of The WEFA Group, shows the recession of 1990 and 1991 and then a

TABLE 2.1 Base Solution (NNB): Macroeconomic Variables

	1990	1991	1992	1993	1994	1995	1996	1997	1998	1999
Gross national product (billion 1990 $)	5,782.4	5,793.0	5,912.8	6,048.2	6,182.1	6,368.8	6,535.8	6,679.5	6,876.2	7,085.1
% change	1.7	0.2	2.1	2.3	2.2	3.0	.26	2.2	2.9	3.0
Inflation rate % change	6.8	5.4	3.6	3.7	3.3	4.2	4.4	4.5	4.3	3.9
Personal consumption (billion 1990 $)	3,697.9	3,714.0	3,767.6	3,836.3	3,916.3	4,015.6	4,121.2	4,210.1	4,337.2	4,462.4
% change	3.2	0.4	1.4	1.8	2.1	2.5	2.6	2.2	3.0	2.9
Gross private investment (billion 1990 $)	930.8	966.8	1,016.1	1,061.9	1,092.5	1,161.5	1,202.5	1,211.3	1,274.6	1,328.5
% change	-5.8	3.9	5.1	4.5	2.9	6.3	3.5	0.7	5.2	4.2
Net exports of goods and services (billion 1990 $)	-115.8	-135.1	-152.4	-165.2	-175.6	-193.9	-210.2	-195.9	-231.5	-240.4
Exports of goods and services (billion 1990 $)	582.5	497.9	626.2	651.4	678.0	704.1	728.2	750.9	769.7	795.1
% change	4.9	2.7	4.7	4.0	4.1	3.9	3.4	3.1	2.5	3.3
Imports of goods and services (billion 1990 $)	698.3	733.0	778.7	816.6	853.6	898.0	938.4	946.8	1,001.2	1,035.5
% change	3.0	5.0	6.2	4.9	4.5	5.2	4.5	0.9	5.7	3.4
Employment (million people)	117.2	118.1	118.5	119.1	119.7	120.7	121.9	122.5	123.2	123.8
% change	0.9	0.7	0.4	0.5	0.5	0.8	1.0	0.5	0.5	0.5
Unemployment rate % change	5.8	6.5	6.3	6.8	6.7	6.7	6.3	6.6	6.6	6.8
Federal surplus/deficit (billion $)	-153.3	-110.2	-97.1	-95.6	-98.9	-80.3	-74.9	-73.9	-78.1	-85.4
Money supply (M2) (billion $)	3,508.6	3,719.0	3,893.8	4,171.0	4,351.5	4,561.3	4,807.1	5,130.4	5,460.9	5,836.4
% change	7.4	6.0	4.7	7.1	4.3	4.8	5.4	6.7	6.4	6.9
3-month certificate of deposit rate	9.69	7.91	7.65	6.07	6.14	7.12	7.88	7.22	7.25	7.18

moderate recovery to an annual growth rate of between 2 and 3 percent over the remainder of the decade. The forecast suggests moderation of inflationary pressures to around 4 percent and unemployment rates near 6.5 percent. Although there is an improvement in the federal budget deficit, NIPA basis, annual deficits continue to be $75–100 billion throughout the decade. The trade balance remains sharply negative, representing a troubling element in the forecast simulation.

It is important to note that defense expenditures have not been reduced in these baseline projections from earlier growth estimates. Defense spending grows at 2.8 percent per year in real terms (see Table 2.2), so that by the end of the decade defense spending increases 25 percent over the level attained at the end of the previous decade.[3] The same base simulation has been used as a basis of comparison for all of our alternate simulations. Over a fairly wide margin, so long as the base solution used for comparison is the same, the specifics of the base solution do not greatly affect our primary concern, the differences between it and the alternative solutions.

The intent of the simulations is to examine the extent of the impact of a reduction in defense spending on the aggregate economy and on the sectoral composition of output. It was apparent from preliminary simulations that reductions in defense spending would not automatically lead to fully offsetting adjustments returning the economy to its base solution level of production. The Keynesian demand effects dominate the first few years of the simulation. Moreover, although there are significant endogenous offsetting changes in interest rates and in the foreign trade balance, reduced defense spending leaves the economy with a significantly higher unemployment rate for a long period of time. It is clearly necessary to consider alternative policies that will offset the reduction in government spending. Some of these are themselves expenditures; for example, increases in nondefense government spending. Others involve shifting the gain to consumers through tax cuts. Finally, there is the option of relying on monetary policy stimulus as a way of offsetting the expenditure reductions. All of these are examined in the simulations presented next. (The simulation assumptions are summarized in Table 2.2.)

The alternative solutions compared are:

- *NNB Base Simulation*—the base solution, as discussed above.
- *NN2.5 Defense Cuts, No Offset*—an alternative solution, which assumes that federal defense spending and manpower in the armed forces will be reduced from the level shown in NNB by 2.5 percent annually beginning in 1992.

- *NN2.5ND Defense Cuts, Nondefense Offset*—the same solution as NN2.5 except that the reduction of defense spending is reallocated to federal nondefense spending.
- *NN2.5TX Defense Cuts, Tax Cut Offset*—the same assumptions as NN2.5 except that the reduction in defense spending is translated into an equivalent reduction in personal and corporate income taxes.
- *NN2.5M2 Defense Cuts, Monetary Offset*—the same assumptions as NN2.5 except that an offsetting stimulus is generated through a 0.8 percent per year increase in money supply.

Alternative Simulation Results: Macroeconomic Variables

The macroeconomic results of alternative arms reduction scenarios are summarized in Table 2.3. In each case we show only the percent deviation (arithmetic deviation where appropriate) of the alternative from the base solution (NNB), beginning in 1992, the first year of arms reduction.

NN2.5 Arms Reduction Without Policy Offsets

The impact on GNP of continued arms reductions without policy offsets is systematically negative. Economic growth is reduced by approximately 0.7 percent annually during the first three simulation years (1992–1994), but the negative impact decelerates, so that the shortfall from baseline GNP increases by only 0.2 percent annually after 1995 even though the rate of arms reduction has not been reduced. By 1999, GNP is 3.1 percent below the comparable base simulation value. In this example, arms reduction causes a stretched-out growth recession. The absolute level of GNP does not decline, but the economy is growing more slowly than potential. By 1999 the unemployment rate is 2.6 percent higher than in the base solution. Endogenous offsets account for the reduced impact after several years. Inflation is reduced by approximately 1 percent per year. Net exports show substantial improvement, in large part because of a significant reduction in imports, which are highly sensitive to economic activity. Arms reduction without offsetting government expenditures results in a significant improvement in the federal budget, which moves slightly into surplus at the end of the simulation period. Interest rates fall, endogenously, by 1.25 percent in this period. Nevertheless, the accelerator effect reduces gross private investment.

To summarize, an extended period of gradual arms reduction does not bring about sufficient endogenous offsets, at least within the

TABLE 2.2 Assumptions of Alternate Arms Reduction Simulations

	1990	1991	1992	1993	1994	1995	1996	1997	1998	1999
Total federal defense spending (billion 1990 $)										
NNB	388.0	381.8	393.4	404.5	415.9	427.2	439.1	451.4	464.0	476.9
% change	0.8	-1.6	3.0	2.8	2.8	2.7	2.8	2.8	2.8	2.8
NN2.5	388.0	381.8	372.3	363.0	353.9	345.0	336.4	328.0	319.8	311.8
% change	0.8	-1.6	-2.5	-2.5	-2.5	-2.5	-2.5	-2.5	-2.5	-2.5
NN2.5ND	388.0	381.8	372.3	363.0	353.9	345.0	336.4	328.0	319.8	311.8
% change	0.8	-1.6	-2.5	-2.5	-2.5	-2.5	-2.5	-2.5	-2.5	-2.5
NN2.5TX	388.0	381.8	372.3	363.0	353.9	345.0	336.4	328.0	319.8	311.8
% change	0.8	-1.6	-2.5	-2.5	-2.5	-2.5	-2.5	-2.5	-2.5	-2.5
NN2.5M2	388.0	381.8	372.3	363.0	353.9	345.0	336.4	328.0	319.8	311.8
% change	0.8	-1.6	-2.5	-2.5	-2.5	-2.5	-2.5	-2.5	-2.5	-2.5
Total government military employment (armed forces) (million people)										
NNB	2.25	2.25	2.25	2.25	2.25	2.25	2.25	2.25	2.25	2.25
% change	0.0	0.0	0.0	0.0	0.0	0.0	0.0	0.0	0.0	0.0
NN2.5	2.25	2.25	2.19	2.14	2.09	2.03	1.98	1.93	1.88	1.84
% change	0.0	0.0	-2.5	-2.5	-2.5	-2.5	-2.5	-2.5	-2.5	-2.5
NN2.5ND	2.25	2.25	2.19	2.14	2.09	2.03	1.98	1.93	1.88	1.84
% change	0.0	0.0	-2.5	-2.5	-2.5	-2.5	-2.5	-2.5	-2.5	-2.5
NN2.5TX	2.25	2.25	2.19	2.14	2.09	2.03	1.98	1.93	1.88	1.84
% change	0.0	0.0	-2.5	-2.5	-2.5	-2.5	-2.5	-2.5	-2.5	-2.5
NN2.5M2	2.25	2.25	2.19	2.14	2.09	2.03	1.98	1.93	1.88	1.84
% change	0.0	0.0	-2.5	-2.5	-2.5	-2.5	-2.5	-2.5	-2.5	-2.5
Total federal government civilian employment in defense sector (million people)										
NNB	1.29	1.15	1.16	1.17	1.19	1.21	1.23	1.25	1.26	1.28
% change	-4.5	-11.0	1.4	0.9	1.1	2.3	1.4	1.4	1.3	1.3
NN2.5	1.29	1.15	1.04	0.93	0.84	0.76	0.68	0.61	0.54	0.47
% change	-4.5	-11.0	-9.7	-9.9	-10.2	-8.8	-10.6	-11.0	-11.7	-12.3
NN2.5ND	1.29	1.15	1.04	0.93	0.84	0.76	0.68	0.61	0.54	0.47
% change	-4.5	-11.0	-9.7	-9.9	-10.2	-8.8	-10.6	-11.0	-11.7	-12.3
NN2.5TX	1.29	1.15	1.04	0.93	0.84	0.76	0.68	0.61	0.54	0.47
% change	-4.5	-11.0	1.4	0.9	1.1	2.3	1.4	1.4	1.3	1.3
NN2.5M2	1.29	1.15	1.04	0.93	0.84	0.76	0.68	0.61	0.54	0.47
% change	-4.5	-11.0	-9.7	-9.9	-10.2	-8.8	-10.6	-11.0	-11.7	-12.3

Total federal nondefense spending (billion 1990 $)

NNB	113.9	105.7	108.4	111.1	113.8	116.7	119.6	122.6	125.7	128.8
% change	8.5	-7.2	2.5	2.5	2.5	2.5	2.5	2.5	2.5	2.5
NN2.5	113.9	105.7	108.4	111.1	113.8	116.7	119.6	122.6	125.7	128.8
% change	8.5	-7.2	2.5	2.5	2.5	2.5	2.5	2.5	2.5	2.5
NN2.5ND	113.9	105.7	127.1	147.9	168.9	189.6	210.8	232.1	253.6	275.3
% change	8.5	-7.2	20.2	16.4	14.2	12.3	11.2	10.1	9.3	8.6
NN2.5TX	113.9	105.7	108.4	111.1	113.8	116.7	119.6	122.6	125.7	128.8
% change	8.5	-7.2	2.5	2.5	2.5	2.5	2.5	2.5	2.5	2.5
NN2.5M2	113.9	105.7	108.4	111.1	113.8	116.7	119.6	122.6	125.7	128.8
% change	8.5	-7.2	2.5	2.5	2.5	2.5	2.5	2.5	2.5	2.5

Total federal government receipts (tax and others) (billion 1990 $)

NNB	1,198.9	1,237.0	1,275.6	1,303.3	1,321.9	1,364.3	1,392.1	1,420.7	1,443.3	1,462.5
% change	1.9	3.2	3.1	2.2	1.4	3.2	2.0	2.1	1.6	1.3
NN2.5	1,198.9	1,237.0	1,260.9	1,271.5	1,269.8	1,292.3	1,301.7	1,312.5	1,320.2	1,320.9
% change	1.9	3.2	1.9	0.8	-0.1	1.8	0.7	0.8	0.6	0.1
NN2.5ND	1,198.9	1,237.0	1,276.2	1,306.1	1,328.5	1,376.1	1,410.2	1,446.7	1,478.1	1,506.2
% change	1.9	3.2	3.2	2.3	1.7	3.6	2.5	2.6	2.2	1.9
NN2.5TX	1,198.9	1,237.0	1,258.2	1,266.3	1,263.4	1,285.6	1,294.6	1,304.5	1,312.0	1,315.4
% change	1.9	3.2	1.7	0.6	-0.2	1.8	0.7	0.8	0.6	0.3
NN2.5M2	1,198.9	1,237.0	1,263.0	1,279.8	1,290.7	1,332.2	1,364.3	1,393.1	1,417.9	1,436.3
% change	1.9	3.2	2.1	1.3	0.8	3.2	2.4	2.1	1.8	1.3

Money supply (M2) (billion $)

NNB	3,508.6	3,719.0	3,893.8	4,171.0	4,351.5	4,561.3	4,807.1	5,130.4	5,460.9	5,836.4
% change	7.4	6.0	4.7	7.1	4.3	4.3	5.4	6.7	6.4	6.9
NN2.5	3,508.6	3,719.0	3,868.9	4,107.6	4,236.3	4,386.1	4,564.7	4,812.7	5,067.4	5,355.7
% change	7.4	6.0	4.0	6.2	3.1	3.5	4.1	5.4	5.3	5.7
NN2.5ND	3,508.6	3,719.0	3,896.4	4,179.4	4,371.2	4,597.7	4,866.1	5,218.9	5,586.9	6,005.9
% change	7.4	6.0	4.8	7.3	4.6	5.2	5.8	7.3	7.1	7.5
NN2.5TX	3,508.6	3,719.0	3,877.7	4,128.9	4,275.7	4,447.5	4,652.6	4,930.0	5,217.0	5,542.0
% change	7.4	6.0	4.3	6.5	3.6	4.0	4.6	6.0	5.8	6.2
NN2.5M2	3,508.6	3,719.0	3,931.0	4,250.1	4,476.5	4,737.2	5,039.8	5,429.2	5,833.2	6,292.7
% change	7.4	6.0	5.7	8.1	5.3	5.8	6.4	7.7	7.4	7.9

NNB: Base solution

NN2.5:   2.5% change annual reduction of federal defense spending and armed forces under NNB beginning 1992.

NN2.5ND: NN2.5 plus same amount increase in federal nondefense spending.

NN2.5TX: NN2.5 plus same amount reduction in federal receipts (tax and others).

NN2.5M2: NN2.5 plus 0.8% increase in money supply (M2).

TABLE 2.3 Comparison of Macroeconomic Variables Under Different Scenarios
(percentage change from base solution NNB)

	1992	1993	1994	1995	1996	1997	1998	1999
Real GNP								
NN2.5	−0.8	−1.4	−2.0	−2.3	−2.5	−2.8	−2.9	−3.1
NN2.5ND	0.0	0.1	0.1	0.1	0.2	0.3	0.4	0.4
NN2.5TX	−0.5	−0.9	−1.3	−1.4	−1.5	−1.7	−1.7	−1.8
NN2.5M2	−0.7	−1.0	−1.0	−0.6	−0.2	−0.1	0.1	0.1
Real GNP growth rate								
NN2.5	−0.8	−0.6	−0.6	−0.3	−0.2	−0.3	−0.2	−0.2
NN2.5ND	0.0	0.0	0.0	0.1	0.1	0.1	0.1	0.1
NN2.5TX	−0.6	−0.4	−0.3	−0.2	−0.1	−0.2	0.0	−0.1
NN2.5M2	−0.7	−0.3	0.0	0.4	0.4	0.2	0.2	0.1
Inflation[a]								
NN2.5	−0.1	−0.4	−0.7	−1.0	−1.0	−1.0	−0.9	−0.9
NN2.5ND	0.1	0.2	0.3	0.4	0.4	0.4	0.5	0.5
NN2.5TX	0.0	−0.3	−0.5	−0.6	−0.7	−0.6	−0.5	−0.5
NN2.5M2	−0.1	−0.3	−0.5	−0.4	−0.2	0.0	0.2	0.1
Real personal consumption expenditure								
NN2.5	−0.5	−1.0	−1.6	−2.1	−2.6	−3.0	−3.3	−3.7
NN2.5ND	0.1	0.1	0.2	0.3	0.5	0.6	0.8	1.0
NN2.5TX	−0.2	−0.4	−0.6	−0.8	−0.9	−1.0	−1.1	−1.2
NN2.5M2	−0.4	−0.7	−0.9	−0.9	−0.8	−0.7	−0.5	−0.5
Real gross private investment								
NN2.5	−1.4	−1.9	−2.1	−1.7	−1.1	−0.8	−0.4	−0.2
NN2.5ND	0.0	−0.1	−0.2	−0.5	−0.7	−1.1	−0.9	−1.4
NN2.5TX	−0.7	−1.0	−1.1	−0.8	−0.4	−0.2	0.2	0.1
NN2.5M2	−0.9	−0.2	1.7	4.5	7.2	9.1	10.5	11.7
Net exports of goods and services[a]								
NN2.5	5.4	13.3	25.0	40.8	56.7	74.3	96.6	109.0
NN2.5ND	0.3	0.6	0.8	0.9	1.3	5.4	0.2	2.5
NN2.5TX	3.5	9.1	17.2	28.4	39.8	52.1	66.3	79.9
NN2.5M2	4.6	9.6	14.3	17.7	18.3	16.8	14.2	7.9
Real exports of goods and services								
NN2.5	−0.1	−0.1	0.0	0.1	0.2	0.2	0.4	0.5
NN2.5ND	0.0	−0.1	−0.2	−0.3	−0.4	−0.5	−0.8	−0.9
NN2.5TX	0.0	−0.1	0.0	0.0	0.1	0.1	0.2	0.1
NN2.5M2	−0.1	0.0	0.0	0.2	0.2	0.2	0.2	0.1
Real imports of goods and services								
NN2.5	−0.8	−1.7	−3.0	−4.5	−5.9	−7.7	−9.3	−10.1
NN2.5ND	−0.1	−0.1	−0.2	−0.3	−0.4	−1.2	−0.6	−0.9
NN2.5TX	−0.5	−1.2	−2.0	−3.1	−4.2	−5.4	−6.5	−7.6
NN2.5M2	−0.7	−1.3	−1.8	−2.1	−2.2	−2.3	−2.1	−1.8
Employment (percentage change)								
NN2.5	−0.4	−0.9	−1.4	−1.8	−2.2	−2.6	−3.0	−3.3
NN2.5ND	0.2	0.3	0.5	0.6	0.8	1.1	1.2	1.4
NN2.5TX	−0.3	−0.6	−0.9	−1.2	−1.4	−1.6	−1.8	−1.9
NN2.5M2	−0.3	−0.7	−0.9	−0.9	−0.7	−0.6	−0.5	−0.5
Unemplyoment rate[a]								
NN2.5	0.4	0.8	1.3	1.6	1.9	2.2	2.4	2.6
NN2.5ND	−0.1	−0.3	−0.4	−0.5	−0.6	−0.7	−0.8	−0.9
NN2.5TX	0.3	0.6	0.9	1.1	1.2	1.4	1.5	1.6
NN2.5M2	0.3	0.7	0.8	0.8	0.6	0.5	0.4	0.3

(Continues)

TABLE 2.3   *(Continued)*

	1992	1993	1994	1995	1996	1997	1998	1999
Federal surplus/deficit[a]								
NN2.5	7.9	16.7	26.5	41.3	60.6	82.2	109.4	130.7
NN2.5ND	3.0	6.6	10.9	15.7	21.9	30.3	39.3	49.5
NN2.5TX	3.6	6.9	11.0	19.0	30.3	42.2	59.2	75.3
NN2.5M2	10.8	28.8	57.0	99.0	148.7	191.4	238.5	279.4
Money supply (M2)								
NN2.5	−0.6	−1.5	−2.6	−3.8	−5.0	−6.2	−7.2	−8.2
NN2.5ND	0.1	0.2	0.5	0.8	1.2	1.7	2.3	2.9
NN2.5TX	−0.4	−1.0	−1.7	−2.5	−3.2	−3.9	−4.5	−5.0
NN2.5M2	0.8	1.5	2.3	3.1	3.9	4.6	5.4	6.2
3-Month certificate of deposit rate[a]								
NN2.5	−0.18	−0.42	−0.81	−1.06	−1.23	−1.30	−1.26	−1.23
NN2.5ND	0.05	0.14	0.26	0.38	0.48	0.58	0.65	0.72
NN2.5TX	−0.12	−0.28	−0.50	−0.68	−0.77	−0.79	−0.72	−0.68
NN2.5M2	−1.02	−2.03	−3.00	−3.67	−3.96	−4.18	−4.34	−4.58

[a]Absolute differences from base solution.
NN2.5:   2.5% annual reduction of federal defense spending and armed forces under NNB beginning 1992.
NN2.5ND: NN2.5 plus same amount increase in federal nondefense spending.
NN2.5TX: NN2.5 plus same amount reduction in federal receipts (tax and others).
NN2.5M2: NN2.5 plus 0.8% increase in money supply (M2).

simulation period, to bring the economy back to a full employment equilibrium.

NN2.5ND and NN2.5TX Arms Reductions
with Expenditure Offsets

The idea that all defense expenditure cutbacks would go to improve the deficit is extreme in view of the pressures for civilian spending or for tax reduction. In the next two simulations, we have maintained the level of the budget at base solution levels by substituting nondefense spending for cutbacks in military spending in NN2.5ND and by providing comparable cutbacks in individual and corporate income taxes in NN2.5TX.

The substitution of civilian for military expenditures wipes out the negative macroeconomic impacts of arm reduction and even provides a small stimulus. But the tax cuts do not! Tax reductions are only partially translated into demand increases, so growth remains reduced. In 1999, with the tax cut offset, GNP is 1.8 percent below its base solution level. The impacts on other macroeconomic variables are consistent with the results for GNP.

NN2.5M2 Arms Reduction With Monetary Policy Offset

The monetary policy offset to arms reduction spread over the simulation period represents a less flexible policy measure than would occur in reality, although a 0.8 percent per year more rapid growth of M2 than in the base solution is not a radical step.

The impact of monetary expansion is long in coming but substantial. Although the systematic expansion in money supply begins the same year as the first reduction in military spending, its effect is delayed. In 1992 the negative impact of arms reduction is not offset by increased money supply, even though there is already a significant reduction in the interest rate. In subsequent years, lower interest rates are a powerful stimulus to private investment, and that in turn causes the economy to return to its original track by 1998. The recovery of the economy has the anticipated impacts on other macroeconomic variables.

To summarize, monetary policy is an effective means to stimulate demand and to redirect it toward investment, but, as is well known, the monetary instruments act with a lag, and in the meantime economic growth sags.

Sectoral Impacts of Alternative Arms Reduction Simulations

Arms reduction has sectorally differentiated economic impacts and, in turn, so does the recovery of the economy as a result of policy actions. We consider the sectoral impacts in Table 2.4, which shows the effects of the alternative simulations as percentage deviation from the corresponding base solution values. The results, particularly in the simulations where policy offsets are not sufficient to return the economy to its base-level output (NN2.5 and NN2.5TX, for example) are affected by macroeconomic forces as well as by the results of changes in composition of final demand. The most powerful effects are apparent in simulation NN2.5, which assumes arms reduction without policy offset. The impact on manufacturing as a whole increases gradually to approximately minus 3 percent, corresponding to the impact on GNP. Effects of about the same magnitude occur in agriculture, and somewhat smaller impacts are apparent in services. Construction, which has countercyclical components, comes back toward its base solution levels after five years. The distribution of output losses within manufacturing is consistent with the reduction of purchases by the defense sector; the largest output losses (some 6 to 8 percent) occur fairly quickly in aircraft, other transportation equipment, electrical machinery, and automobiles. The iron and steel industry, which provides input to these sectors, is also seriously affected.

The simulations that provide alternative demand offsets, such as NN2.5ND, which substitutes nondefense spending for arms reduction, show much smaller sectoral impacts—for example, a manufacturing reduction of only 0.5 percent in the middle of the simulation period and 1.1 percent at the end. This is offset by increases above base solution levels in certain sectors, such as services and construction. Differential effects are also observable within manufacturing where substantial negative effects persist in other transportation equipment and electrical machinery but where automobiles benefit over the entire simulation period. The differential effects, obscured in the calculation of aggregates such as GNP, are important as an indication of the dislocations caused by arms reduction, even when macroeconomic performance is maintained near its base solution level, as in simulation NN2.5ND (nondefense spending offset). Resource shifts between sectors can, and do, occur but they are not costless. Some sector outputs are below their base solution values, others above.

To show the magnitude of the effects, we computed separately the sums of positive and of negative deviations from base solution values over the various sectors (Table 2.5). The magnitude of the dislocations depends greatly on the assumptions about offsets to arms reduction and on the timing of their effects. There are substantial negative effects for some industries even when the negative demand effects of arms reduction are largely offset, as in simulation NN2.5ND. The negative industrial effects persist in some industries even when monetary policy stimulus creates substantial positives in some sectors (Simulation NN2.5M2). The dislocations are, of course, larger and one sided when GNP is away from its base solution level, as in simulation NN2.5 (no offset).

Comparison with CGE Results

How do these macro model simulation results compare with the CGE calculations of HDS? A comparison is possible for only one point in time because the CGE calculations do not yield the time path, and for only simulation NN2.5ND (nondefense offset) because it alone fully offsets defense spending cuts with alternative expenditures. We chose to compare the figures for 1996 because at that time the cumulative reduction in defense expenditures from the base solution assumption is approximately 25 percent, as in the DHS computation.[4]

The results of the two approaches have significant similarities, but also many differences (Table 2.6). In particular we note that industries

TABLE 2.4 Sectoral Impacts of Alternative Arms Reduction Scenarios
(% deviation of gross output from base solution NNB, based on 1990 dollars)

	1992	1993	1994	1995	1996	1997	1998	1999
Agriculture, forestry, and fishery								
NN2.5	−0.8	−1.4	−2.0	−2.4	−2.6	−3.0	−3.1	−3.3
NN2.5ND	−0.2	−0.5	−0.7	−0.8	−1.0	−1.1	−1.1	−1.4
NN2.5TX	−0.4	−0.8	−1.1	−1.2	−1.2	−1.3	−1.2	−1.4
NN2.5M2	−0.6	−1.0	−0.9	−0.6	−0.1	0.0	0.1	0.0
Mining, total								
NN2.5	−0.6	−1.0	−1.3	−1.4	−1.4	−1.4	−1.0	−0.7
NN2.5ND	0.0	−0.1	−0.2	−0.3	−0.4	−0.6	−0.6	−1.0
NN2.5TX	−0.4	−0.6	−0.8	−0.8	−0.8	−0.8	−0.5	−0.3
NN2.5M2	−0.5	−0.7	−0.6	−0.2	0.3	0.5	0.8	0.9
Construction, total								
NN2.5	−1.6	−1.8	−1.7	−1.0	−0.3	0.1	0.1	0.0
NN2.5ND	0.3	0.5	0.5	0.5	0.4	0.2	0.5	0.1
NN2.5TX	−0.7	−0.9	−0.8	−0.3	0.1	0.1	0.3	−0.2
NN2.5M2	−1.0	0.2	2.6	5.1	6.8	7.0	6.5	6.1
Manufacturing, total								
NN2.5	−1.4	−2.3	−3.1	−3.2	−3.3	−3.3	−3.1	−3.3
NN2.5ND	−0.2	−0.3	−0.5	−0.7	−0.8	−0.9	−1.0	−1.1
NN2.5TX	−0.9	−1.6	−2.1	−2.1	−2.1	−2.1	−1.9	−2.0
NN2.5M2	−1.2	−1.6	−1.4	−0.5	0.5	1.1	1.6	1.7
Manufacturing: food, beverage, tobacco								
NN2.5	−0.6	−1.2	−1.8	−2.3	−2.6	−3.0	−3.2	−3.5
NN2.5ND	0.1	0.2	0.3	0.4	0.6	0.7	0.9	1.0
NN2.5TX	−0.3	−0.6	−0.9	−1.1	−1.1	−1.2	−1.2	−1.3
NN2.5M2	−0.5	−0.9	−1.0	−0.9	−0.6	−0.4	−0.3	−0.3
Manufacturing: textile apparel								
NN2.5	−1.2	−2.1	−2.9	−3.4	−3.8	−4.2	−4.3	−4.6
NN2.5ND	0.0	0.1	0.1	0.1	0.2	0.2	0.4	0.4
NN2.5TX	−0.6	−1.0	−1.3	−1.4	−1.4	−1.6	−1.5	−1.6
NN2.5M2	−1.0	−1.4	−1.4	−0.9	−0.3	−0.1	0.0	0.0
Manufacturing: paper, pulp, printing, publishing								
NN2.5	−0.8	−1.4	−2.0	−2.4	−0.6	−2.9	−3.0	−3.3
NN2.5ND	0.1	0.2	0.2	0.3	0.4	0.5	0.6	0.7
NN2.5TX	−0.4	−0.8	−1.1	−1.2	−1.3	−1.3	−1.3	−1.4
NN2.5M2	−0.7	−1.0	−1.0	−0.7	−0.2	−0.1	0.1	0.1
Manufacturing: chemical, petro/coal, rubber, plastic, leather								
NN2.5	−0.9	−1.7	−2.4	−3.0	−3.4	−3.3	−3.2	−5.5
NN2.5ND	0.1	0.1	0.1	0.0	−0.1	0.3	−0.1	0.4
NN2.5TX	−0.5	−1.0	−1.5	−1.8	−2.0	−1.9	−1.7	−2.1
NN2.5M2	−0.7	−1.2	−1.3	−1.0	−0.6	−0.2	0.1	−0.1
Manufacturing: lumber, wood, furniture, cement, stone, clay, glass								
NN2.5	−1.6	−2.1	−2.4	−1.9	−1.4	−1.0	−0.8	−0.9
NN2.5ND	0.1	0.0	−0.1	−0.3	−0.4	−0.7	−0.7	−1.2
NN2.5TX	−0.8	−1.2	−1.2	−0.9	−0.5	−0.4	−0.1	−0.4
NN2.5M2	−1.1	−0.6	1.0	3.1	4.5	4.8	4.5	4.0
Manufacturing: iron, steel								
NN2.5	−3.1	−5.1	−6.4	−6.1	−5.5	−5.1	−4.0	−3.6
NN2.5ND	−0.4	−0.8	−1.4	−1.8	−2.3	−2.7	−3.0	−3.7
NN2.5TX	−2.1	−3.6	−4.5	−4.3	−3.9	−3.7	−3.0	−2.9
NN2.5M2	−2.6	−3.4	−2.5	0.2	3.0	4.7	5.9	6.3

(Continues)

TABLE 2.4 *(Continued)*

	1992	1993	1994	1995	1996	1997	1998	1999
Manufacturing: aluminum, other nonferrous metal, fabric metal								
NN2.5	−1.4	−2.2	−2.5	−2.1	−1.5	−0.9	0.1	0.8
NN2.5ND	−0.1	−0.3	−0.4	−0.6	−0.8	−1.1	−1.3	−1.9
NN2.5TX	−0.9	−1.5	−1.7	−1.4	−1.0	−0.6	0.1	0.4
NN2.5M2	−1.2	−1.3	−0.6	0.9	2.5	3.4	4.1	4.4
Manufacturing: nonelectrical machinery								
NN2.5	−1.0	−1.6	−2.1	−2.2	−2.1	−1.9	−1.6	−1.5
NN2.5ND	−0.2	−0.5	−0.7	−1.0	−1.2	−1.3	−1.5	−1.6
NN2.5TX	−0.7	−1.2	−1.6	−1.7	−1.6	−1.5	−1.3	−1.2
NN2.5M2	−0.8	−1.0	−0.6	0.5	1.7	2.6	3.4	3.8
Manufacturing: electrical machinery								
NN2.5	−2.1	−3.8	−5.2	−6.0	−6.6	−7.1	−7.2	−7.2
NN2.5ND	−0.9	−1.9	−2.9	−3.8	−4.8	−5.9	−6.9	−8.0
NN2.5TX	−1.7	−3.2	−4.4	−5.2	−5.8	−6.4	−6.6	−7.0
NN2.5M2	−1.9	−3.1	−3.6	−3.3	−2.8	−2.6	−2.5	−2.7
Manufacturing: aircraft								
NN2.5	−4.3	−6.8	−7.1	−3.7	−3.4	−3.1	−1.0	2.4
NN2.5ND	−2.1	−3.6	−4.3	−3.7	−1.2	2.7	5.0	8.5
NN2.5TX	−3.9	−6.1	−6.6	−4.0	−2.6	−2.4	−2.7	2.6
NN2.5M2	−4.1	−6.0	−5.6	−2.1	1.5	2.6	5.0	8.7
Manufacturing: other transportation equipment								
NN2.5	−3.6	−6.0	−7.8	−8.2	−8.2	−9.4	−10.5	−11.6
NN2.5ND	−1.0	−1.8	−2.5	−3.0	−3.3	−3.5	−3.3	−3.1
NN2.5TX	−3.0	−5.2	−6.8	−7.4	−7.5	−8.0	−9.0	−10.1
NN2.5M2	−3.3	−5.1	−5.8	−5.3	−4.7	−4.5	−4.6	−5.3
Manufacturing: automobiles								
NN2.5	−2.4	−4.2	−5.4	−5.5	−5.4	−5.1	−4.1	−3.3
NN2.5ND	0.2	0.4	0.4	0.4	0.4	0.2	0.3	−0.1
NN2.5TX	−1.2	−2.3	−3.0	−3.0	−2.8	−2.6	−1.9	−1.7
NN2.5M2	−2.0	−2.8	−2.1	0.2	2.8	4.8	6.5	7.5
Manufacturing: instrument								
NN2.5	−1.1	−2.0	−2.7	−3.1	−3.5	−3.8	−4.0	−4.3
NN2.5ND	−0.3	−0.6	−0.9	−1.2	−1.4	−1.6	−1.7	−1.9
NN2.5TX	−0.9	−1.5	−2.1	−2.4	−2.6	−2.8	−2.9	−3.2
NN2.5M2	−1.0	−1.5	−1.6	−1.2	−0.6	−0.2	0.1	0.4
Manufacturing: miscellaneous								
NN2.5	−0.8	−1.4	−1.8	−1.8	−1.7	−1.7	−1.4	−1.1
NN2.5ND	−0.1	−0.3	−0.7	−1.2	−1.7	−2.2	−2.8	−3.5
NN2.5TX	−0.5	−0.8	−1.1	−1.1	−1.0	−1.1	−1.1	−1.2
NN2.5M2	−0.7	−1.0	−1.0	−0.7	−0.5	−0.8	−1.1	−1.6
Service, total								
NN2.5	−0.5	−0.9	−1.4	−1.7	−2.1	−2.4	−2.6	−2.9
NN2.5ND	0.1	0.1	0.2	0.2	0.3	0.4	0.5	0.6
NN2.5TX	−0.3	−0.5	−0.7	−0.9	−1.0	−1.1	−1.1	−1.2
NN2.5M2	−0.4	−0.6	−0.7	−0.5	−0.3	−0.1	0.0	0.1
Government, total								
NN2.5	−0.8	−1.6	−2.5	−3.2	−3.7	−4.3	−4.7	−5.2
NN2.5ND	−0.2	−0.4	−0.6	−0.8	−0.9	−1.1	−1.2	−1.3
NN2.5TX	−0.6	−1.2	−1.7	−2.1	−2.5	−2.8	−3.0	−3.3
NN2.5M2	−0.8	−1.3	−1.7	−1.8	−1.7	−1.7	−1.7	−1.8

NN2.5:   2.5% annual reduction of federal defense spending and armed forces under NNB beginning 1992.
NN2.5ND: NN2.5 plus same amount increase in federal nondefense spending.
NN2.5TX: NN2.5 plus same amount reduction in federal receipts (tax and others).
NN2.5M2: NN2.5 plus 0.8% increase in money supply (M2).

TABLE 2.5 Sectoral Dislocation of Arms Reduction Scenarios (billion 1990 $)

	1992	1993	1994	1995	1996	1997	1998	1999
Simulation NN2.5								
Sum of positives	0.0	0.0	0.0	0.0	0.0	0.0	0.3	4.9
Sum of negatives	−39.9	−69.5	−93.2	−101.4	−105.8	−108.4	−103.0	−118.2
Simulation of NN2.5ND								
Sum of positives	1.9	3.0	3.8	4.2	5.3	10.4	11.8	16.8
Sum of negatives	−6.6	−13.1	−19.8	−26.1	−32.0	−38.9	−45.3	−56.2
Simulation of NN2.5TX								
Sum of positives	0.0	0.0	0.0	0.0	0.0	0.0	0.4	3.6
Sum of negatives	−26.1	−47.3	−62.9	−66.9	−67.3	−68.8	−64.0	−71.4
Simulation of NN2.5M2								
Sum of positives	0.0	0.0	2.1	12.9	39.0	55.9	73.9	83.6
Sum of negatives	−34.3	−48.1	−44.9	−28.4	−22.8	−21.0	−21.5	−24.5

NN2.5:   2.5% annual reduction of federal defense spending and armed forces under NNB beginning 1992.
NN2.5ND: NN2.5 plus same amount increase in federal nondefense spending.
NN2.5TX: NN2.5 plus same amount reduction in federal receipts (tax and others).
NN2.5M2: NN2.5 plus 0.8% increase in money supply (M2).

TABLE 2.6 Percentage Changes in Employment by Sector Due to Reduction in Military Spending

Industry	CGE	NN2.5ND (1996)
Traded goods		
Agriculture, forestry, fishing	0.70	−1.13
Food, beverage, tobacco	−0.22	0.14
Textiles	−0.76	0.02
Apparel	−0.61	0.26
Leather products	−1.26	0.25
Lumber and wood products	0.55	−0.28
Furniture and fixtures	0.25	−0.05
Paper and paper products	−0.07	0.09
Printing and publishing	0.80	0.42
Chemicals	−0.46	−0.06
Petroleum and related products	−0.37	0.19
Rubber products	−1.25	−0.31
Glass and glass products	−1.32	−0.55
Iron and steel	−2.31	−2.03
Metal products	−1.91	−0.60
Nonelectric machinery	−1.46	−2.29
Electric machinery	−3.35	−4.06
Transportation equipment	−3.44	0.36
Nontraded goods		
Mining	−0.07	−0.31
Electrtic, gas and water	0.59	0.02
Construction	1.31	0.70
Wholesale and retail	−0.47	0.20
Communication	1.02	0.27
Total, all private sectors	0.01	0.06

that are directly or indirectly linked closely to defense (i.e., iron and steel, transportation equipment, and machinery) show roughly comparable negative effects. This follows directly from the demand adjustments made in both models. The results from other sectors that are influenced more broadly by the offsetting adjustment in nondefense spending and through relative prices and other demand forces are much less well matched. In one case—construction—an explanation would require further study of the models, coefficients, and structure. In many other cases, the percentage effects are small and may be within the error bounds of the models.

International Repercussions

The effects of U.S. arms reduction on other countries are computed in the framework of the LINK world model system (Table 2.7). We show the effects on Japan separately because it was linked on a sector-by-sector basis to the U.S. model in the simulations. We assume for illustration that the United States is the only country practicing arms reduction. Trade flows are the mechanism for international transmission; trade with the world at large is affected perceptibly more than trade with Japan.

The effects on other countries depend greatly, as in the United States, on whether or not there are offsetting demand policies. Simulation NN2.5ND (nondefense spending offset) has only very small (negative) effects on Japan and the rest of the world. On the other hand, the impact of NN2.5 (without demand offset) is perceptible and worldwide, although percentage-wise the effect on GNP in other countries is less than half as great as in the United States. Not surprisingly, the impact is greater in Japan and other industrial countries than in the Third World.

Conclusions

A number of conclusions emerge from our analysis of the arms reduction simulations.

1. In the absence of offsetting demand policy, a gradual but continued reduction in defense spending causes economic activity to fall below its base simulation path, with adverse effects on employment.
2. After the first few years, built-in stabilizers go partway toward offsetting the declining trend, so that after 1996 the growth rate

TABLE 2.7 International Impacts of U.S. Arms Reduction Under Various Scenarios
(percentage changes from base solution NNB)

	1992	1993	1994	1995	1996	1997	1998	1999
Real GNP								
Japan								
NN2.5	−0.1	−0.3	−0.5	−0.7	−1.0	−1.2	−1.5	−1.7
NN2.5ND	0.0	0.0	−0.1	−0.1	−0.1	−0.2	−0.2	−0.2
NN2.5TX	−0.1	−0.2	−0.3	−0.5	−0.7	−0.9	−1.1	−0.3
NN2.5M2	−0.1	−0.2	−0.3	−0.3	−0.4	−0.4	−0.3	−0.3
Other industrialized countries (excluding U.S., Japan)								
NN2.5	−0.06	−0.16	−0.32	−0.54	−0.74	−0.95	−1.23	−1.33
NN2.5ND	0.00	−0.01	−0.02	−0.03	−0.05	−0.12	−0.10	−0.10
NN2.5TX	−0.04	−0.11	−0.23	−0.39	−0.54	−0.69	−0.88	−1.00
NN2.5M2	−0.05	−0.13	−0.22	−0.27	−0.24	−0.16	−0.07	0.10
Developing countries								
NN2.5	−0.04	−0.08	−0.15	−0.24	−0.34	−0.44	−0.55	−0.60
NN2.5ND	0.00	−0.01	−0.01	−0.02	−0.03	−0.06	−0.04	−0.07
NN2.5TX	−0.02	−0.06	−0.10	−0.17	−0.23	−0.31	−0.38	−0.45
NN2.5M2	−0.01	−0.02	−0.04	−0.06	−0.07	−0.08	−0.07	−0.05
World total								
NN2.5	−0.23	−0.44	−0.66	−0.84	−1.00	−1.17	−1.33	−1.45
NN2.5ND	0.01	0.01	0.02	0.02	0.02	0.00	0.04	0.03
NN2.5TX	−0.15	−0.29	−0.43	−0.55	−0.65	−0.77	−0.86	−0.96
NN2.5M2	−0.20	−0.31	−0.35	−0.28	−0.17	−0.10	−0.03	0.04
Real trade								
Japan (exports)								
NN2.5	−0.3	−0.7	−1.2	−1.9	−2.5	−3.1	−3.7	−4.1
NN2.5ND	0.0	−0.1	−0.1	−0.2	−0.2	−0.4	−0.4	−0.5
NN2.5TX	−0.2	−0.5	−0.9	−1.4	−1.9	−2.4	−2.8	−3.2
NN2.5M2	−0.3	−0.5	−0.7	−0.8	−0.8	−0.8	−0.7	−0.4
World total								
NN2.5	−0.2	−0.5	−0.8	−1.2	−1.6	−2.0	−2.5	−2.7
NN2.5ND	0.0	0.0	−0.1	−0.1	−0.2	−0.4	−0.3	−0.4
NN2.5TX	−0.1	−0.3	−0.6	−0.9	−1.2	−1.5	−1.8	−2.1
NN2.5M2	−0.2	−0.3	−0.5	−0.6	−0.6	−0.6	−0.6	−0.5

NN2.5: 2.5% annual reduction of federal defense spending and armed forces under NNB beginning 1992.
NN2.5ND: NN2.5 plus same amount increase in federal nondefense spending.
NN2.5TX: NN2.5 plus same amount reduction in federal receipts (tax and others).
NN2.5M2: NN2.5 plus 0.8% increase in money supply (M2).

is only 0.2 percent lower in arms reduction scenario NN2.5 (without demand offsets) than in the base solution.

3. Offsetting defense-spending reductions with nondefense spending can maintain the economy on its base solution path.

4. Offsetting arms-spending reductions with comparable cuts in personal and corporate income taxes does not suffice to return the economy to its base simulation level because not all tax cuts enter the demand stream.

5. Monetary policy is a powerful instrument but its delayed action initially cause the economy to decline relative to the base solution. The monetary stimulus is sufficiently strong to return the economy to the base solution level in the end.

6. The effects of arms reduction vary greatly by industry. Dislocations are apparent even when macroeconomic activity is maintained at the base solution level.

7. Comparisons with the CGE calculation of HDS show comparable effects for the sectors affected heavily by arms reduction, but the effects vary greatly among other sectors for no obvious reasons.

8. U.S. arms reduction that is not offset by effective demand policies has worldwide impacts on trade and economic activity.

Notes

1. For this reason HDS presents only simulations that assume that reductions in military spending are offset by other types of final demand.

2. The differences observed, of course, also reflect differences between the coefficients in the two systems.

3. Spending related to the Gulf War will make the 1990–1991 figures unrealistic, but it may not throw off the longer term projections.

4. We are comparing effect on gross product by sector with effect on employment in percentage terms in the CGE calculations. Because the latter shows long-run results, the effects should be roughly comparable in terms of percentages.

Bibliography

Adams, F. Gerard, B. Gangnes, and S. Shishido (1992) Economic Activity, Trade, and Industry in the US-Japan-World Economy: A Macro Model Study of Economic Interactions.

3

Defense Expenditures in the 1980s: A Macroeconomic, Interindustry, and Regional Analysis

Ralph M. Doggett

During the 1980s, expenditures for defense increased at a rate unprecedented in peacetime. The level of expenditures, in real terms, peaked in 1988, declined slightly in 1989, and is projected to decline precipitously over the next five years. The consequences for the economy as a whole are likely to be fairly neutral—the decreased expenditure levels will take a great deal of pressure off the federal budget deficit, which should increase the borrowing potential of consumers and investors. However, the consequences for key defense industries and their suppliers will be quite negative. Selected states that have developed a dependence on the defense market will also experience adverse impacts.

This chapter briefly presents the results of an analysis of the economic impacts of reduced expenditures for defense over the coming decade. Included is a discussion of the levels and distribution of defense expenditures assumed in the analysis, the macroeconomic context in which the analysis was undertaken, the impacts on individual industries, and the impacts on each of the 50 states and the District of Columbia. The analysis presented here is distinguished from other empirical studies in this book by the use of a disaggregated input-output/econometric model and detailed disaggregation matrixes to break down defense expenditure cutback assumptions to industrial sectors and to the fifty states.

Methodology and Data Sources

The estimates were developed within the Interindustry Economic Research Fund's (IERF) integrated macroeconomic-interindustry forecasting models, supplemented by data bases provided by the Department of Defense. The IERF Long-term Interindustry Forecasting Tool was the cornerstone upon which the analysis was built. This model combines econometric forecasting equations for personal consumption expenditures, investment in producers' durable equipment, construction investment, exports and imports, along with exogenously supplied estimates of federal, state and local government purchases of goods and services, for 78 industries. These equations and exogenous assumptions are embodied within a dynamic interindustry (input-output) forecasting system that estimates interindustry sales and output. The model produces macroeconomic forecasts from the bottom up by summing the estimates of detailed final demands generated by the econometric equations, to arrive at estimates of GNP and its components. Through the interindustry framework, the model also produces estimates of gross output by each industry, as well as producer prices, employment, labor compensation and other components of value added. Results from the interindustry component, particularly the producer price estimates, play an important role within the econometric equations used to estimate final demands.

For the defense impact analysis, the LIFT model was supplemented by two defense data bases. Both were provided to IERF by DOD's Office of Program Analysis and Evaluation, which developed and maintains an economic forecasting and analysis capability called the Defense Economic Impact Modeling System (DEIMS). The key component of DEIMS is the "Defense Translator," which provides detailed estimates of the distribution of defense expenditures by major budget category and industry. This data base was combined with IERF estimates defense expenditures by major budget category, derived from the Defense Authorization Act, to develop estimates of direct purchases for defense from each of the 78 industries delineated in the LIFT model. The industry level estimates of defense purchases were then used along with the econometric equations of LIFT to estimate macroeconomic variables, the industry level variables listed above, plus the estimates of indirect and total output for defense by each of the 78 industries.

For the purpose of developing state level estimates, the DEIMS regional model data base was used. This data base is built upon estimates of the distribution of prime contract awards by budget category, industry and state, supplemented by state shares of total national output by industry based on County Business Patterns data from the Bureau of the Census.

The Defense Budget

The Defense Appropriations Act for fiscal year 1991 provides for total budget authority and outlays for fiscal years 1990 through 1995 as shown in Table 3.1. The Act also provides for an Operation Desert Shield supplement. The budget estimates were deflated to 1982 dollars and converted to a calendar year basis for use in the Interindustry Economic Research Fund's economic forecasting models. The estimates were also distributed among broad budget expenditure categories, as shown in Tables 3.2 and 3.3, on the basis of estimates provided in the administration's unified budget request submitted to Congress in January 1990. All of the estimates were extended to the year 2000 by assumption.

The Macroeconomic Context

The economic outlook for the U.S. economy is one of slow growth through the decade. Real GNP is projected to grow at an average annual rate of only 1.8 percent from 1990 to 2000 (see Table 3.4). The rate is slowest during the period 1993–1995 (1.55 percent per year) but

TABLE 3.1   Defense Budget Authority and Outlays, With Operation Desert Shield Supplement (billion dollars, selected fiscal years)

	1990	1991	1992	1993	1994	1995	2000
Defense Authorization Act							
Budget authority	301.6	289.1	291.6	291.8	292.0	295.0	344.5
outlays	296.3	297.0	295.0	292.0	290.0	291.0	332.8
Operation Desert Shield supplement							
Budget authority	—	15.0	—	—	—	—	—
Outlays		11.5	2.8	0.6	—	—	—
Contributions from other countries							
Budget authority	—	7.5	—	—	—	—	—
Outlays	—	5.8	1.4	0.6	—	—	—
Defense budget with supplement							
Budget authority	301.6	296.6	291.6	291.8	292.0	295.0	344.5
Outlays	296.3	302.8	296.4	292.3	290.0	291.0	332.8

TABLE 3.2 Defense Expenditures by Major Budget Category
(billion 1982 dollars, selected calendar years)

Expenditure Category	1990	1993	1995	1997	2000
Military personnel	66.5	61.3	56.8	53.8	52.6
Operation and maintenance	75.8	68.5	63.2	59.9	58.8
Procurement	70.1	56.0	50.4	48.6	49.3
Aircraft	23.3	19.2	17.2	16.3	16.0
Missiles	13.3	9.8	8.7	8.3	8.1
Weapons and tracked vehicles	2.6	1.8	1.6	1.5	1.5
Ammunition	1.9	1.4	1.2	1.1	1.1
Ships and conversions	9.5	8.4	7.6	7.9	9.0
Other	19.5	15.4	14.1	13.5	13.6
Research and development	32.8	23.8	21.9	20.9	20.5
Military construction and other	7.4	5.6	4.9	4.6	4.3
Total	252.6	215.2	197.2	187.8	185.5

TABLE 3.3 Defense Expenditures by Major Budget Category
(percent of total, selected calendar years)

Expenditure Category	1990	1993	1995	1997	2000
Military personnel	26.3	28.5	28.8	28.6	28.4
Operation and maintenance	30.0	31.8	32.0	31.9	31.7
Procurement	27.8	26.0	25.6	25.9	26.6
Aircraft	9.2	8.9	8.7	8.7	8.6
Missiles	5.3	4.6	4.4	4.4	4.4
Weapons and tracked vehicles	1.0	0.8	0.8	0.8	0.8
Ammunition	0.8	0.7	0.6	0.6	0.6
Ships and conversions	3.8	3.9	3.9	4.2	4.9
Other	7.7	7.2	7.2	7.2	7.3
Research and development	13.0	11.1	11.1	11.1	11.1
Military construction and other	2.9	2.6	2.5	2.4	2.3
Total	100.0	100.0	100.0	100.0	100.0

TABLE 3.4 Key Macroeconomic Variables (units as shown, selected years)

	1990–1993	1993–1995	1990–1995	1995–2000	1990–2000
Real GNP (expected growth rates)	1.65	1.55	1.61	1.92	1.77
PCE Deflator (expected growth rates)	3.76	3.23	3.55	2.80	3.17
Productivity (expected growth rates)	0.79	0.87	0.82	1.03	0.93
	1990	1993	1995	1997	2000
Unemployment rate (percent)	5.13	4.97	5.25	5.32	5.23
3-month Treasury Bill rate (%)	7.60	6.57	5.99	5.56	6.29
Foreign crude oil price ($/barrel)	18.37	19.74	22.09	23.65	26.01
Average domestic/foreign price	0.96	0.92	0.90	0.89	0.87
Defense share of GNP (percent)	6.10	4.96	4.40	4.03	3.76
Federal government surplus/deficit (billion 1982 $)	−212.54	−141.41	−65.81	−2.00	63.49

picks up to almost 2 percent per year in the second half of the decade. Slow growth in private sector labor productivity is a key factor, not mitigated by improvements in the terms of trade or by the relatively low inflation rates. Unemployment rates hover around the 5 percent level. The average annual foreign crude oil price climbs nearly $8 a barrel over the decade. The decline in defense expenditures, whose share of GNP falls from 6.1 percent in 1990 to 3.8 percent by 2000, is the main factor reducing the federal government budget deficit from more than $200 billion in 1990 to $2 billion in 1997. Surpluses are projected for the second half of the decade.

Direct and Indirect Impacts on Industrial Output

The distribution of expenditures across the major budget categories dictates the distribution of expenditures across supplying industries. For example, expenditures from the military personnel account are largely wages and salaries paid to the uniformed services and hence do not directly affect suppliers of goods and services. However, the indirect effects through personal consumption expenditures from these wages and salaries are an important component of the estimates of total defense impacts. Operations and maintenance (O&M) expenditures are for travel and transportation, energy, spare parts, other supplies, and civilian personnel pay. The O&M purchases of goods and services are directed to suppliers of defense capital equipment of which the aerospace, electronics and ordnance industries are the largest. Business services and the research arms of major defense industries are the primary recipients of expenditures for research and development. Suppliers of construction materials and the construction industry itself benefit from military construction expenditures.

Table 3.5 shows the estimated direct purchases for defense from individual industries in 1990 and 1995. The table also shows the total impact of defense expenditures on each industry after taking into account both the direct and indirect consequences. For example, the total impact measures not only the amount of ferrous metals purchased directly by the Department of Defense, but also the amount of ferrous metals embodied in all other purchases for defense—in aircraft, ships, communications equipment, and so on. The total impact also measures purchases arising indirectly as the result of personal consumption expenditures from wages and salaries paid to military and civilian personnel.

Table 3.5 also displays the total output of each industry and the defense share of that total output. As can be seen, for some industries

TABLE 3.5 Summary of Defense Expenditures and Industry Output, 1990 and 1995 Defense Budget Resolution Forecast—December 1990 (billion 1990 dollars, except as noted)

Industry	1990				1995			
	Defense Direct	Defense Total	Total Output	Defense Share of Total Output (%)	Defense Direct	Defense Total	Total Output	Defense Share of Total Output (%)
Agriculture	34.2	3,703.3	245,507.2	1.5	27.6	2956.5	266,380.8	1.1
Iron mining	0.0	190.2	4,105.8	4.6	0.0	133.5	4,157.5	3.2
Nonferrous metals	13.9	185.8	4,693.2	4.0	10.4	146.1	4,921.8	3.0
Coal mining	53.8	913.5	29,060.3	3.1	31.4	691.0	30,804.8	2.2
Crude petroleum natural gas	0.0	6,191.3	105,995.6	5.8	0.0	4,939.5	103,684.5	4.8
Nonmetallic mining	0.0	524.9	13,800.9	3.8	0.0	397.5	14,760.2	2.7
Construction	15,611.7	22,127.4	344,117.1	6.0	11,661.0	16,733.9	406,534.1	4.1
Food and tobacco	298.4	8,197.9	435,323.4	1.9	241.2	6,611.0	461,483.2	1.4
Textiles	113.3	2,038.5	62,311.9	3.3	93.8	1,630.9	70,702.0	2.3
Knitting	0.0	1,599.1	15,744.2	10.2	0.0	1,308.0	16,195.7	8.1
Apparel	1,096.2	1,689.1	68,994.8	2.4	900.2	1,358.0	75,601.7	1.8
Paper	118.9	3,531.1	119,232.7	3.0	96.8	2,831.5	130,086.3	2.2
Printing	548.7	4,089.7	172,334.5	2.4	443.8	3,317.7	185,069.3	1.8
Chemicals	3,100.8	11,359.6	279,164.5	4.1	2,375.4	9,012.9	316,903.0	2.8
Petroleum refining	7,648.3	14,028.5	194,914.6	7.2	6,594.0	11,554.7	201,303.2	5.7
Ordnance accessor	21,791.5	23,737.9	31,672.7	74.9	14,715.7	16,224.2	25,463.8	63.7
Rubber plastic	498.6	4,517.8	110,870.4	4.1	378.7	3,684.9	133,218.9	2.8
Shoes	14.1	561.9	7,934.9	7.1	11.5	457.2	7,343.7	6.2
Lumber	94.3	1,747.3	77,645.9	2.3	87.0	1,398.9	89,945.9	1.6
Furniture	197.3	929.4	42,507.0	2.2	158.0	753.8	46,573.8	1.6
Stone, clay, glass	111.0	2,611.2	62,926.7	4.1	96.0	2,058.0	70,530.7	2.9
Ferrous metals	503.8	4,709.7	77,239.0	6.1	405.5	3,369.7	79,165.0	4.3
Nonferrous metals	24.7	4,034.3	61,478.2	6.6	20.8	3,070.8	71,043.5	4.3
Metal products	2,414.6	8,887.6	163,042.4	5.5	1,958.3	7,120.8	187,132.6	3.8
Engines and turbines	1,209.4	1,676.4	17,850.3	9.4	862.8	1,262.9	23,228.1	5.4

	30.5	99.3	14,237.1	0.7	25.6	83.7	18,785.4	0.4
Agricultural machinery	296.6	598.0	22,666.3	5.6	229.6	480.9	30,786.0	1.6
Construction, mining, oilfield equipment	203.4	1,321.3	26,756.9	4.9	146.9	1,014.2	32,324.9	3.1
Metalworking machinery	106.3	277.3	18,231.1	1.5	70.1	210.3	21,111.1	1
Special incustry machinery	770.1	3,898.8	67,955.2	5.7	594.1	3,096.8	83,351.1	3.7
Non electrical machinery	943.1	1,228.3	68,639.6	1.8	740.8	977.6	90,735.1	1.1
Computers, office equipment	111.7	668.3	27,771.2	2.4	86.2	532.5	30,873.6	1.7
Service, industry machinery								
Radio, TV, communication equipment	26,542.9	36,551.1	144,456.7	25.3	19,097.4	27,715.8	185,205.1	15.0
Electrical appliances	1,597.8	2,834.2	39,465.6	7.2	1,210.6	2,222.0	46,763.6	4.8
Household appliances	28.5	424.4	19,228.5	2.2	21.1	349.6	226,730	1.5
Electrical lighting and wiring	793.6	1,930.9	41,613.1	4.6	633.1	1,538.0	50,221.7	3.1
Motor vehicles	2,005.6	5,936.4	223,965.4	2.7	1,463.0	4,625.0	238,462.2	1.9
Aerospace	35,380.4	51,308.3	98,894.5	41.8	24,945.8	29,091.6	104,398.5	27.9
Other transportation equipment	11,339.5	11,844.6	23,912.6	49.5	8,971.2	9,375.6	22,937.9	41.1
Instruments	3,202.1	4,601.5	69,422.6	6.6	2,538.9	3,662.5	82,584.3	4.4
Miscellaneous manufacturing	118.7	1,179.0	34,451.9	3.4	97.1	953.8	37,966.9	2.5
Transportation services	8,205.4	19,706.0	340,539.6	5.8	6,441.9	15,827.3	377,316.8	4.2
Communication services	1,302.7	6,441.2	215,631.2	3.0	1,005.4	5,400.1	247,865.8	2.2
Utilities	2,833.2	11,500.4	314,760.2	3.7	2,293.5	9,191.2	331,350.2	2.8
Wholesale, retail trade	3,996.3	29,748.6	1,013,314.4	2.9	3,139.4	23,846.3	1,105,574.9	2.2
Eating and drinking	812.7	5,435.8	213,190.6	2.5	682.5	4,484.6	215,160.1	2.1
Finance and insurance	94.6	13,313.0	497,576.0	2.7	80.0	10,803.4	528,257.6	2.0
Real estate rental	1,112.2	26,508.2	908,236.1	2.9	740.0	21,435.2	981,170.0	2.2
Hotels	1,835.4	6,414.9	146,647.7	4.4	1,516.0	5,174.1	155,729.5	3.3
Business services	15,551.6	44,950.8	792,301.4	5.7	12,627.5	36,961.9	902,503.1	4.1
Auto repairs	902.0	5,118.3	148,364.0	3.4	764.9	42,136	162,407.2	2.6
Movies and amusements	631.3	2,326.4	95,440.6	2.4	539.6	1,960.8	105,283.3	1.9
Medicine education npo	4,103.7	18,307.7	655,799.7	2.8	2,974.0	14,624.9	691,295.6	2.1
Government enterprises	563.8	2,169.4	70,457.6	3.1	436.0	1,622.6	70,899.4	2.3
Unimportant industrial	0.0	1,575.2	14,703.5	10.7	0.0	1,207.8	14,402.1	8.4
Scrap and used	56.3	172.9	22,851.1	0.8	36.7	115.0	27,501.3	0.4
Government industry	106,125.7	106,125.7	565,814.8	18.8	92,659.7	92,659.7	571,504.9	16.2

the estimated 1990 defense share of total output is quite large—75 percent of the ordnance and accessories industry output; 50 percent of the other transportation equipment industry output; 42 percent of the aerospace industry output; and 25 percent of the radio, TV and communication equipment industry output. The estimates for 1995 indicate that the defense share of industry output is projected to decline for all industries. For two industries the decline is substantial and largely accounts for declines in total industry output. These are the ordnance and accessories and other transportation equipment industries. The latter produces ships and tanks. In addition, the aerospace and communications equipment industries will struggle as a result of the declines in defense purchases.

Regional Impacts

Table 3.6 shows state shares of national direct, indirect and total defense expenditures, along with state shares of total national output, and the defense shares of total state output in 1990. As can be seen, California is the runaway winner with more than 20 percent of total direct purchases for defense—nearly double the state's share of total output nationwide. California's share of total indirect impacts of defense expenditures is also large, more than 14 percent. Defense accounts directly and indirectly for more than 8 percent of California's total output. Other large suppliers of defense goods and services are Texas (7.2 percent), Virginia (6.8 percent), Florida (4.7 percent), and New York (4.5 percent). These same states receive the largest indirect impacts as well. With regard to the relative importance of defense to the individual state economies, a slightly different ordering of states emerges. Alaska, Hawaii and Virginia rely on direct and indirect purchases for defense for more than 12 percent of total output in their states. Other states in which defense plays a particularly important role are Washington (9.5 percent), Mississippi (8.7 percent), Maryland (8.3 percent), and California (8.2 percent). Defense expenditures are least important to the economies of Iowa, West Virginia, and Wisconsin, where they account for less than 3 percent of total state output.

Tables 3.7 and 3.8 translate the assumptions about declining defense spending into annual percentage growth rates for direct defense expenditure and for the impact (direct and indirect) of defense spending at the state level. While the percentage paths differ between states, the figures show greater uniformity than the absolute figures shown in Tables 3.5 and 3.6. Even if the cutbacks are made with the objective of making them proportional so that the growth rates

TABLE 3.6 Summary of Defense Expenditure Impacts by State, 1990

State	Percent of Defense Direct	Percent of Defense Indirect	National Defense Total	Percent of Total Output	Defense Percent of State
Alabama	1.50	1.68	1.58	1.40	6.35
Alaska	0.55	0.45	0.50	0.23	12.12
Arizona	1.41	1.24	1.33	1.29	5.81
Arkansas	0.58	0.75	0.66	0.88	4.22
California	20.02	14.16	17.23	11.79	8.24
Colorado	1.78	1.53	1.49	1.56	5.39
Connecticut	2.63	1.84	2.26	1.61	7.88
Delaware	0.22	0.34	0.28	0.38	4.13
District of Columbia	0.78	0.69	0.74	0.72	5.76
Florida	4.68	3.68	4.20	4.44	5.33
Georgia	2.86	2.80	2.83	2.69	5.92
Hawaii	1.20	1.01	1.11	0.51	12.32
Idaho	0.15	0.24	0.19	0.35	3.08
Illinois	1.85	3.47	2.62	4.63	3.19
Indiana	1.65	2.14	1.88	2.22	4.79
Iowa	0.38	0.64	0.49	1.08	2.55
Kansas	1.35	1.23	1.29	1.03	7.05
Kentucky	0.94	1.22	1.07	1.21	5.00
Louisiana	1.51	1.71	1.60	1.5	5.68
Maine	0.63	0.57	0.60	0.44	7.74
Maryland	2.95	2.66	2.81	1.92	8.25
Massachusetts	2.95	2.66	2.81	2.68	5.91
Michigan	1.38	2.81	2.06	3.73	3.11
Minnesota	0.94	1.23	1.08	1.82	3.33
Mississippi	1.37	1.14	1.26	0.82	8.65
Missouri	2.92	2.13	2.55	2.12	6.76
Montana	0.15	0.19	0.17	0.26	3.69
Nebraska	0.35	0.52	0.43	0.64	3.77
Nevada	0.26	0.25	0.25	0.41	3.46
New Hampshire	0.40	0.43	0.41	0.44	5.28
New Jersey	2.26	3.01	2.62	3.42	4.32
New Mexico	0.66	0.60	0.63	0.50	7.14
New York	4.52	4.30	4.42	7.16	3.47
North Carolina	1.85	2.83	2.32	2.81	4.64
North Dakota	0.19	0.21	0.20	0.22	5.07
Ohio	2.82	3.86	3.31	4.38	4.27
Oklahoma	1.11	1.54	1.31	1.19	6.23
Oregon	0.32	0.58	0.44	0.95	2.62
Pennsylvania	3.08	4.15	3.59	4.58	4.41
Rhode Island	0.34	0.44	0.36	0.40	5.50
South Carolina	1.51	1.76	1.63	1.34	6.85
South Dakota	0.14	0.20	0.17	0.26	3.60
Tennessee	0.94	1.44	1.18	1.80	3.69
Texas	7.21	7.47	7.34	7.17	5.77
Utah	0.74	0.82	0.78	0.64	6.87
Vermont	0.11	0.17	0.14	0.20	4.04
Virginia	6.78	5.55	6.19	2.90	12.04
Washington	3.26	2.45	2.87	1.71	9.46
West Virginia	0.17	0.35	0.26	0.49	2.94
Wisconsin	0.61	1.35	0.96	0.98	2.75
Wyoming	0.13	0.21	0.17	0.21	4.54

TABLE 3.7   Summary of Direct Purchases for Defense by State, 1990 to 1995
(exponential annual growth rates)

	1990	1991	1992	1993	1994	1995
Alabama	−1.05	−1.96	−5.58	−5.15	−4.34	−3.14
Alaska	−2.35	−0.75	−5.52	−5.54	−4.96	−3.87
Arizona	−1.56	−3.57	−6.01	−5.22	−4.03	−3.24
Arkansas	−1.32	−2.21	−4.90	−4.99	−4.05	−3.13
California	−1.35	−4.89	−7.35	−6.09	−4.65	−3.70
Colorado	−1.45	−2.47	−5.64	−4.86	−4.07	−3.11
Connecticut	−1.86	−4.45	−6.60	−7.83	−5.18	−3.86
Delaware	−0.96	−0.14	−4.43	−4.66	−4.04	−3.21
District of Columbia	−0.74	−1.15	−5.91	−5.61	−5.07	−3.71
Florida	−1.32	−2.79	−5.35	−4.95	−3.96	−2.98
Georgia	−2.31	−1.72	−6.06	−5.64	−4.52	−3.49
Hawaii	−2.64	−0.23	−4.96	−5.32	−4.89	−3.71
Idaho	−2.34	−0.30	−3.82	−3.94	−3.52	−2.62
Illinois	−1.69	−2.20	−5.79	−5.55	−4.67	−3.54
Indiana	−2.55	−4.88	−6.67	−5.94	−4.90	−3.69
Iowa	−1.19	−3.78	−6.16	−5.59	−4.43	−3.38
Kansas	−2.39	−3.17	−6.88	−5.97	−4.68	−3.80
Kentucky	−1.88	−0.01	−4.70	−4.98	−4.53	−3.47
Louisiana	−1.01	−1.47	−3.23	−6.69	−4.79	−3.15
Maine	−0.41	−1.64	−2.60	−7.34	−5.15	−3.01
Maryland	−0.58	−2.50	−6.01	−5.70	−4.72	−3.40
Massachusetts	−0.47	−6.03	−7.80	−6.10	−4.82	−3.84
Michigan	−2.30	−4.97	−6.75	−5.62	−4.54	−3.64
Minnesota	−1.04	−6.00	−7.21	−5.87	−4.46	−3.79
Mississippi	−0.83	−2.02	−2.84	−7.40	−5.13	−3.17
Missouri	−2.15	−4.57	−7.86	−6.64	−4.83	−3.95
Montana	−1.86	−0.26	−4.70	−4.68	−4.03	−3.06
Nebraska	−2.49	−0.12	−4.29	−4.50	−4.08	−3.17
Nevada	−1.85	−0.15	−3.35	−3.37	−2.99	−2.24
New Hampshire	−0.88	−4.40	−6.43	−5.74	−4.58	−3.30
New Jersey	−0.63	−3.26	−6.19	−5.81	−4.88	−3.57
New Mexico	−1.14	−1.09	−5.22	−4.79	−4.13	−3.12
New York	−1.31	−4.80	−7.03	−6.60	−4.97	−3.80
North Carolina	−2.99	−0.61	−4.25	−4.56	−4.25	−3.31
North Dakota	−3.34	−0.67	−5.07	−5.18	−4.74	−3.84
Ohio	−1.26	−4.63	−7.36	−6.11	−4.82	−3.73
Oklahoma	−1.70	0.02	−4.67	−4.92	−4.38	−3.20
Oregon	−0.81	−1.12	−3.86	−4.30	−3.34	−2.27
Pennsylvania	−0.43	−2.97	−5.64	−6.13	−4.81	−3.50
Rhode Island	−1.12	−1.99	−5.76	−5.33	−4.44	−3.34
South Carolina	−2.16	0.16	−4.57	−4.74	−4.10	−3.18
South Dakota	−3.00	−0.41	−4.74	−4.86	−4.35	−3.45
Tennessee	−0.16	−1.52	−4.68	−4.79	−4.06	−2.96
Texas	−1.60	−2.01	−5.72	−5.21	−4.21	−3.33
Utah	−0.23	−1.15	−5.58	−5.57	−4.93	3.41
Vermont	−1.50	−4.48	−6.01	−5.43	−3.95	−3.58
Virginia	−1.19	−1.05	−4.30	−5.68	−4.69	−3.26
Washington	−1.18	−4.81	−6.48	−6.00	−4.54	−3.39
West Virginia	−0.44	−1.70	−4.74	−4.67	−3.98	−2.77
Wisconsin	−2.12	−3.93	−3.81	−5.92	−4.66	−3.24
Wyoming	−1.81	0.53	−4.74	−4.66	−4.00	−3.23
United States	−1.41	−3.18	−6.05	−5.79	−4.58	−3.48

TABLE 3.8 Summary of Total Impacts of Expenditures for Defense by State, 1990 to 1995 (exponential annual growth rates)

	1990	1991	1992	1993	1994	1995
Alabama	−1.83	−1.94	−5.59	−5.41	−4.59	−3.44
Alaska	−2.40	−0.65	−5.09	−5.27	−4.75	−3.59
Arizona	−2.13	−3.31	−6.09	−5.49	−4.31	−3.47
Arkansas	−2.14	−2.24	−5.51	−5.57	−4.67	−3.57
California	−1.76	−3.96	−6.66	−5.79	−4.50	−3.54
Colorado	−2.08	−2.26	−5.70	−5.29	−4.49	−3.40
Connecticut	−1.99	−4.26	−6.54	−6.89	−4.69	−3.58
Delaware	−1.65	−1.30	−5.15	−5.24	−4.58	−3.45
District of Columbia	−1.12	−1.00	−5.22	−5.13	−4.57	−3.28
Florida	−1.87	−2.60	−5.69	−5.45	−4.46	−3.43
Georgia	−2.34	−1.76	−5.81	−5.59	−4.66	−3.53
Hawaii	−2.37	−0.13	−4.61	−5.06	−4.69	−3.44
Idaho	−2.49	−1.30	−5.09	−5.16	−4.48	−3.38
Illinois	−2.19	−2.51	−5.70	−5.46	−4.47	−3.41
Indiana	−2.70	−3.99	−6.34	−5.78	−4.63	−3.59
Iowa	−2.04	−3.13	−6.01	−5.64	−4.59	−3.42
Kansas	−2.44	−2.86	−6.46	−5.77	−4.68	−3.66
Kentucky	−2.20	−0.85	−5.00	−5.21	−6.63	−3.49
Louisiana	−2.27	−1.80	−4.53	−6.24	−4.85	−3.51
Maine	−1.26	−1.73	−3.81	−6.45	−4.90	−3.19
Maryland	−1.23	−2.36	−5.73	−5.51	−4.56	−3.32
Massachusetts	−1.26	−4.77	−6.79	−5.68	−4.41	−3.46
Michigan	−2.51	−3.60	−6.22	−5.57	−4.60	−3.59
Minnesota	−1.65	−4.38	−6.56	−5.69	−4.37	−3.55
Mississippi	−1.50	−2.07	−4.00	−6.61	−4.93	−3.31
Missouri	−2.17	−3.80	−7.03	−6.15	−4.62	−3.70
Montana	−2.40	−0.98	−5.21	−5.30	−4.62	−3.50
Nebraska	−2.51	−1.00	−4.90	−5.05	−4.47	−3.36
Nevada	−2.38	−1.03	−4.82	−4.90	−4.33	−3.30
New Hampshire	−1.78	−3.86	−6.18	−5.65	−4.41	−3.35
New Jersey	−1.48	−2.82	−5.78	−5.50	−4.56	−3.38
New Mexico	−1.82	−1.27	−5.32	−5.16	−4.50	−3.38
New York	−1.65	−4.31	−6.62	−6.06	−4.53	−3.50
North Carolina	−2.71	−1.10	−4.81	−5.04	−4.58	−3.44
North Dakota	−2.96	−0.76	−4.93	−5.12	−4.67	−3.56
Ohio	−2.00	−3.76	−6.62	−5.85	−4.66	−3.61
Oklahoma	−2.63	−0.78	−5.07	−5.24	−4.64	−3.46
Oregon	−1.97	−2.39	−5.41	−5.49	−4.39	−3.31
Pennsylvania	−1.56	−2.75	−5.65	−5.78	−4.62	−3.46
Rhode Island	−1.82	−2.08	−5.50	−5.36	−4.45	−3.42
South Carolina	−2.33	−0.63	−4.91	−5.10	−4.49	−3.39
South Dakota	−2.70	−0.96	−4.98	−5.16	−4.68	−3.45
Tennessee	−1.58	−2.19	−5.53	−5.45	−4.58	−3.45
Texas	−2.43	−2.08	−5.75	−5.49	−4.55	−3.57
Utah	−1.24	−1.45	−5.39	−5.35	−4.69	−3.33
Vermont	−2.48	−4.13	−6.07	−5.41	−3.88	−3.42
Virginia	−1.59	−0.97	−4.51	−5.46	−4.67	−3.30
Washington	−1.66	−3.89	−6.35	−5.88	−4.56	−3.48
West Virginia	−2.22	−2.59	−5.81	−5.70	−4.75	−3.61
Wisconsin	−2.42	−3.15	−5.19	−5.74	−4.61	−3.36
Wyoming	−3.25	−0.55	−5.21	−5.29	−4.65	−3.67
United States	−1.93	−2.79	−5.87	−5.65	−4.57	−3.48

will not differ much, their absolute impact will differ greatly between states.

This chapter has demonstrated an input-output–based calculation of the impacts of arms reduction in the U.S. economy. The input-output tool and related data disaggregation permit a highly detailed measurement of the impact of reduced defense spending by industry and by state.

4

Computational Analysis of the Sectoral Effects on U.S. Trade and Employment of Unilateral and Multilateral Reductions in Military Expenditures

Jon D. Haveman, Alan V. Deardorff, and Robert M. Stern

Introduction

The original impetus for our research was to analyze some possible economic effects of a "peace dividend." While the onset of armed conflict in the Gulf diverted attention away from the idea of a peace dividend, there is reason to believe—now that the conflict is over—that there will be continuing pressure to reduce and to restructure defense spending. The purpose of this chapter is to investigate the possible sectoral impacts on trade and employment in the United States that might be experienced as a result of an across-the-board reduction in military spending.[1] We do not address the effects of a restructuring of military expenditures.

Using the computational general equilibrium (CGE) Michigan Model of World Production and Trade, we first investigate the impact of a 25 percent unilateral reduction in military spending for the United States alone and subsequently examine a 25 percent multilateral reduction in military spending in all of the major Western industrialized and developing countries. An important advantage in using the Michigan Model is the sectoral detail that it provides. In this chapter, we perform a variety of computational experiments that take into account different compensating macroeconomic policies and that enable us to compare the sectoral effects involved. Further, the Michigan Model allows us to extend previous studies by incorporating the effects of international trade and by allowing for price and exchange rate responses as well as primary input substitution possibilities. It is hoped that these additional elements will provide a richer insight into the sectoral effects stemming from possible reductions in military expenditures than has been provided by earlier research.[2]

Previous work has generally compensated for changes in military expenditures by changing nonmilitary government purchases. However, as discussed below, prior episodes of substantial reductions in U.S. military expenditures did not follow this path. We therefore assume that reductions in government military spending will be compensated by shifting expenditures to various components of final demand including nondefense government spending, private consumption, investment, and a pro rata reallocation across all nondefense sectors.

The chapter is divided as followes. In the next section, we present a brief review of previous research. The following section presents a brief description of the Michigan Model and elements of it that are of particular importance to our study. The succeeding sections contain an explanation of and results for the unilateral reductions for the United States, and present the results for the multilateral experiments. We then provide some discussion of the implications of the results in the final section.

Previous Research

For the past 30 years, there have been a number of studies assessing the impact of defense spending on a nation's economy. The pioneer work was done by Leontief and associates in the early 1960s. The results of these studies have been fairly consistent, even though there has been a great deal of variation in methodology and country of analysis. Most studies find that reductions in military expenditures have a positive effect on an economy in terms of increased employment and, where modeled, increased GNP. The rest of this section will discuss several representative studies.

Leontief and Hoffenberg (1961) used input-output analysis to estimate the impact of a change in military expenditures on employment in 58 broad sectors of the U.S. economy. They analyzed a 20 percent reduction in military expenditures coupled with a compensating increase in nonmilitary forms of government spending. The net result was an increase of 288,040 workers in "business employment." This increase stemmed from a transfer of spending but no reduction in military personnel. The same experiment including a cut in personnel of 20 percent yielded a net reduction in employment of 120,758 workers. They, as do we, also provided results to facilitate the analysis of a shift toward other sectors of final demand, including consumption and investment among others. Their study was, however, performed in a framework with no modeling of international effects, price changes, or substitution possibilities.

Leontief et al. (1965) presented an analysis of the regional impact of a 20 percent reduction in military expenditures. This model assumed that final demand adjusts to maintain a constant level of employment in the aggregate U.S. economy. It therefore concentrated on the changing industrial and regional composition of employment.

Dunne and Smith (1984) used the econometrically based Cambridge Growth Project to calculate the impact of military spending on the U.K. economy. Their experiments involved a cut in military expenditures from 5 percent to 3.5 percent of GDP, the European average. These cuts were accompanied by matching increases in other forms of government spending. Their general conclusion was that this reduction in military expenditures would increase total employment by approximately 100,000 jobs.

There have been other studies, like ours that have employed CGE in an international framework. Liew (1985) used the ORANI model of Australia to assess the impact on international trade, prices, and GNP of a 10 percent increase in military expenditures. This increase was assumed to be compensated by a reduction in one of three other categories of government spending (i.e., health, education, or welfare), thereby holding total government expenditure constant. Although the results of these three experiments differed somewhat in direction and magnitude, the general message, although quantitatively small in each case, was that an increase in military expenditure would tend to reduce GNP and employment, and create a small merchandise trade deficit. The experiments were consistent in suggesting increased imports, and two of the three experiments suggested a reduction in exports. Liew's results are in line with the other studies mentioned, given the direction of change in military spending.

Overview of the Michigan Model

The theoretical structure and equations of the Michigan Model are described in detail in Deardorff and Stern (1986, pp. 9–36, 235–247; 1990, pp. 9–35). For our purposes here, we present a brief overview of the model and call attention to some of its features that are pertinent to the present analysis.

In designing the Michigan Model, the objective was to take into account as many of the microeconomic interconnections among industries and countries as possible. This disaggregated general equilibrium framework enables us to examine a variety of economic issues that most other computational models cannot address, either because they are too highly aggregated or because they are specified only in partial equilibrium terms. The current version of the model includes 22 tradable and 7 nontradable industries in 18 industrialized and 16 developing countries, plus an aggregate sector representing the rest of the world.[3] We use a base of 1980 data on trade, production, and employment for all 34 countries, plus constructed measures of the coverage of nontariff barriers (NTBs) for the 18 industrialized countries.

The model is best thought of as being composed of two parts: the country system and the world system. The country system contains separate blocks of equations for the individual tradable and nontradable sectors for each country, and the world system contains a single set of equations for individual tradable sectors for the world as a whole. The country blocks are used first to determine each country's supplies and demands for goods and currencies on world markets as functions of exogenous variables, world prices, and exchange rates. The supply and demand functions for each country are then combined to provide the input to the world system that permits world prices and exchange rates to be determined.

The world system is the less complicated of the two systems. We start with the export supply and import demand functions from the country equations, which depend on world prices and exchange rates. To get world prices we add these supplies and demands across all countries and set the difference equal to net demand from the rest of the world. To obtain exchange rates, where these are flexible, we add the value of excess supply across all of the industries in a country and equate the resulting trade balance to an exogenously given capital flow. Once we obtain the world prices for each tradable industry and the exchange rate for each country, we enter them back into the separate country blocks in order to determine the rest of the relevant country-specific variables.

The Michigan Model can be used to analyze the price and quantity responses to a number of exogenous changes in the world trading environment. These changes can be represented through the use of some 18 exogenous variables, each referring to a different change in the trading environment. For the current analysis, we use only two exogenous change variables, both representing particular kinds of shifts in demand. One is an interindustry shift variable that describes a reallocation of final demand across industries. The other is an intraindustry shift variable that captures a shift of demand within an industry from home-produced goods to imports.[4]

U.S. Unilateral Reductions in Military Expenditures

In this section, we consider the sectoral effects on U.S. trade and employment of a 25 percent unilateral reduction in military expenditures in the United States and discuss the implications of different assumptions regarding the macroeconomic policies accompanying such a reduction. The effects of a multilateral 25 percent reduction in military expenditures simultaneously in all of the major Western industrialized and developing countries included in the Michigan Model are considered in the following section. The results presented in this section are intended to facilitate the analysis of a broad spectrum of scenarios concerning the macroeconomic policies accompanying a reduction in U.S. military expenditures. We first provide some background of previous periods of reduced defense spending and then a description of the assumptions and theoretical implementation of the scenarios within the Michigan Model. The results of the various scenarios are presented at the end of this section.

Substantial reductions in defense spending are not new to the United States (Steuerle and Wiener 1990). The periods immediately following World War II, the Korean conflict, and the Vietnam War each saw a substantial de-emphasis of defense spending within the government budget and as a share of GNP. The immediate post–World War II years represent the largest decline, when defense spending fell from 39.1 percent to 3.7 percent of GNP between 1945 and 1948. The five years following the Korean and Vietnam wars each saw defense spending decline, but by the more modest amount, in both cases, of approximately 4 percent of GNP.

In periods of substantial restructuring of government spending, a question naturally arises: What happens to nonmilitary expenditures when military expenditures are reduced? There are principally three macroeconomic policies that could accompany a reduction in military expenditures: (1) increase other spending; (2) reduce taxes; or (3) reduce government borrowing. That is, first, policymakers could redistribute the expenditure to other forms of government spending such as human or physical resources. Second, the reduction in expenditure could be matched by a reduction in government receipts, thus increasing civilian consumption. Finally, the reduced expenditure could be used to reduce (increase) a budget deficit (surplus), reducing interest rates, and thereby stimulating investment. The three postwar periods experienced each of these policies, but in rather different combinations.

Table 4.1 provides a detailed account of the macroeconomic policies accompanying the demilitarization in each of the three periods noted above and the present period of reduced defense expenditures.

Column (1) shows the change in defense spending, and columns (2)–(4) display the accompanying changes in the other major components of the government budget. From column (4), it can be seen that each period is associated with falling budget deficits. In each of the postwar periods, 30 percent or more of the reduction in military spending was used to reduce the budget deficit. In the current period, the decline in the deficit exceeds the reduction in military spending.

In the years immediately after World War II and the Korean conflict, a significant portion of the reduced defense spending was used to offset federal government receipts, as displayed in column (3) of Table 4.1. The latter two time periods have, however, been associated, respectively, with a zero and positive change in receipts as a percent of GNP. The propensity for shifting expenditure from defense to human resources increased throughout the first three periods, whereas the current demilitarization is accompanied by a fall in human resources spending.[5]

As Steuerle and Wiener note, the late-Reagan–early-Bush era of reduced defense spending is rather uncharacteristic. The period from 1986 to 1989 witnessed a reduction in defense spending as a percent of GNP, a reduction in spending on human resources, an increase in total revenue, and a reduction in the deficit of almost four times the reduction in defense spending. The uncharacteristic nature of this period is not surprising given that this is the first large-scale peacetime demilitarization.

It is evident from these experiences that there have been a variety of macroeconomic responses to reductions in military expenditures. This

TABLE 4.1   Changes in the Composition of Postwar Government Spending

	Change in Percent of GNP			
Period	Military Expenditures (1)	Human Resources Spending (2)	Government Receipts (3)	Government Deficit (4)
World War II				
1945–1948	−35.4	3.1	−4.5	−27.1
Korean War				
1953–1958	−4.0	1.7	−1.4	−1.2
Vietnam War				
1968–1973	−3.6	2.3	0.0	−1.8
Recent				
1986–1989	−0.6	−0.5	0.8	−2.3

Source: Steuerle and Wiener (1990).

makes it difficult to determine what the appropriate strategy should be in modeling such expenditure reductions. The effect on the sectoral composition of trade and employment due to a reduction in defense spending depends crucially on the assumptions one makes about the accompanying macroeconomic policies. Because the Michigan Model does not formally allow for changes in interest rates or domestic taxes, the individual scenarios are implemented by exogenously altering the composition of final demand. In what follows, we make allowances accordingly for shifts in defense spending to several categories of final demand, including consumption, investment, nonmilitary government spending, and a pro rata shift across all sectors of nonmilitary final demand. We then examine separately the results of each shift.

Computational Experiments and Assumptions

We shall concentrate on the four scenarios just mentioned. Each scenario is based on an alternative redistribution of $64.8 billion in military expenditures, or 25 percent of the 1985 U.S. national defense budget.[6] This reduction is taken as a uniform percentage of the defense budget allocated to each of the 29 sectors being modeled. In the first scenario, the reduction in military spending is assumed to be absorbed proportionally by all three sectors of final demand: consumption, investment, and nonmilitary government expenditure. The second scenario redistributes spending from defense to other forms of government expenditure, maintaining constant levels of consumption and investment. The third scenario redistributes the spending across consumption while keeping other sources of final demand constant, and the fourth redistributes the spending across investment[7] while, again, maintaining a constant level of consumption and nonmilitary government purchases. In all runs, the $64.8 billion is allocated to each sector according to that sector's share in demand.[8] Although we do not suggest that any one of these experiments captures exactly what is likely happen, the linear nature of the model allows one to approximate any in-between cases.

In interpreting the results to follow, it is important to note the assumptions that are common to all scenarios:

1. The level of aggregate expenditure is constant.
2. Capital stocks are fixed for each industry, on the grounds that the time period under investigation is too short for changes in investment to be realized as additions to the capital stock.
3. Real wages are assumed to be flexible, i.e., labor markets are permitted to clear.

4. The U.S. Department of Defense is assumed to follow a "buy American" policy. All defense expenditure is assumed to have been allocated to domestic industry.
5. Exchange rates are modeled as flexible, except for a number of developing countries.

Some of these assumptions are in need of further explanation or justification. First, the assumption that aggregate expenditure is held constant is necessary because the microeconomic orientation of the Michigan Model makes it inappropriate for discussing macroeconomic phenomena such as the determination of aggregate expenditure or employment. Implicit within this assumption, and the form of each scenario, is that a dollar-for-dollar transfer is made. For example, with a reduction in the budget deficit it is assumed that investment changes by exactly the amount of the change in the deficit. Further effects of the changed interest rate would likely be changes in consumers' savings-consumption choices. Such effects are not represented explicitly in the Michigan Model.

A further consequence of the microeconomic nature of the model is assumption (3). Our results are all dependent on constant aggregate employment, which is assured by allowing for flexibility in real wages. There are alternative methods of maintaining constant employment, such as allowing the composition of final demand to adjust appropriately, but these adjustments would de-emphasize the role played by the differences in the distribution of military spending and the distribution of other sources of final demand.

Assumption (4), representing the "buy American" or "buy domestic" policy of the U.S. Department of Defense (DOD), is designed to reflect the preference given to domestic manufacturers and suppliers when contracts are signed and purchases are made. Given this preference, we believe that the average propensity of the DOD to import is significantly less than that of final and intermediate demand in the aggregate. Zero imports are thus assumed to be a more accurate representation of reality than is the aggregate average propensity to import.

Implementation of the policy experiments is conceptualized as a shift in the final demand for the output of each of the 29 sectors. The first step in each of the scenarios is to redistribute the reduction in military spending appropriately.[9] As noted above, defense purchases are assumed to be made entirely from domestic production. The shift of expenditure away from defense will therefore be accompanied by an exogenous increase in imports. As a result, we need to adjust the fraction of new expenditure that now goes toward the purchase of imported goods. We assume that each category of total demand in an industry purchases imports in the same percentages as that of final demand in that industry as a whole. More precise estimates could be made if a breakdown of imports by consumption, investment, and government purchases could be used, but unfortunately such data are not available.

Some Theoretical Considerations

Before looking at our computational results, it may be useful to describe some of the interactions that are present in the Michigan Model. A cut in defense expenditure has two effects. First, depending upon where defense expenditure was concentrated compared to the pattern of expenditure in the category of final demand to which that expenditure is shifted, total demand in some industries will rise and in other industries will fall. We will look at both cases in turn. Second, even in industries where total demand declines, and certainly in ones where demand expands, there is a shift from defense spending, which was devoted exclusively to home goods, to other demand that is spent partly on imports.

Consider, then, an industry in which there has been no defense spending in other sectors. The cut in defense spending will therefore, at initial prices, unambiguously increase total demand in that industry, as well as increase demands for both imported and home-produced goods there. As long as the world price and the exchange rate do not change, the prices of exports and imports in the sector will remain constant. However, the shift in demand in the home sector requires a price increase there, and this induces a further shift in both supply and demand for exports and imports. The demand for imports shifts up due to substitution away from higher priced home goods, and the supply of exports shifts down due to the higher prices of inputs from the home sector. Thus the result at this point is a rise in output in the home sector, a fall in exports, and a rise in imports.

These results could change somewhat, however, if there is a change in prices of exports and imports. If the country is large in the world market, then its increased net demand for imports will raise the world price. In addition, if the increase in net imports here applies to other industries as well, then the worsening of the trade balance will lead to a depreciation of the currency, which will also raise the domestic currency prices of traded goods. On the export side, a price increase for either of these reasons will tend to offset the decline in exports noted above, and may even lead exports in certain sectors to increase overall. On the import side, the possible price increase for these two reasons may in addition be enhanced by still another possibility. If the industry being considered is covered by a nontariff barrier, then the attempt to increase imports will lead to a rise in the tariff equivalent of the barrier, thus raising the price of imports still further. Thus, for three reasons the price of imports may rise, and if it does the changes will be further complicated and the end result therefore cannot be determined with certainty.

Consider now the opposite extreme case, where defense expenditure in an industry is cut substantially and only a small amount of new final demand is created in the same industry, thus reducing total demand. The demand curve in the home sector therefore shifts down while the demand curve for imports shifts slightly to the right. The price in the home market therefore falls in this case, and this shifts both the supply of exports and the demand for imports down. The results, therefore, are a rise in exports and a fall in imports (assuming that the initial increase in import demand is small compared to the effect of the drop in the home price).

Here again, there could be further adjustment of prices if there are changes in world prices, the exchange rate, or the tariff equivalent of a nontariff barrier, and in this case the effects would tend to go in the opposite direction from what we discussed earlier. However, because over the entire economy the defense cut replaces spending that was only in home sectors with other spending that goes partly to imports, the case of an exchange rate depreciation that was considered seems the much more likely one.

To sum up, our theoretical analysis suggests that home-sector prices will rise in some sectors and fall in others due to a shift of expenditure out of defense, with corresponding changes in home-sector outputs. As a first approximation, imports rise and exports fall in sectors where demand expands, and the opposite is likely where demand contracts. However, because of the overall shift toward imports with the cut in defense, the currency is likely to depreciate, and this tends to raise prices across the board.

Computational Results

The Michigan Model produces results for a wide range of variables that emerge from the calculations as percentage changes for each of the 29 sectors. Base-year data—from 1980 in this study—are then used to compute absolute changes for selected variables (e.g., exports, imports, and employment). In what follows we discuss all four scenarios, but emphasize the results of the first experiment, that of a shift from defense to all other sources of final demand. The other three scenarios will be discussed subsequently.

Scenario 1: Redistributing Spending Across Total Final Demand.
The aggregate results for the United States for each of the four
scenarios are presented in Table 4.2. Column (1) refers to the results of
redistributing spending across total civilian demand (i.e., consumption,
investment and nonmilitary government spending combined). It
appears that a 25 percent reduction in defense spending is fairly
painless in the aggregate. That is, there is a marginal reduction in
both exports and imports,[10] and only 0.6 percent of the U.S. labor force
would experience some dislocation.

The reduction in U.S. exports is not surprising. Domestic demand
increases in a majority of the tradable sectors. This increase in demand
will cause an increase in the home price for that industry, leading to a
substitution from production for export to production for home use, thus
reducing total exports. To understand the decrease in aggregate
imports, recall that defense expenditure is assumed to be spent entirely
in home sectors. Given that the shift of expenditure therefore involves
an exogenous increase in imports, it is somewhat surprising that
imports decline in the aggregate. One possible explanation is that the

TABLE 4.2 Summary of Effects on the United States Due to Shifts of 25 Percent
in Defense Spending

	Total Civilian Demand (1)	Nondefense Government (2)	Consumption (3)	Investment (4)	Multilateral Demilitarization (5)
Change in exports					
value (million $)	−380.4	−1197.9	−887.8	2303.1	−1531.0
percent	−0.2	−0.6	−0.4	1.1	−0.7
Change in imports					
value (million $)	−169.3	−912.0	−663.5	−2398.9	427.2
percent	−0.1	−0.5	−0.4	1.3	0.2
Labor dislocations[a]					
thousand person-years	575.6	456.7	734.5	808.2	596.2
percent	0.6	0.5	0.7	0.8	0.6
Terms of trade (percentage change)	0.05	0.07	0.05	0.02	0.12
Effective exchange rate (percentage charge)[b]	0.1	0.1	0.1	−0.2	0.2
Prices (percentage change)[c]	0.1	0.1	0.1	−0.1	0.2

[a]Refers to the sum of positive changes in home and export sectors within all industries.
[b]Positive = Appreciation.
[c]Index of import and home prices.

fall in the home price for a sector experiencing a reduction in demand is large enough to cause sufficient substitution away from imports in that sector so as to overwhelm the exogenously imposed increase. We will demonstrate in what follows that this is indeed what is happening.

The results discussed thus far are aggregates of the changes that take place in the underlying sectors of the U.S. economy. Tables 4.3 and 4.4 contain the sectoral results for the four experiments. Again, looking at the first scenario, it does not appear that any one industry will be seriously impacted.

Basic metal industries (ISIC 371 and 372), durable goods sectors (ISIC 381, 382, 383, 384, and 38A) and community, social and personal services (ISIC 9, which includes government employment) are the only sectors in which employment decreases significantly in percentage terms, as can be seen in partition (1) of Table 4.3. Only three sectors experience a significant decline in absolute employment. Employment in ISIC 9 falls by 329 thousand person-years, which is 1 percent of that sector's 1980 employment. Electric machinery (ISIC 383) and transport equipment (ISIC 384) each fall by roughly 2.8%, or 63 and 64 thousand person-years, respectively.

The aggregate figures for the change in imports, it turns out, tell a very misleading story, as can be seen in partition (1) of Table 4.4. Although imports fall in the aggregate, at the sectoral level imports actually rise, as expected, in all but a handful of sectors. It turns out, as documented in Haveman, Deardorff, and Stern (1990), that all sectors in which imports decline had a decrease in domestic demand. For two sectors in which demand falls, miscellaneous manufacturing (ISIC 38A) and nonelectric machinery (ISIC 382), the increases in imports are enough to outweigh the substitution effect resulting from the reduced home price. As a result, they each experience an increase in imports. This is the case for 16 of the 22 sectors modeled. Of the six remaining sectors experiencing a reduction in demand, five show a negligible decline in imports. The sixth, transportation equipment (ISIC 384), shows a decline of 4.4 percent or $1.4 billion. The decline in this sector alone is enough to offset the combined increase in the other sectors.

The sectoral changes in exports are much less surprising. As can be seen from partition (1) of Table 4.4, 19 of the tradable sectors experience a small decline in exports, with leather products (ISIC 323) experiencing the largest decline in percentage terms, 1.6 percent. The response of these sectors is consistent with the intuition described above. The remaining three sectors—agriculture (ISIC 1), footwear (ISIC 324), and electrical machinery (ISIC 382)—each produce more for export once expenditures are redistributed. Intuition would suggest that exports should increase in sectors experiencing a decrease in

TABLE 4.3 Net Changes in Employment in the United States Due to Shifting 25 Percent of Defense to Each of Four Scenarios

Industry	ISIC	Total Civilian Demand (1)		Nondefense Government (2)		Consumption (3)		Investment (4)	
		%	Thousand Person-years	%	Thousand Person-years	%	Thousand Person-years	%	Thousand Person-years
Traded goods									
Agriculture, forestry, and fishing	1	1.16	40.70	0.70	24.73	1.43	50.20	0.48	16.86
Food, beverage, and tobacco	310	1.53	27.75	-0.22	-4.06	2.26	40.80	0.19	3.38
Textiles	321	0.33	3.68	-0.76	-8.59	0.30	3.42	1.35	15.10
Wearing apparel	322	1.00	13.06	-0.61	-8.08	1.62	21.12	-0.06	-0.73
Leather products	323	0.40	0.37	-1.26	-1.16	0.56	0.51	1.19	1.09
Footwear	324	1.51	2.49	-0.35	-0.58	2.22	3.64	0.34	0.57
Wood products	331	0.33	1.93	0.55	3.23	-0.84	-4.96	4.89	27.91
Furniture and fixtures	332	1.40	6.91	0.25	1.22	0.99	4.91	4.01	19.55
Paper and paper products	341	0.31	2.32	-0.07	-0.50	0.36	2.68	0.45	3.31
Printing and publishing	342	0.57	8.25	0.80	11.53	0.70	10.11	-0.13	-1.82
Chemicals	35A	-0.31	-3.29	-0.46	-5.00	-0.38	-4.11	0.13	1.37
Petroleum and related products	35B	0.05	0.09	-0.37	-0.63	0.30	0.50	-0.56	-0.94
Rubber products	355	-0.74	-1.97	-1.25	-3.35	-0.82	-2.20	0.03	0.09
Nonmetallic mineral products	36A	0.25	1.28	0.61	3.09	-0.96	-4.90	4.86	24.03
Glass and glass products	362	-0.52	-1.00	-1.32	-2.59	-0.62	-1.20	0.57	1.10
Iron and steel	371	-1.63	-14.02	-2.31	-20.01	-2.13	-18.39	0.97	8.23
Nonferrous metals	372	-2.26	-7.67	-3.58	-12.27	-2.81	-9.56	1.10	3.67
Metal products	381	-1.68	-29.18	-1.91	-33.16	-2.30	-40.10	0.99	17.04
Nonelectric machinery	382	-0.65	-18.79	-1.46	-42.16	-1.56	-45.09	3.69	104.23
Electric machinery	383	-2.75	-63.26	-3.35	-77.21	-3.24	-74.69	-0.29	-6.60
Transportation equipment	384	-2.89	-64.11	-3.44	-76.38	-3.04	-67.47	-1.84	-40.53
Miscellaneous manufacturing	38A	-2.04	-35.27	-2.48	-42.86	-2.46	-42.61	0.00	-0.03
Total traded		-0.50	-129.74	-1.14	-294.80	-0.68	-177.39	0.79	196.87
Nontraded goods									
Mining and quarrying	2	0.10	0.93	-0.07	-0.73	0.08	0.80	0.29	2.83
Electric, gas, and water	4	1.23	17.24	0.59	8.33	1.80	25.13	-0.44	-6.17
Construction	5	0.70	43.30	1.31	80.99	-0.67	-42.00	5.73	346.42
Wholesale and retail trade	6	1.30	260.72	-0.47	-95.28	1.79	357.71	0.90	180.59
Transportation, storage, commerce	7	0.15	7.53	-0.39	-20.21	0.33	16.89	-0.11	-5.83
Finance, insurance, and real estate	8	1.56	129.11	0.03	2.28	2.26	186.25	0.14	11.85
Communications, social and personal services	9	-1.04	-329.09	1.02	319.41	-1.16	-367.40	-2.28	-726.56
Total nontraded		0.18	129.74	0.40	294.80	0.25	177.39	-0.24	-196.87
Total, all industries		0.01	0.00	0.01	0.00	0.01	0.00	0.02	0.00

TABLE 4.4 Net Percentage Changes in Trade in the United States Due to Shifting 25 Percent of Defense to Each of Four Scenarios

Industry	ISIC	Total Civilian Demand (1)		Nondefense Government (2)		Consumption (3)		Investment (4)	
		Exports	Imports	Exports	Imports	Exports	Imports	Exports	Imports
Traded goods									
Agriculture, forestry, and fishing	1	0.02	2.96	0.11	4.86	-0.01	3.27	0.08	0.21
Food, beverage, and tobacco	310	-1.35	2.13	-1.39	0.46	-1.84	3.05	0.67	-0.05
Textiles	321	-1.28	1.35	-2.09	0.23	-2.02	1.55	2.37	1.50
Wearing apparel	322	-1.08	2.98	-4.35	0.49	-1.71	4.53	4.33	-0.85
Leather produces	323	-1.61	2.95	-3.80	0.10	-2.61	4.38	4.41	-0.12
Footwear	324	0.18	2.52	-3.12	0.22	-0.17	3.76	4.48	-0.33
Wood products	331	-0.53	0.98	-0.83	1.16	-0.55	0.71	-0.19	1.91
Furniture and fixtures	332	-0.16	3.39	-1.57	1.65	-0.49	2.67	2.37	7.81
Paper and paper products	341	0.06	2.05	-0.82	2.59	-0.13	2.46	1.57	-0.02
Printing and publishing	342	-0.13	2.30	-0.73	4.05	-0.42	2.74	1.55	-0.87
Chemicals	35A	-0.05	1.42	-0.36	1.52	-0.20	1.89	0.78	-0.49
Petroleum and related products	35B	-0.15	1.11	-0.48	0.98	-0.27	1.55	0.62	-0.46
Rubber products	355	-0.27	1.15	-0.97	0.97	-0.52	1.90	1.33	-1.58
Nonmetallic mineral products	36A	-0.26	2.09	-0.96	2.44	-0.51	1.58	1.34	3.83
Glass and glass products	362	-0.23	1.50	-0.73	4.00	-0.51	1.44	1.28	-0.30
Iron and steel	371	-0.51	-0.68	-1.37	1.61	-1.18	-1.59	2.93	0.98
Nonferrous metals	372	-0.34	-0.56	-0.25	2.79	-1.30	-1.74	3.46	1.33
Metal products	381	-0.02	0.51	-0.71	-0.70	-0.30	-1.46	1.68	3.45
Nonelectric machinery	382	0.21	0.88	-0.35	-0.82	-0.08	-1.39	1.81	11.87
Electric machinery	383	-0.21	-1.73	-0.94	-2.96	-0.57	-2.72	1.85	3.36
Transportation equipment	384	-0.16	-4.35	-0.54	-5.74	-0.25	-4.79	0.55	-1.42
Miscellaneous manufacturing	38A	-0.04	0.09	-0.38	-0.27	-0.19	-0.46	0.84	2.61
Total traded		-0.19	-0.07	-0.58	-0.47	-0.43	-0.33	1.14	1.41

domestic demand. As noted above, this increase is a result of the fall in the home price. However, this only happens in one of the seven traded sectors in which domestic demand falls. In six of these sectors, the appreciation of the currency, combined with a fall in the world price, is sufficient to offset the effects of the fall in the home price.

Scenario 2: Redistributing Spending Across Nondefense Government Spending. The second scenario again reduces military expenditures by 25percent, but includes a compensating policy of increasing only nondefense-related government spending. In the aggregate, the employment effects of this alternative redistribution are not qualitatively different. This more directed distribution does, however, impact the traded sectors to a much larger extent than does the previous scenario. Exports fall by $1,197.9 million, three times the fall in scenario 1, and imports fall by $912.0 million, more than five times the reduction in scenario 1.

At the sectoral level, from partition (2) of Table 4.3, we can make several general comments regarding the employment changes. First, the burden of such a reduction appears to fall disproportionately on the traded sectors. There is a net transfer of 294,800 person-years from traded industries to nontraded industries. ISIC 9 appears to be driving this shift. These results reflect the larger fraction of nondefense government purchases that come from nontraded industries.[11] Second, it should be noted that the burden borne by the traded industries is heavier and more evenly distributed across industries than in scenario 1.

The sectoral impact on exports is more evenly distributed than previously and of a larger magnitude in each industry. The aggregate reduction in imports remains concentrated in the durable goods industries and is largely due to the disproportionately large reduction in demand for goods produced by the transportation equipment industry (ISIC 384).

Scenario 3: Redistributing Spending Across Consumption. The results of the third scenario reflect a shift in spending from defense to consumption. This shift is intended to represent a reduction in taxes as a response to reduced military expenditures.

The aggregate results in Table 4.2 are once again larger than those reported for scenario 1. The effect on employment is a dislocation of 734,500 workers. The impact on imports and exports is less severe than in scenario 2, but still larger than for the shift in scenario 1. Imports and exports each fall by 0.4 percent, or $663.5 million and $887.8 million, respectively.

This restructuring of final demand shows a slightly weaker impact on traded goods than did the previous scenario. As reported in Table 4.3, there is a shift of 177,400 person-years from traded to nontraded industries. This is, again, a reflection of the higher propensity of consumers to purchase nontraded goods relative to that of the DOD. Private consumers place a much greater emphasis on purchases from wholesale and retail trade (ISIC 6), and finance, insurance, and real estate (ISIC 8) than does the DOD. Partition 4.3 of Table 4.3 shows that employment in wholesale and retail trade (ISIC 6), and finance, insurance, and real estate (ISIC 8) increase significantly, whereas workers in the durable goods industries (ISIC 381, 382, 383, 384, and 38A) and ISIC 9 bear the brunt of the dislocations.

The sectoral impact on exports is uniformly negative, reflecting the currency appreciation and increased demand in most sectors. The impact on imports conforms to a priori expectations. In sectors where demand increases, imports increase and, conversely, imports fall in sectors with decreasing demand.

Scenario 4: Redistributing Spending Across Private Fixed Investment. The final unilateral scenario is a shift in spending to private fixed investment. This scenario is intended to mimic a reduction in the budget deficit accompanying a reduction in military expenditures. The reduced budget deficit presumably causes interest rates to fall and consequently encourages private fixed investment. The results for this scenario are strikingly different from the preceding ones. The increase in investment demands leads to an increase in both exports and imports. The number of worker dislocations is also largest for this type of a shift. It is noteworthy that demand increases significantly in only four sectors: furniture and fixtures (ISIC 332), nonelectric machinery (ISIC 382), construction (ISIC 5), and wholesale and retail trade (ISIC 6). This is due to the high level of concentration of investment expenditures. The expenditure in these four sectors is significantly greater than that of the remaining sectors.

The sectoral results present a very interesting picture. Partition (4) of Table 4.3 indicates that employment increases in 17 of the 22 traded sectors. This happens despite a decline in demand for 20 of the traded sectors. There is also a net transfer of 196,900 person-years from the nontraded sectors to the traded sectors.

The phenomenon of increasing employment accompanying decreasing domestic demand can be explained by the resulting change in exports, noted in partition (4) of Table 4.4. The declining domestic demand, resulting in a lower home price for the good, combined with a depreciation of the dollar leads to an increase in exports in all sectors, with the exception of wood products (ISIC 331). This increase in exports is in most cases sufficient to offset the employment effects of the reduced domestic demand.

The sectoral effects on imports are driven, to a large extent, by the exogenous increase caused by the shift away from defense purchases. Sectors not receiving an exogenous increase in imports generally experience a decline and, conversely, those with an exogenous increase generally experience increased imports.[12]

Summary. The results of the first three scenarios are qualitatively similar whereas the fourth is significantly different from the others. The first three scenarios suggest that the burden of shifting expenditures is disproportionately borne by the traded goods industries, whereas the fourth shifts the burden to nontraded industries. The linear nature of the model is reflected in the first scenario, which is a weighted average of the other three.

It should be noted in all the scenarios that military personnel are included in ISIC 9, which means that we assume the military employs workers in the same proportion as all other components of ISIC 9. The results presented above will thus under- or overstate the results according to the difference in labor as a fraction of spending in each component of ISIC 9. Nonetheless, correction for these inaccuracies would not change the qualitative nature of the results.

Multilateral Reductions in Military Expenditure

In this section, we present the results of an experiment similar to scenario 1 in the last section. This experiment involves a pro rata shift of 25 percent of 1985 military expenditures across all categories of final demand for 33 of the 34 countries included in the model.[13] The assumption that military expenditures in most countries are biased toward home-produced goods is less applicable for many countries than it is for the United States. Countries such as Australia simply do not possess the necessary industry to satisfy the demands of its government's military. The "buy domestic" assumption is, therefore, assumed to hold only for the United States.

In order to calculate the demand shift parameters for each of the 29 industries in each country, it was necessary to distribute the aggregate military expenditure and GNP data obtained across the industries modeled.[14] The distribution of GNP was accomplished through the use of the input-output tables already employed in the model. The aggregate obtained was distributed to replicate the share in final demand for each of the 29 sectors.

Leontief and Duchin (1983) provide estimates of the proportion of the ACDA data on aggregate military expenditures that correspond to 12 categories. We, in turn, concorded these categories to our industrial classification. They also provide estimates of the decomposition of the ACDA data by sector for 15 regions of the world. We used these regional breakdowns for each of the 33 countries to correspond to their location within the individual regions.[15]

Computational Results

The aggregate results for the United States of the multilateral 25 percent reduction in military expenditures are listed in column (5) of Table 4.2.[16] The employment dislocation of 596,200 person-years is quite similar to the case in unilateral scenario 1. The effects on U.S. exports and imports are, however, quite different. Exports decline more significantly, by $1,531.0 million, whereas imports increase by $427.2 million. The response of imports and exports is partially due to the larger appreciation of the dollar.

The sectoral results for the United States of the unilateral and multilateral experiments are presented for comparative purposes in Table 4.5. The direction of change in employment evidently remains the same, but the magnitudes are different. Within traded goods, the declines in employment are now larger and the increases in employment are smaller. There is an increase in the amount of labor (155,200 person-years) shifted from traded to nontraded industries, due primarily to the larger reduction in exports. The reduction in exports reflects the dollar appreciation and a decline in world prices. Global defense spending is primarily focused on the purchase of goods that are traded internationally, especially durable goods and basic metal industries. The multilateral reduction in defense spending thus reduces the world demand for traded goods. This reduced demand is then translated into lower world prices. In response to the lower prices, domestic producers shift away from export production to home production, thereby reducing exports.

The sectoral results for imports, partition (4) of Table 4.5, to the extent that they differ from those of the unilateral simulations, also reflect the lower world prices. Imports increase in 17 of the 22 sectors. Sectors with a decline in imports experience a smaller decline; the opposite holds true for sectors with a rise in imports. Recall that ISIC 384 was responsible for the bulk of the reduction in imports in the unilateral runs. The multilateral scenario produces a greater decline in the world price for ISIC 384, and consequently reduces the decline in imports by approximately 25 percent.

In the aggregate, a multilateral reduction in military spending thus appears to have a somewhat larger impact on the U.S. economy than does a unilateral reduction. At the sectoral level, although some industries may experience a larger impact, the differences appear to be fairly small.

TABLE 4.5 Comparison of Unilateral and Multilateral Results for the United States

Industry	ISIC	Employment (Percent Change)		Employment (Thousand Person-years)		Exports (Percent Change)		Imports (Percent Change)	
		Unilateral	Multilateral	Unilateral	Multilateral	Unilateral	Multilateral	Unilateral	Multilateral
Traded goods									
Agriculture, forestry, and fishing	1	1.16	1.50	40.70	52.50	0.02	0.20	2.96	2.67
Food, beverage, and tobacco	310	1.53	1.61	27.75	29.24	-1.35	-0.79	2.13	2.05
Textiles	321	0.33	0.22	3.68	2.51	-1.28	-1.53	1.35	1.33
Wearing apparel	322	1.00	0.86	13.06	11.21	-1.08	-4.06	2.98	3.45
Leather produce	323	0.40	0.15	0.37	0.14	-1.61	-2.65	2.95	3.02
Footwear	324	1.51	1.53	2.49	2.52	0.18	-0.51	2.52	2.62
Wood products	331	0.33	0.32	1.93	1.84	-0.53	-0.52	0.98	0.97
Furniture and fixtures	332	1.40	1.39	6.91	6.84	-0.16	-0.81	3.39	3.63
Paper and paper products	341	0.31	0.01	2.32	0.06	0.06	-1.88	2.05	2.27
Printing and publishing	342	0.57	0.54	8.25	7.73	-0.13	-1.08	2.30	2.74
Chemicals	35A	-0.31	-0.43	-3.29	-4.68	-0.05	-0.33	1.42	1.57
Petroleum and related products	35B	0.05	0.04	0.09	0.06	-0.15	-0.66	1.11	1.32
Rubber products	355	-0.74	-1.14	-1.97	-3.04	-0.27	-1.28	1.15	1.89
Nonmetallic mineral products	36A	0.25	0.18	1.28	0.91	-0.26	-0.96	2.09	2.43
Glass and glass products	362	-0.52	-0.97	-1.00	-1.90	-0.23	-1.16	1.50	1.67
Iron and steel	371	-1.63	-1.92	-14.02	-16.61	-0.51	-2.28	-0.68	-0.65
Nonferrous metals	372	-2.26	-2.88	-7.67	-9.82	-0.34	-2.13	-0.56	-0.65
Metal products	381	-1.68	-1.85	-29.18	-32.17	-0.02	-0.89	-0.51	-0.14
Nonelectric machinery	382	-0.65	-0.84	-18.79	-24.13	0.21	-0.45	0.88	1.01
Electric machinery	383	-2.75	-3.03	-63.26	-69.67	-0.21	-1.77	-1.73	-1.16
Transportation equipment	384	-2.89	-3.21	-64.11	-71.27	-0.16	-1.15	-4.35	-3.22
Miscellaneous manufacturing	38A	-2.04	-2.17	-35.27	-37.47	-0.04	-0.19	0.09	0.19
Total traded		-0.50	-0.59	-129.74	-155.19	-0.19	-0.74	-0.07	0.26
Nontraded goods									
Mining and quarrying	2	0.10	0.01	0.93	0.07				
Electric, gas and water	4	1.23	1.23	17.24	17.22				
Construction	5	0.70	0.75	43.30	46.15				
Wholesale and Retail Trade	6	1.30	1.23	260.72	265.77				
Transportation, storage, commerce	7	0.15	0.16	7.53	7.97				
Finance, insurance and real estate	8	1.56	1.61	129.11	133.57				
Communication, social and personal services	9	-1.04	-0.99	-329.09	-315.56				
Total nontraded		0.18	0.22	129.74	155.19				

Conclusions and Implications

In the long run, a reduction in defense spending is generally regarded to have a positive impact on the economy. In the short run, however, a reduction in defense outlays could result in unemployment and adjustment pressures in at least some sectors of the economy. In order to facilitate a smooth transition, government assistance, if deemed necessary, should be pointed in the right direction. The computational general equilibrium results that we have reported based on the Michigan Model are useful in assessing the sectoral impact of a reduction in military expenditures.

Public officials may be able to influence whether nondefense government, consumption, or investment spending expands in response to reductions in military spending. The decision of which policy to follow is largely outside the scope of this chapter. That is, whether reduced military spending is used to meet other federal spending needs, to reduce taxes and thus allow for higher consumption or personal savings, or to cut the federal deficit and thus increase domestic investment must be decided on the basis of many considerations not discussed here.

Although the impacts of a 25 percent unilateral or multilateral reduction in military expenditures do not appear to be large in the aggregate, our computational results suggest that the sectoral impacts differ significantly depending on the accompanying macroeconomic policy. It also appears that certain specific sectors may bear the brunt of the adjustment costs and therefore would be in need of assistance in the event that reduced military spending may in fact be carried out.

Notes

We are grateful to members of the Research Seminar in International Economics at the University of Michigan, Janet Netz, Peter Pauly, and Kenneth Reinert, for their helpful comments on earlier versions of this chapter. Financial assistance was provided in part by a grant from the Ford Foundation in support of a program of research in trade policy in the Institute of Public Policy Studies at the University of Michigan.

1. As will become clear from the discussion that follows, we can use our modeling framework to analyze increases as well as reductions in military spending.

2. There may, of course, be other effects at both the micro and aggregate levels that our modeling approach cannot capture. These effects include the dynamics of adjustment in goods and factor markets and possible impacts working through financial markets and changes in aggregate savings and

investment behavior. This suggests the need for a broader and more integrated modeling effort, which is unfortunately something beyond our capability at present.

3. The industries are listed in Table 4.3.

4. See Haveman, Deardorff, and Stern (1990) for a formal statement of the roles that these two shift parameters play in the model.

5. Human resources include spending on health and Medicare, income maintenance, Social Security, and education programs.

6. The use of a 1985 sectoral breakdown in military expenditures reflects the availability of the most recent input-output table for the United States. In performing the experiments we use the more disaggregated 1977 input-output table to represent technology. It is assumed that the technology represented there still held for 1985.

7. Investment is taken to be only gross private fixed investment. Changes in business inventories are considered to be of a more transitional nature and less sensitive to interest rate fluctuations, and hence not affected by a reduction in the budget deficit.

8. For example, in scenario 1, suppose sector 310 is 10 percent of total civilian demand. Then spending in sector 310 is assumed to increase by $6.48 billion. Similarly in scenario 3, if sector 310 is 10 percent of *consumption*, spending in sector 310 increases by $6.48 billion.

9. See Haveman, Deardorff, and Stern (1990) for details on the 1985 levels of consumption, investment, government nondefense, and defense spending and the sectoral changes in demand brought about by each of the scenarios.

10. Other experiments in which no "buy American" policy for defense is assumed yield similar but slightly stronger impacts on imports and exports.

11. Recall that the assumption regarding defense purchases was that, within industries, defense purchases were disproportionately from home suppliers. That a greater proportion of defense spending is from traded sectors is consistent with this assumption.

12. Recall that industries with positive investment purchases will receive an exogenous increase in imports, whereas those with no investment demand will not.

13. Data for Hong Kong are not available, so there is assumed to be no shift in demand within Hong Kong.

14. Data on aggregate military expenditures and gross national product for each country for 1985 were obtained from the U.S. Arms Control and Disarmament Agency (ACDA) publication, World Military Expenditures and Arms Transfers, 1987 edition. In some cases, the most recent available data were for 1984.

15. See Grobar and Stern (1989) and Grobar, Stern, and Deardorff (1990) for further details and estimates and analysis of the effects of international trade in armaments for 1980.

16. The effects on the other countries included in the Michigan Model will be addressed in future work.

References

Deardorff, Alan V. and Robert M. Stern. 1986. The Michigan Model of World Production and Trade: Theory and Applications. Cambridge, MA: MIT Press.

Deardorff, Alan V. and Robert M. Stern. 1990. Computational Analysis of Global Trading Arrangements. Ann Arbor, MI: University of Michigan Press.

Dunne, J. Paul and Ron P. Smith. 1984. "The Economic Consequences of Reduced UK Military Expenditure," Cambridge Journal of Economics 8: 297-310.

Grobar, Lisa M. and Robert M. Stern. 1989. "A Data Set on International Trade in Armaments for the Western Industrialized and Developing Countries for 1980: Sources and Methodological Issues," Weltwirtschaftliches Archiv 125: 748- 762.

Grobar, Lisa M., Robert M. Stern, and Alan V. Deardorff. 1990. "The Economic Effects of International Trade in Armaments in the Major Western Industrialized and Developing Countries," Defence Economics 1: 97-120.

Haveman, Jon D., Alan V. Deardorff, and Robert M. Stern. 1990. "Some Economic Effects of Unilateral and Multilateral Reductions in Military Expenditures in the Major Industrialized and Developing Countries," presented at the Annual Meeting of the American Economic Association, Conflict and Peace Economics II: Disarmament Effects and National Protection (Joint Session with the Peace Science Society), Washington, D.C. (December 28).

Leontief, W., and F. Duchin. 1983. Military Spending. New York: Oxford University Press.

Leontief, Wassily W., and Marvin Hoffenberg. 1961. "The Economic Effects of Disarmament," Scientific American 204.

Leontief, Wassily W., Alison Morgan, Karen Polenske, David Simpson, and Edward Tower. 1965. "The Economic Impact-Industrial and Regional-of an Arms Cut," The Review of Economics and Statistics 47.

Liew, L.H. 1985. "The Impact of Defence Spending on the Australian Economy," Australian Economic Papers 24: 326-36.

Steuerle, Eugene C. and Susan Wiener. 1990. "Spending the Peace Dividend: Lessons From History," Urban Institute Policy Paper.

United States Arms Control and Disarmament Agency. 1988. World Military Expenditures and Arms Transfers 1987. U.S. Government Printing Office.

5

Defense Burden Sharing and the Japanese Macroeconomy

Robert Dekle and John Makin

Introduction

International security arrangements are in flux. The advent of perestroika gave rise to hopes of decreased defense expenditures for the Allies, but the hopes appear partly dashed. If defense spending cannot be cut as much as we had hoped or if total Allied defense expenditures remain high, a re-examination of the existing security arrangements among the Allied nations seems to be in order.

This chapter focuses on Japan's role in providing for an Allied defense and on the impact of higher Japanese defense spending on Japanese economic growth. Currently, by the Japanese government's own calculations, Japan spends approximately 1 percent of its GNP on defense-related expenditures. Using a simple theory of public goods, this chapter suggests that for there to be an optimal supply of total allied defense, Japan should spend somewhat more on measures to promote world peace, and other Western countries might spend less.

In the next section, we consider theoretically the level of defense spending appropriate to Japan. We find that a country's defense spending will be higher, the lower the "costs" and the higher the "benefits" of such spending. The benefits of defense spending appear to be higher, the higher the productive capacity of a country. A country with a large productive capacity will have more to lose if its economy is destroyed by war. In the third section, we estimate one important "cost"—the impact of defense spending on economic growth. By diverting capital and labor from the private sector, defense spending may lower private sector output. We find that had Japan spent 6.5 percent of its GNP on defense, its annual economic growth rate would have been lower by between 0.5 and 1.0 percentage points.

The "Appropriate" Level of
International Burden Sharing for Japan

When Japan's defense expenditures are made consistent with the NATO definition of defense spending, Japan's defense/GNP share comes close to 2 percent, which is below that of Italy (2.7 percent) and Canada (2.2 percent), but above that of the non-NATO European nations, Austria (1.3 percent) and Finland (1.4 percent). The NATO definition of defense spending includes (1) all spending on regular military forces, (2) military aid (including equipment and training) to other nations, (3) military pensions, (4) host government expenses for U.S. forces, and (5) host country infrastructure and staff costs. The Japanese defense budget omits items (2) and (3), and probably underestimates items (4) and (5). The U.S. definition of the defense budget is roughly consistent with the NATO definition.

Is the 2 percent of GNP "enough" for Japan's defense spending? The theory of public goods gives a partial answer.[1] Public goods are goods desired by all members of an organization. These goods satisfy the common interests of the organization members. Public or collective goods differ from other kinds of goods in the following two respects. First, if the good exists, then everyone who desires it automatically benefits. Nonpurchasers of the collective good cannot be feasibly prohibited from consuming the good (the principle of nonexclusivity). Second, if the good is available to any one person in a group, the incremental cost of providing it to all other members is zero or negligible (the principle of "nonrivalness" of consumption). Examples of collective goods are traffic lights, public schools, and toll-free roads in towns and villages.

A collective good need not be tangible; it may be an abstract concept like a general sense of well-being and security. Since the time of Adam Smith, defense has been considered an international good among allied nations. Allied countries have a common interest in their collective security. Excluding one country is difficult. If international security exists, any Western bloc country may enjoy the fruits of world peace without any additional expenditures. In addition, the incremental cost of providing international security to any one country is often negligible. If Germany and Austria are allied, the protection of Germany automatically protects Austria.

Assuming that international security is a public good, how should the cost of achieving the optimal level of international security be allocated among Western allies? The appendix to this chapter presents a model that is a modification of that by Olson and Zeckhauser (1966). The model shows that the benefits a country gets from world security are proportional to the country's potential output, defined as the maximum GNP a country can attain given its natural resources, population, level of technology, and human capital. This proportionality condition arises when the marginal benefit of defense is made equal to its marginal costs. If a nation has great potential to produce goods and services, then the nation has more to lose by the disruption of its productive capacity. In the extreme case of complete defeat in a war, the entire productive capacity of a nation will be in the hands of the enemy. The importance of international security seems to rise as a country becomes more economically productive.

The theory of public goods predicts, however, that if all nations acted in their own self-interest, there would be an undersupply of total allied defense. The reason for the suboptimal supply of security for the Western alliance is as follows. If all nations independently decided on their level of defense expenditures, then (as shown in the model in the appendix) the optimal level of defense in each country will be the point where the marginal benefit of defense equals its marginal cost. The optimal supply of a public good occurs, however, only when the sum of the marginal benefits of the good equals its marginal cost. Because defense is a collective good, a one-unit increase in defense increases the benefits of security for all Western bloc countries, not just for the country undertaking the expenditures. For there to be an optimal supply of defense, the effect of the defense expenditures of one country on other countries must be taken into account. When the United States spends for defense, for example, other countries with national goals similar to those of the United States automatically benefit. Because the United States has the world's largest potential output, its optimal level of defense expenditures will be very large. These large defense expenditures may enable other nations to free-ride on international security, which is likely to result in an inadequate provision of total Western bloc defense.

To resolve the suboptimal defense problem, assume that it is feasible to tax each country according to the increment to GNP the country receives from world security. It is straightforward to show that the country with the higher output should be assessed a higher tax. When countries in an alliance are taxed in proportion to their marginal benefits from defense, there will be an optimal supply of total allied security. Because the taxes will add up to the marginal cost of defense, the optimality condition that the sum of the marginal benefits of the public good equals its marginal cost is satisfied.

This scheme for optimal defense burden sharing suggests that Japan should spend somewhere between 4.1 and 6.5 percent of GNP on security-related activities. Germany spends 4 percent and the United States 6.5 percent of GNP on defense.[2] Assuming that Japan's potential output is between that of United States and Germany, and assuming that the United States and Germany are already contributing their share to the Western alliance, Japan should be spending between 4.0 and 6.5 percent of its GNP on defense to make the total supply of allied defense sufficient.

This does not imply that Japan should simply purchase more military hardware. Any expenditure that decreases international tension is appropriate. Such spending might include overseas economic assistance and scholarships for students from developing countries.[3] In addition, it should be emphasized that these GNP proportions are not necessarily "moral" or "fair." To arrive at some "fair" level of defense contributions, we must specify how incomes are to be distributed among nations. Such specifications can only be arbitrary.

The above international public goods model assumes that defense spending does not give rise to benefits that are strictly national in addition to the common, external security benefits. de Strihou (1968) argues that defense expenditures provide benefits that are strictly national and not shared with the allies, such as purely domestic political and economic gains. The value to each country of these national benefits should be subtracted from total defense expenditures to calculate the burden borne by each country.

In Japan's case, political benefits to increased defense expenditures do not exist. In fact, defense spending may entail a heavy political cost. The Japanese Constitution prohibits full-scale conventional militarization, and the Japanese population seems to be vehemently opposed to a large-scale military buildup.[4] In addition, if Japan were to heavily rearm, its Asian neighbors would be extremely uncomfortable.

If both the United States and Germany are presently contributing optimal amounts to world stability, then the theory of public goods suggests that there is presently a Western bloc underprovision of measures to promote international peace. It may be, however, that the U.S. and German fears of the Soviet Union and Third World military adventurism were exaggerated, thereby magnifying their estimates of the benefits arising from protecting the Western allies from aggression. If the "correct" total benefits are substantially lower, as is now likely, both the United States and Germany can spend smaller proportions of their GNPs on defense, and Japan may not have to increase its present GNP share by much.

The Relationship Between Defense
Spending and Economic Performance

The previous section showed that the level of defense spending appropriate to a country depends crucially on the benefits and costs of such spending. In this section, we review recent work that has attempted to quantify the economic costs of defense expenditures.

Changes in a country's defense spending affect the country's economic performance from both the demand and the supply sides. The demand side effects predominate in the short and meduim runs when the economy is adjusting to a different employment level. For example, most large-scale econometric models emphasize the demand side, and these models usually predict the following effects when, say, the United States runs a fiscal or defense expansion without monetary accommodation.[5] The dollar, the U.S. real GNP, and the real interest rates rise, and the U.S. multilateral current account deteriorates. Imports increase due to higher GNP and higher prices for domestically produced goods. Exports fall because of more expensive exportables. Depending on the model, the current account worsens more than the trade balance; the higher interest rate on foreign debt raises investment payments abroad. For example, the Japanese Economic Planning Agency predicts that an increase of 1 percentage point in the U.S. government spending–GNP ratio sustained over six years will worsen the U.S. current account–GNP ratio by 0.77 percentage points (Economic Planning Agency, 1988).

In the medium to long runs, most economists would argue that the supply side effects dominate in the world. Makin (1989), Wong (1989), and Dekle (1989) have separately examined the supply-side effects of increases in defense spending. Their models have assumed full employment and have simulated the effects of increased defense spending on the aggregate production function's inputs, namely, capital stock and labor supply.

From the aggregate production function, making some simplifying assumption, we know that growth in output is equal to[6]:

Output growth = (capital share) x (growth in capital input)
+ (labor share) x (growth in labor input) + residual

$$(5.1)$$

Defense spending draws capital and labor from productive use, but output growth may not be greatly affected because of the large size of the residual, which accounts for more 55 percent of the Japanese economic growth rate (Denison and Chung, 1976). A large component of the residual is "technical progress."

Makin (1989) examined the relationship between gross fixed capital formation and defense spending in a cross section of seven major industrial economies and found a persistent negative correlation.[7] The negative relationship is anchored at its extremes by Japan and the United States. With time-series data for the United States and Japan, Makin found that a 1 percent annual increase in defense spending reduces annual gross fixed capital formation by 0.13 percent in the United States and 0.82 percent in Japan.[8] Assuming a constant capital share of output of one-quarter as in Wong (1989), had Japan spent 6.5 percent of its GNP on defense, Japanese annual output growth between 1955 and 1986 would have been lower by about 1 percent.[9]

Dekle (1989) borrows the growth accounting framework of Denison and Chung (1976) and shows that if Japan's defense-GNP ratio had been approximately the U.S. level of 6.5 percent, Japan's national income would have grown between 1961 and 1971 at 8.76 percent a year instead of the actual 9.29 percent. The reason for the relatively small fall is that many other factors besides the growth of capital were responsible for the rapid growth of Japanese national income. Dekle assumes that defense spending "crowds out" investment in nonresidential structures and equipment one-for-one. Unlike Wong (1989), Dekle assumes that investment in different years is uncorrelated, and declines in capital stock are not cumulative.

Wong's (1989) study is the only one that takes into account changes in both capital and labor. He finds that an increase in defense expenditures seriously dampens the accumulation of capital stock in the private sector, which is similar to Makin's result. An increase in the Japanese defense expenditure–GNP share to the U.S. share of 6.5 percent lowers Japanese capital stock by 37 percent between 1970 and 1985. The reason the capital stock falls so much is that in Wong's model, investment is a function of GNP. A fall in investment this year is said to lower current GNP, which lowers investment next year.[10] That is, the damage to the capital stock is cumulative. Private sector labor also falls as more people are enlisted in the Japanese armed forces. Because labor supply is less plausibly related to GNP, next period's labor supply is unaffected by this period's labor, so the fall in labor supply is not cumulative and is negligible, declining by only 2 percent between 1970 and 1985. The combined effects of the annual declines in both capital and labor result in Japan's 1985 GNP being lower by about 7 percent than otherwise. The reason for the rather small decrease in GNP relative to the large decline in capital is that the capital share of output in Japan is only about one-quarter.

In the three studies, the effect of defense spending on the growth rate of Japanese annual aggregate output ranges from 0.5 percent

(Dekle 1989) to 1 percent (Makin 1989). However, it appears that the studies have neglected the relationship between defense and technical progress, an important component of the defense spending–economic growth nexus.[11] As mentioned above, growth accounting studies usually have a large unexplained residual, much of which is related to technological progress. We will now turn to some of the possible effects of defense expenditures on technical progress.

It has often been maintained that defense research and development (R&D) may have large potential civilian spillovers. In the United States, the military support of the cargo transport plane Boeing 367-80 has led to the rapid and relatively inexpensive development of the successful commercial jet aircraft, the Boeing 707. Other notable examples of defense R&D spillovers are the General Electric jet engine, supercomputers, and the Teflon coating on household utensils. On the other hand, the development of military hardware may have indirect negative effects on the competitiveness of an economy by consuming the time and energies of highly skilled engineers and scientists. In the United States, for example, it has been argued that the "deep pockets" of the defense contractors have raised the cost of attracting technicians, engineers, and scientists to the nonmilitary sector; this, in turn, raised the production costs of domestic commercial goods, making them more expensive than those of competing countries. Defense-related research has also typically been characterized by inefficient featherbedding and cost-plus-profit procurement.

It is very difficult to assess the potential economic impact of military R&D spillovers. The main problems are the unavailability of direct measures of R&D productivity and the necessity of using imperfect proxies such as total factor productivity growth. Despite the measurement problems, Zvi Griliches (1987) cites econometric results showing that all R&D spending increases the annual growth rate of U.S. corporate output by 33–62 percent, depending on the year. Basic R&D spending has a premium over general R&D spending by several hundred percent. Griliches, however, shows that basic research undertaken by the private sector has a higher return than basic research supported by the government.

The impact of R&D spending on corporate output in Japan is similarly large. Kazuyuki Suzuki and Tsutomu Miyagawa (1986) show for manufacturing firms that all R&D spending raises the growth rate of output by 40–55 percent. They do not have figures for the returns to basic research, but it can probably be assumed that over the long run, the premium of basic research over general research is as high in Japan as in the United States.

Concluding Comments

This chapter has examined Japan's role in providing international public goods and the effects of the provision of such goods on the Japanese economic growth rate. We found that by diverting capital and labor from the private sector, defense spending will lower private sector output. The magnitude of the decline in output will depend greatly on the effect of defense expenditures on technological progress.

Appendix

This appendix shows that the benefits a nation gets from world security are proportional to the country's potential output.

Assume that international security is a strictly increasing function of allied common defense expenditures represented by vector $D = (D(1), D(2),...,D(i),..,D(N))$ where i is a given country.

Define country i's actual gross national output as international security times potential output, Y, minus defense expenditures: $GNP(i) = F(D)Y(i) - cD(i)$, where c is the constant unit cost of defense. c should be interpreted as the financial wealth and human capital diverted from the productive sector of the economy to the military sector to create a unit of defense. The diversion of resources from the productive sector results in a fall in actual GNP. $cD(i)$ will be positively related to the amount a nation spends on defense as reported in the official government budget statistics.

The model above assumes full employment; if the economy is not fully employed, then defense spending will have the usual stimulative effects. Potential output is the maximum GNP a country can attain given the country's natural resources, population, level of technology, and human capital. The assumption is that as international tension rises, a country will have greater difficulty achieving its economic potential. An increase in country i's defense spending, which is an increase in world security, makes a country better able to reach its full-employment output. Assuming that other allies do not react to a change in country i's defense spending (the Nash assumption), the GNP of country i will be maximized when the marginal benefit of defense $F'(D)Y$ equals its marginal cost c. Let this level of optimum defense expenditures be $cD^*(i)$.

A straightforward application of the envelope theorem demonstrates that.

$$d[cD^*(i)/GNP]/dY(i) = F(D(1), ...,D^*(i), ...D(N))$$

is positive. As a country's potential output rose, it would desire a higher level of output.

Notes

In his role as editor, Professor Gerard Adams greatly improved both the content and the style of this work. The authors thank the Pew Charitable Trusts for financial assistance. Mary-Ellen Glynn and John McGlynn provided superb research assistance. Portions of this chapter appeared in Robert Dekle, "The Relationship between Defense Spending and Economic Performance in Japan" in John Makin and Donald Hellmann, eds. *Sharing World Leadership*, 1989, Washington, D.C.: American Enterprise Institute.

1. Atkinson and Stiglitz (1980, lecture 16) and Boadway (1979, chapter 4) provide good introductions to the theory of public goods.
2. Before reunification with East Germany, West Germany was spending 4.0 percent of GNP on defense. Here it is assumed that the united Germany will be spending the same GNP share of defense as the former West Germany.
3. However, not all expenditures have equivalent "defense" payoffs.
4. According to a recent prime minister's office's poll, only 7.8 percent of the Japanese population support strengthening the military.
5. See Chapter 2 by Adams and Huang.
6. The identity in the text can be derived from the aggregate production function (see Solow, 1957). Assume that production is characterized by

$$Y(t) = A(t) \times K(t)^a \times L(t)^{(1-a)},$$

where $Y(t)$ is output, $A(t)$ is Harrod-neutral technical progress, $K(t)$ is capital stock, $L(t)$ is labor, and a is capital's share of output. Taking natural logarithms and time derivatives, we get equation (5.1). The residual corresponds to the logarithmic derivative of $A(t)$. Note that (5.1) is not a structural equation. Determinants of the growth in capital and labor are not specified. The growth accounting literature pioneered by Denison (1967, 1974) has found that for almost every country, output growth cannot be explained by the growth in capital and labor. There are often difficulties in accurately measuring the growth in capital and labor, and the size of the residual may partly reflect measurement error in addition to technical change.
7. Cross-section regressions were run on the data of the United States, the United Kingdom, Japan, Germany, Canada, France, and Italy. The negative correlation between defense spending and investment was apparent in all years (1955–1985 in five-year intervals) that the regressions were run.
8. For both the United States and Japan, annual national accounts data between 1955 and 1986 are used.
9. The difference between Japan's defense spending–output share of approximately 1 percent and 6.5 percent is 5.5 percent. Multiplying 5.5 percent

by 0.82 results in an annual fall in gross fixed capital formation of 4.51 percent. Multiplying 4.51 by 0.25 gives approximately 1 percent.

10. With full-employment assumed, it is surprising that a fall in investment will lower current GNP.

11. For example, Dekle's growth accounting exercise has assumed that technical progress is disembodied from new capital inputs. It is well known that Japanese technological progress has proceeded by the rapid introduction of the latest vintage of capital equipment. The Japanese steel industry, for example, became highly efficient by incorporating oxygen-processing and large-scale open-hearth furnaces.

References

Atkinson, A.B. and Joseph Stiglitz (1980). *Lectures on Public Economics.* (New York: McGraw Hill).

Boadway, R. (1979). *Public Sector Economics* (Cambridge, MA: Winthrop).

Dekle, R. (1989). "The Relationship between Defense Spending and Economic Performance in Japan," *Sharing World Leadership,* (Washington, D.C.: American Enterprise Institute for Public Policy Research).

Denison, E. (1967). *Why Growth Rates Differ: Postwar Experience in the Western Countries.* (Washington: Brookings.)

Denison, E. (1974). *Accounting for United States Economic Growth: 1929-1969.* (Washington: Brookings.)

de Strihou, J. (1968). "Sharing the Defense Burden Among Western Allies." unpublished doctoral dissertation, Yale University.

Economic Planning Agency (1988). "External Balance Effects of Exchange Rate Changes and Macroeconomic Policies," paper presented at the Fourth EPA International Symposium.

Griliches, Z. (1987). "R and D and Productivity: Measurement Issues and Econometric Results," *Science,* July 3, 1987, pp. 31-35.

Makin, J.H. (1989). "Americna Economic and Military Leadership in the Postwar Period," *Sharing World Leadership,* (Washington, D.C.: American Enterprise Institute.)

Olson, Mancur and Richard Zeckhauser (1966). "An Economic Theory of Alliances," *Review of Economics and Statistics,* pp.206-   79.

Solow, R. (1957). "Technical Change and the Aggregate Production Function." *Review of Economics and Statistics,* pp. 104-111.

Suzuki, K. and Tsutomu Miyagawa, (1986). *Corporate Investment and R and D Strategy* (Tokyo: Toyo Keizai).

Wong, K. (1989). "National Defense and Foreign Trade: The Sweet and Sour Relationship Between the United States and Japan," *Sharing World Leadership,* (Washington, D.C.: American Enterprise Institute).

PART TWO

Arms Reduction and the Developing Economies

The perspective of the developing economies on issues of economics and national security is very different from that of the industrial countries. The role of the military in the political and economic life of many developing countries has been far greater than in the developed free-market economies of Europe, North America and Japan. Many LDCs have security problems with their neighbors. Some have sought geopolitical dominance in their region. Some are fighting off internal insurgencies. Iraq, India and Pakistan, the Philippines, South Korea and North Korea, and numerous countries of Latin America and Africa are but some of the countries that come to mind. The strategic relationships between these countries and the industrial countries are also highly complex, some of the links dating back to the colonial period and others arising out of strategic allegiances in the face of broad international disputes—the East-West or the Arab-Israeli conflicts, for example.

It would be simplistic, consequently, to assume that arms reductions will take place in the Third World in parallel with such developments in the industrial countries. And, similarly, it would be simplistic to anticipate that savings from military expenditures made in the industrial countries will be automatically diverted toward development aid and/or that such aid will be distributed among many developing countries in a simple systematic fashion, in inverse proportion to their per capita income, for example.

The changes occurring in the political relations between the major powers may ultimately enable some developing countries also to reduce their military spending. But an increased concern for regional issues may even force some of the LDCs to increase their military outlays. What is likely to happen to defense spending in the developing world must be appraised on a country-by-country basis, and that is clearly beyond the scope of this book. Our concern, consequently, is on the more general issue: How do military expenditures affect growth in the Third World? What are the quantitative dimensions of these impacts?

Whether military expenditures help or hinder economic development is still, somewhat surprisingly, a matter of controversy. The traditional approach to economic development (Chenery and Strout 1966) sees growth constrained by a lack of resources, particularly capital and educated workers. The diversion of resources from investment or from the educated civilian labor force that is implied by building stocks of armaments and armed forces can naturally be expected to reduce a country's growth potential. But alternative approaches point in a different direction. Military spending can provide a stimulus that will utilize otherwise underutilized resources. Moreover, evolutionary and externality perspectives of economic development focusing on the linkages between sectors (Harberger) and the externalities from advanced (frequently export or defense) sectors (Feder 1982, Ram 1987), also imply positive relationships between military spending and economic growth. Because these influences may all be at work at the same time, the historical evidence can well be expected to be inconclusive. In some cases military expansion may correlate positively with growth, in others there may be negative relationships.

The two chapters that follow illustrate the empirical approaches that have been taken to examine these questions: a cross-section view using data from many countries at the same time and a time series perspective considering the impact of defense spending in one country over time. In this part of the book we compare these two perspectives.

A Cross-Section View

A cross-section view, looking at the same time at many countries at various stages of economic development, has a long tradition in development economics (Chenery and Syrquin 1975). An extensive literature testing the impact of government and defense spending followed Benoit's (1972, 1973, 1978) studies, which showed, in cross-section data, a positive relationship between economic growth and defense spending.

The basic equation of this approach is:

$$\dot{Y}_i = f(\dot{G}_i, X_{i1}, \ldots, X_{ij})$$

where
$\dot{Y}_i$ = growth rate of real GDP in country i
$\dot{G}_i$ = growth rate of government spending in country i
X_{ij} = a number of other relevant variables from 1 to j affecting growth $i1 \ldots ij$

Much of the work of this type has been nontheoretic in approach but, as Feder (1982) illustrates, it is possible to introduce substantial theory into this framework. Nevertheless, the theoretical structure is thin at best. The equation may also be visualized as reduced forms from a variety of underlying theoretical constructs. Even the direction of causation is not clear. High defense expenditures are associated with high levels of GNP (Landau 1986). The structural linkages between aggregate growth and defense spending are sure to be highly complex.

Econometricians have been aware that a number of conditions must be fulfilled for a set of cross-section data to reveal relationships that are meaningful for measuring behavior in a single country over time.[1] The use of internationally consistent data is a particularly important consideration in this regard.[2] And assumptions about common behavioral coefficients among different countries in the cross section are also important.

Nevertheless, the cross-section view is suggestive of the role of defense spending in economic development. And it is from this perspective that the unanticipated finding of Benoit (1972, 1973, 1978) that economic growth is positively associated with defense spending represents a particular challenge. Is the finding valid? Does it follow that increased defense spending is beneficial to development? We suspect not! These are the concerns of Adams, Behrman, and Boldin in chapter 6.

The Macro Model Approach

An alternative approach to examining the quantitative relationships between economic development and military expenditures is to trace them over time within a particular country. Such a perspective makes possible a more theoretically structured approach, estimating the parameters of the relevant structural relationships and integrating them into an econometric model of the entire economy. Simulation analysis of such a model with various assumptions about defense spending provides a means to measure the economy-wide effect of defense spending. Such an approach is followed by Adams, Mariano, and Park in Chapter 7 on the Philippines.

The macro model approach has some substantial advantages, but it also poses significant difficulties. The theory underlying a macro model need not be different from that behind the cross-section perspective. In practice the emphasis on national accounts data and the structural detail of a macroeconometric model causes model builders to take a more detailed but often also more rigid approach than the students of cross-section data. The models often emphasize short-term demand considerations though recent models and the Adams, Mariano, and Park study presented in Chapter 7 put equal emphasis on supply (Klein 1978).

A critical issue here is the need to recognize properly the treatment of defense spending in national accounts. One must not lose sight of the fact that government employment, including the military, makes a contribution to GDP on a factor cost basis and that purchases of military equipment are typically treated as public consumption expenditures (Reich 1986). The interactions between sectors must be taken into account. This is straightforward for traditional input relationships, assuming that adequate input-output data are available. But it is not so readily accomplished when dealing with externalities that extend from the military sector to the civilian economy.

From an empirical perspective, macro modeling of developing economies has been making great strides. Macro models are traditionally based on empirically estimated parameters, in contrast to simulation models and some CGE models. They can be tested against the historical performance of the economy, and as a result, simulations of counterfactual history represent an interesting way to appraise the impact of defense on the economy. On the other hand, the estimation of the structural parameters often poses severe difficulties. In many countries, the data are insufficient or inaccurate. Sometimes some of the relevant information with regard to the movement of different dimensions of defense spending is "top secret." As most practicing econometricians realize, the long-term perpectives are difficult to pin down with relatively short consistent time series of data. Often collinearity in the data means that a number of competing hypothesis could represent the process observed in the data. The single-country macro model approach makes it possible to adapt the model to the specifics of particular countries, albeit at the cost of building many models for many different countries.[3]

Chapter 7 by Mariano, Adams, and Park represents a careful effort to integrate the military sector into an econometric macro model of the Philippine economy. It demonstrates that defense spending affects the economy through numerous channels and that its impact on growth depends greatly on the nature of the military effort, on the linkages between the military sector and the rest of the economy, and on the fiscal and monetary policies that accompany mobilization or demobilization.

Notes

1. For a discussion, see Pindyck and Rubinfeld (1981).
2. The data produced by the International Comparison Project (ICP) (Kravis, Heston and Summers (1982) are an important contribution in this regard.
3. There are possibilities for building a standardized country model distinguishing between countries only with respect to country-specific data using a common structure, but this may lose some of the advantages of country specificity.

References

Benoit, Emile (1972), "Growth and Effects of Defense in Developing Countries," *IDR*, Vol. 1, pp. 2–10.

Benoit, Emile (1973), *Defense and Economic Growth in Developing Cournties*, Boston: D.C. Heath.

Benoit, Emile (1978), "Growth and Defense in Developing Countries," *Economic Development and Cultural Change*, Vol. 26

Chenery, H. and A. Strout (1966), "Foreign Assistance and Economic Development," *American Economic Review*, Vol. 56 No. 4, pp. 679–733.

Chenery, H. and Syrquin (1975), *Pattern of Development*, London: Oxford Univ. Press.

Feder, G. (1982), "On Exports and Economic Growth," *Journal of Development Economics*, 12:1/2, 59–73.

Klein, L.R. (1978), "The Supply Side," *American Economic Review*, Vol. 68, No. 1, pp. 1–7.

Kravis, I., A. Heston, and R. Summers (1982), *World Product and Income: International Comparisons of Real Gross Product*, Baltimore: Johns–Hopkins University Press.

Landau, D. (1986), "Government and Economic Growth in the Less Developed Countries: An Empirical Study for 1960–1980," *Economic Development and Cultural Change*, Vol. 35, No. 1, pp. 35–75.

Pindyck, R., and D. Rubinfeld (1981), *Econometric Models and Economic Forecasts*, New York: McGraw–Hill, second edition.

Ram, R. (1987), "Government Size and Economic Growth: A New Framework and Some Evidence from Cross–Section and Time–Series Data: Comment 1989," *American Economic Review*, Vol. 79, No. 1, pp. 272–280.

Reich, (1986), "Treatment of Government Activity on the Production Account," *Review of Income and Wealth*, 32, 1, pp. 69–86.

6

Defense Spending and Economic Growth in the LDCs: The Cross-Section Perspective

F. Gerard Adams, Jere R. Behrman, and Michael Boldin

The easing of East-West cold war tensions, which have motivated defense strategy and military spending in the industrial countries since World War II, has shifted the focus of economic, political, and military security issues from the industrial world toward the developing countries. The risk of world war has given way increasingly to concerns about regional conflicts in the Third World.

National security has always played a major role in government policy and resource allocation in the developing countries. There is much room for conflict in the Third World in connection with economic disparities and rivalries—control of natural resources, environmental issues, and demographic pressures, as well as purely political and ethnic disputes. Ever since independence, many LDCs have felt the need to build armed forces to establish a national identity, to protect their frontiers, to deal with insurgency and counterinsurgency, to achieve geopolitical objectives, and to fulfill aggressive aims. As a result, military spending has absorbed a significant share of the total resources of many developing countries. Data from the University of Pennsylvania's International Comparison Project (ICP) would suggest that, after purchasing power parity adjustment, military outlays range from 14.7 percent of GDP in the so-called low-income countries to 15.8 percent in the lower middle-income countries as compared to 9.5 percent in the industrial countries. (see Table 6.1).

That the allocation of scarce resources for defense should have an adverse impact on economic development would evoke considerable

TABLE 6.1   Goverment and Defense Spending as a Share of GDP (percentages), 1974–1986

	Low-Income Countries	Middle-Income Countries	Industrial Countries
Government/GDP	22.3	17.8	17.0
Military/GDP	14.7	15.8	9.5

Source: International Comparison Project, University of Pennsylvania; computed from ICP data tapes.

agreement among economists. Admittedly, the relationships between the military and the civilian economy in developing countries are complex, but on balance one would anticipate that the use of manpower, equipment, and foreign exchange for military purposes would impose measurable costs on the civilian economy. Consequently, Benoit's (1972, 1973, 1978) finding of a positive association between growth and defense caused considerable skepticism and produced a long series of papers seeking either to discredit or to substantiate it.

The observed positive relationship in cross-section data may be an empirical artifact; empirical tests, following Benoit's work, have been inconclusive. On the other hand, if the positive relationship can be supported empirically, we must be able to explain why it occurs because it might have important policy implications. Economic theory should provide an explanation. Furthermore, more focused, empirical tests may be appropriate.

This chapter extends previous work by Ram (1986) and Biswas and Ram (1986) applying the Feder (1982) approach to the defense-spending question. Our objective is to throw additional empirical light on the contribution of government and defense spending to economic growth. Does such spending provide measurable externalities to the growth of the civilian economy?

Empirical work in economic growth has frequently taken a cross-sectional perspective, looking at the development of many countries over a particular time span. We too will be examining the question of government and defense spending impacts from the cross-sectional view, taking advantage of the data set adjusted for purchasing power parity available from the International Comparison Project (Kravis, Heston, and Summers 1982; Summers and Heston, 1988). In the first part of this chapter, we re-examine the empirical evidence on the impact of government spending, military and nonmilitary, on economic growth. In the second part, we introduce the Feder two-sector growth theory and apply it. In the third part, we estimate the parameters of the Feder equation including defense and nondefense components, and evaluate the results. We conclude that the contribution of government spending to GDP can be accounted for largely by the measurement of government production in GDP. There is no evidence of externality effects.

The Empirical Approaches to Determining Defense Expenditure Impacts in the LDCs

The empirical work on the relationship between government/ defense spending and growth exemplifies how a counterintuitive result can lead to an extended stream of controversy and research. Although Benoit considered potentially positive and negative impacts, he expected on balance that allocating resources to defense would negatively influence growth. The "bombshell"[1] was that for a cross section of 44 countries there was a positive correlation between the GDP growth rate and the share of GDP going into defense.

Despite, or perhaps because of, the simplistic nature of Benoit's work, numerous empirical studies followed. These—some dealing specifically with defense spending and others more generally with the role of government—are summarized and brought up to date in Grobar and Porter (1987); Frederiksen and Looney (1983); Chan (1985); Biswas and Ram (1986); Deger (1986); Faini, Annez, and Taylor (1984); Ram (1986); and others. It is apparent from this work that Benoit's result is extraordinarily sensitive to the formulation of the analysis. Cross-sectional correlation studies such as Benoit's are very dependent on the observations included, the time period, and the specification of the equations.

Structural models (for example, that of Deger and Smith [1983]) sometimes show negative impacts of defense spending once other elements of the equation system have been accounted for. But the precise structural role of defense spending in the growth process is far from clear. Granger causality tests of growth on defense and of defense on growth (Joerding 1986; Frederiksen and LaCivita [undated]) suggest that growth "Granger-causes" defense and provides a feedback relationship: "growth leads to defense, which leads to growth, etc." (Frederiksen and LaCivita [undated]). The interaction between military expenditure, exports, and growth has been considerable, as shown by Rothschild (1977). More recent work using a "path analysis" latent variables approach shows that government spending is one of many factors that have direct and indirect growth effects (Scholing and Timmermann 1988).

Our correlations between growth and government/defense variables

(Table 6.1) illustrate the mixed results. Our work differs from similar studies in three basic ways:

- We distinguish, where possible, between military and non-military government spending.
- We separate the experience of the "warring" countries.
- We use more recent data adjusted for international purchasing power parity (PPP).

There was little question about how to treat the data, even though our decisions were likely to have a significant effect on the results. We were uncertain, however, how to handle the countries actively engaged in wars. The underlying data suggested, not surprisingly, that many of the warring nations represented outlier observations. We decided, consequently, to do the bulk of the analysis excluding these countries.[2]

Table 6.2 shows simple correlation coefficients and probabilities for the relationships between economic growth, growth-related factors, and government spending. Results are shown separately for low- and middle-income developing countries.[3] Correlations are shown first with respect to GDP growth rate, then with respect to investment/GDP, and last for growth of exports.

A negative relationship between the share of government expenditures in GDP (governement spending/GDP) and growth is apparent in the table, but the results are not statistically significant and differ in sign among the regions for military expenditures relative to GDP. The positive correlation in the middle-income developing countries, which corresponds to the Benoit results, is worth noting.

The middle part of the table treats the government variables differently, as rates of growth (weighted for the importance of government spending in GDP). There are positive correlations between growth of GDP and growth of government spending, significant in both groups of developing countries. The results are substantially the same for military and nonmilitary government spending. This is the most challenging result.

Another empirical question is whether there are relationships between the military and nonmilitary government expenditures and variables typically associated with economic growth. Rather than presenting an exhaustive analysis, we show only correlations with the principal variables, investment and export growth, which have been associated most closely with economic development in other empirical studies (Adams, Behrman, and Boldin 1989).[4]

The correlations between government spending as a share of GDP

TABLE 6.2 Cross-sectional Correlations Between Growth, Related Variables, and Government Spending in LDCs (1974–1986 average)

	GDP Growth Rate		Investment/GDP		Export Growth Rate	
	Low-Income Countries	Middle-Income Countries	Low-Income Countries	Middle-Income Countries	Low-Income Countries	Middle-Income Countries
Excluding warring countries						
Government spending/GDP						
Pearson correlation coefficient	-0.23	-0.25	0.485	-0.15	-0.29	-0.23
Probability that $R = 0$	0.195	0.143	0.004[a]	-0.381	0.124	0.192
Number of observations	32	34	32	34	29	32
Nonmilitary government spending/GDP						
Pearson correlation coefficient	-0.28	-0.36	0.445	-0.21	-0.34	-0.33
Probability that $R = 0$	0.114	0.036[a]	0.010[a]	0.226	0.067[a]	0.058
Number of observations	32	32	32	34	29	32
Military government spending/GDP						
Pearson correlation coefficient	-0.02	0.235	0.414	0.132	0.010	0.250
Probability that $R = 0$	0.876	0.179	0.018[a]	0.455	0.956	0.166
Number of observations	32	34	32	34	29	32
Government expenditure growth						
Pearson correlation coefficient	0.488	0.474	-0.21	0.096	0.027	0.189
Probability that $R = 0$	0.004[a]	0.004[a]	0.236	0.586	0.888	0.299
Number of observations	32	34	32	34	29	32
Military expenditure growth						
Pearson correlation coefficient	0.456	0.381	-0.21	0.019	0.154	0.190
Probability that $R = 0$	0.008	0.025[a]	0.844	0.913	0.422	0.295
Number of observations	32	34	32	34	29	32
Nonmilitary government expenditure growth						
Pearson correlation coefficient	0.410	0.393	-0.21	0.089	-0.00	0.159
Probability that $R = 0$	0.019	0.021[a]	0.248	0.913	0.974	0.384
Number of observations	32	34	32	34	29	32
Including warring countries						
Military expenditure growth						
Pearson correlation coefficient	0.369	-0.181				
Probability that $R = 0$	0.028[a]	0.275				
Number of observations	35	38				
Nonmilitary government expenditure growth						
Pearson correlation coefficient	0.347	0.257				
Probability that $R = 0$	0.040[a]	0.118				
Number of observations	35	38				

[a] Probability less than 10 percent.

and investment as a share of GDP hardly support the "crowding out" hypothesis in the middle-income countries. (The sign on nonmilitary government spending is negative, but nonsignificant.) In the low-income countries, there is evidence of significant positive correlation between government spending, military and nonmilitary, and investment.

When we turn to the *growth* of government spending, the effects on investment are mixed and nonsignificant. The correlations between government spending as a share of GDP and export growth appear to show largely negative relationships. The significant negative relationships between nonmilitary government spending and export growth are notable, particularly because there is no statistical evidence of such a relationship with respect to military spending.

For the warring countries, which have been excluded from the data above, there are insufficient observations to do a separate statistical analysis. For the most part these countries represent outlier observations and many of them have negative GDP growth rates, as we would anticipate. Including the warring countries in the total sample, we find (see Table 6.2) that the correlation between GDP and growth in military spending turns negative in the middle income countries.

Such a presentation lends little support to the Benoit finding, and raises a multitude of puzzles. By and large, there is not a positive link between the share of government spending in GDP and growth in our data set in the nonwarring countries.[5] However, we cannot show more negative correlations for military spending than for nonmilitary government spending. The growth rate of GDP appears to be positively related to the growth rate of government spending although there is no clear distinction between military and nonmilitary spending.[6]

Theoretical Perceptions of the
Defense Spending/Growth Relationship

Although much of the work on the defense spending/growth relationship has been empirical, if not frankly empiricist, a number of writers, including Benoit, have brought macroeconomic and development theories to bear. The relevant theoretical approaches can be depicted from a structural viewpoint (i.e., demand, supply, and so forth) or from an effect perspective—growth enhancing and growth depressing, for example. We choose a structural perspective, indicating where appropriate the direction of the effect that might be anticipated.

The logical approach, according to the simple theories of Harrod and Domar, has been to associate growth with capital and labor inputs into a one-sector production function. But the theory of development points toward *duality*, the presence of an advanced and of a backward sector and externalities from one to the other. This classic pattern has been implemented by Feder (1982) into a simple two-sector model, which has been widely used to explore the impact of export growth on overall product growth.

The Feder model posits an advanced sector, exports (X), and a domestically oriented sector, nonexports (N). For each sector there is a production function that indicates that output depends on labor (L_N and L_X) and on the capital stock used in that sector (K_N and K_X). In addition, the export sector is assumed to have externalities that positively increase nonexport output so that:

$$N = N(K_N, L_N, X) \tag{6.1}$$

$$X = X(K_X, L_X) \tag{6.2}$$

Therefore, change in total product ($\dot{Y}$) is:

$$\dot{Y} = \dot{N} + \dot{X} = N_K \dot{K}_N + N_L \dot{L}_N + N_X \dot{X} + X_K \dot{K}_X + X_L \dot{L}_X \tag{6.3}$$

Feder makes additional assumptions: (a) that the marginal productivities of labor and capital differ between the sectors by the same proportion, *ü*

$$\frac{X_K}{N_K} = \frac{X_L}{N_L} = 1 + \delta \tag{6.4}$$

(b) that the marginal product of labor in the nonexport sector is proportional to the average product of labor in the whole economy

$$N_L = \beta / L \tag{6.5}$$

and (c) that the marginal product of capital in the nonexport sector is constant:

$$N_K = \alpha \tag{6.6}$$

Under these assumptions, relation (6.3) can be rewritten as:

$$\frac{\dot{Y}}{Y} = \alpha\left(\frac{I}{Y}\right) + \beta\left(\frac{\dot{L}}{L}\right) + \left[\frac{\delta}{(1+\delta)} + N_X\right]\left(\frac{\dot{X}}{X}\right)\left(\frac{X}{Y}\right) \tag{6.7}$$

The terms $\ddot{u}$ and N_X measure, respectively, the productivity differential between the (advanced) export sector and the domestic sector and the externalities provided by the export sector.[7] I, of course, corresponds to $\dot{K}$

Ram (1986) and Biswas and Ram (1986) extended this model to government spending simply by substituting government spending (G) for X in various versions of the Feder model.

We now consider the government sector as an advanced sector additional to export growth in the Feder model. We assume that government, like the export sector, has its own separate production function, and that it makes an external contribution to the nongovernment, nonexport sector in a three-sector economy, which is driven by an export sector and separately by a government sector (G).[8] This yields an equation corresponding to equation (6.7) as follows:

$$\frac{\dot{Y}}{Y} = \alpha\left(\frac{I}{Y}\right) + \beta\left(\frac{\dot{L}}{L}\right) + \left[\frac{\delta}{(1+\delta)} + N_X\right]\left(\frac{\dot{X}}{X}\right)\left(\frac{X}{Y}\right) + \left[\frac{\gamma}{1+\gamma} + N_G\right]\left(\frac{\dot{G}}{G}\right)\left(\frac{G}{Y}\right) \quad (6.8)$$

The assumptions underlying this equation correspond to those assumed for exports above; γ is a term similar to $\ddot{u}$, measuring the excess productivity of the government sector relative to the nongovernment nonexport sectors; and N_G represents the externality effect of government on the nondefense nonexport sector.

Equation (6.8) offers the possibility of testing whether government and/or export growth make special contributions to the rate of growth. These effects would be identified by the two terms on the right side of the equation, which recognize both the productivity differentials and the externalities.[9]

It is possible in the same framework to break down government spending into two components, one representing defense and other encompassing the nondefense spending.[10] This broadens our hypothesis considerably in that government spending on nondefense activities may be expected to have an impact different from that of defense expenditures.

Measurement and Conceptual Treatment of Government Output

An important measurement issue comes up when one extends the model to include government.[11] The notion underlying the Feder model, that export production represents a separate sector, does not quite match the way in which the statistics are collected or available. Exports come from various sectors, some that supply the export market exclusively, others which supply both export and domestic markets, and still others that are entirely domestically oriented (indirect inputs from domestic sectors into exports). It takes a heroic assumption, or a definitional fiction, to argue that exports represent the output of an advanced sector. But there is at least some correspondence between exports production and the product that competes successfully in the world market.

In the case of government, the problem is different. Government expenditures for goods and services are in part production by a government sector and in part purchases from the private economy. The former receive special treatment in the national income accounts because government output is not sold at market prices. The latter clearly represents a product of the other, presumably domestically oriented, sector.

The treatment of government expenditures in the national accounts is at once a source of difficulties and an advantage in this context. Government output is measured at cost in terms of inputs of labor deflated by a wage index (Reich 1986). This would suggest that government production is entirely a matter of labor inputs. An increase in government employment, civilian or military, adds to GDP by computation, so long as it does not crowd out civilian activity. The marginal productivity of labor in government production (N_{GL}) equals unity, and the marginal productivity of capital in government production (N_{GK}) equals zero. This is not consistent with Feder's assumption about the relative marginal productivities of capital and labor in his two-sector economy, as seen in equation (6.4). But it does mean that we can divide government spending (G) into government output on the basis of labor inputs (G_L), and government purchases from the private sector (G_P). We may consequently use available data on government real wage payments to subtract the direct impact of government production activity from the left side of equation (6.8) to yield an equation for civilian GDP (Y_c):

$$\frac{\dot{Y}_c}{Y_c} = \frac{\dot{Y}}{Y} - \frac{G}{Y}\frac{\dot{G}}{G}$$

$$= \alpha\frac{I}{Y_c} + \beta\frac{\dot{L}}{L_c} + \left[\frac{\delta}{1-\delta} + N_X\right]\left(\frac{\dot{X}}{X}\right)\left(\frac{X}{Y_c}\right) + N_G\left(\frac{\dot{G}_L}{G_L}\right)\left(\frac{G_L}{Y_c}\right) + P_G\left(\frac{\dot{G}_P}{G_P}\right)\left(\frac{G_P}{Y_c}\right)$$

$$(6.9)$$

The N_G and P_G terms represent measures of the externality effects of the two components of government spending on nongovernment GDP.

There are probably externalities as the expansion of government production or demand for private sector products offers improved techniques, human capital, and infrastructure that increase output in the nondefense sectors. Although some defense spending undoubtedly goes for equipment that makes no measured contribution to GDP, in many countries the military helps build a critical infrastructure and provides a variety of public services such as police and customs. Thus, externalities may come from military spending as well as from nondefense spending.

An alternate view is to see government spending, military activity in particular, as a burden on a developing country if there is diversion of resources toward defense, but that is taken care of in our equations by the inclusion of the investment and labor terms. There could also be negative externalities.

Empirical Test of the
Feder Hypothesis and Government Expenditure

We now turn to our empirical estimates of the defense expenditure effects. The first part of our computations, presented in Table 6.3, uses equation (6.8) as a basis. Note that we have added a constant term to catch neutral technical change and a K/Y term to allow for capital consumption.[12]

For each of the country groups, we show first an equation including total government spending, and second an equation breaking government spending into military and nonmilitary expenditures. The first line of Table 6.3 shows the intercept, a measure of technical change. Although the coefficients are not statistically significant, it is notable that technical change appears to be negative in the low-income countries and positive (around 1 percent per year) for the middle-income countries. The coefficient of capital/output, which captures capital consumption, is negative as expected.

The investment effect is reasonable and statistically significant in the middle-income category. The labor effects lack statistical significance because many of the developing countries are labor surplus economies. The effect of export growth is important and nearly statistically significant in the low- and middle-income countries, lending support to the thesis that export industries have a productivity differential and/or contribute externalities to the remaining sectors. This result is typical of studies for the middle-income developing economies.[13]

Turning now to the effects of government expenditures, we find that total government spending has positive impacts on growth in both

TABLE 6.3 Cross-sectional Regressions Between Growth and Government Spending in LDCs (Feder-type Models) (1974–1986 average)

Dependent Variable	GDP Growth Rate			
	Low-Income Countries		Middle-Income Countries	
	(a)	(b)	(a)	(b)
Intercept	−0.002	−0.002	0.007	0.006
	(0.10)	(0.11)	(0.60)	(0.49)
Capital/GDP	−0.019	−0.021	−0.034	−0.034
	(1.02)	(0.93)	(4.18)	(4.12)
Investment/GDP	0.141	0.145	0.251	0.263
	(0.92)	(0.78)	(4.10)	(4.17)
Labor growth	0.712	0.809	0.420	0.417
	(0.92)	(1.01)	(1.77)	(1.74)
Export growth	0.963	0.921	0.435	0.431
	(1.97)	(1.80)	(4.15)	(4.04)
Government growth	1.061		1.256	
	(2.29)		(3.45)	
Military growth[a]		1.064		3.203
		(0.49)		(1.68)
Nonmilitary growth[a]		0.984		0.848
		(1.76)		(1.74)
N	29	29	30	30
R^2	0.443	0.430	0.868	0.869
Adjusted R^2	0.322	0.275	0.840	0.835

[a]Inclusion of the warring countries yields coefficients for military and nonmilitary expenditure growth as follows:

	Low-income countries	Middle-income countries
Military expenditure growth	1.106	−2.185
	(0.60)	(1.90)
Nonmilitary expenditure growth	1.180	1.019
	(1.65)	(2.56)

country groups, (the [a] columns in Table 6.3). When government spending is divided into military and nonmilitary expenditures, (the [b] columns in Table 6.3), the positive effects remain, although they are no longer all statistically significant. It is surprising, moreover, that the effects of military spending are larger than the effects of nonmilitary spending.

The military expenditure coefficient is, however, highly sensitive to the countries included. As indicated in Table 6.2, the inclusion of the few warring countries causes the coefficient of military expenditures to turn negative in the middle-income countries at the margin of significance.[14]

We turn next to a modified formulation that focuses on private GDP, that recognizes the measurement issue associated with government production, and that allows for externality effects of government production and government demand on the private sector (equation [6.9]). These equations have been estimated only for the middle-income LDCs. Moreover, they are based on a smaller sample because data on government wages were not available for all countries included in the analysis.

The results are summarized in Table 6.4. In the first column we show an equation comparable to those used in Table 6.3.[15] As noted there, government spending has a significant and positive coefficient.

In the second column, we expand the same equation to show separately government real-wage expenditures and government purchases from the private sector. It is interesting to note that government real-wage payments have a marginally significant coefficient of 1.059 (the coefficient is not significantly different from 1.0), but that the coefficient of other government purchases is not statistically significant (0.816).

In the third and fourth columns, we focus on nongovernment GDP

TABLE 6.4 Cross-sectional Regressions Between GDP and Other Variables in Middle-Income Countries (Feder-type Models) (1974–1986 average)

Dependent Variable	GDP Growth Rate		GDP Private Growth Rate	
	(a)	(b)	(a)	(b)
Intercept	0.012	0.013	0.016	0.013
	(0.811)	(0.794)	(1.102)	(0.794)
GDP/population 1974	−0.000005	−0.0000053	−0.000006	−0.0000053
	(1.423)	(1.317)	(1.765)	(1.317)
Capital/GDP	−0.025	−0.025	−0.025	−0.025
	(2.318)	(2.233)	(2.256)	(2.233
Investment/GDP	0.246	0.246	0.245	0.246
	(3.364)	(2.357)	(3.324)	(3.257)
Labor growth	0.290	0.271	0.213	0.271
	(1.037)	(0.880)	(0.753)	(0.880)
Export growth	0.290	0.605	0.645	0.605
	(4.172)	(3.695)	(4.501)	(3.695)
Government growth	1.005		0.228	
	(2.155)		(0.484)	
Government wage growth		1.059		0.059
		(1.847)		(0.103)
Government purchasing growth		0.816		0.816
		(0.687)		(0.687)
N	23	23	23	23
R^2	0.884	0.885	0.876	0.878
Adjusted R^2	0.841	0.831	0.829	0.821

(Y_C) as the dependent variable. Government spending does not have a significant effect on private GDP and neither of the components of government spending carry a significantly positive sign.[16]

It appears from the comparison that the bulk of the impact of government spending on growth is the result of the inclusion of government production directly in the accounting for GDP. If that is allowed for, as in these equations, the significantly positive impact of $\dot{G}$ on $\dot{Y}$ disappears. The computations do not show evidence of a significant externality effect, either positive or negative, of the government sector on the nongovernment part of the economy. Data were not available to separate military from nonmilitary government wages and purchases, and consequently the separate effect of military spending could not be tested. The measurement of military contributions to GDP is much the same as that for civilian government activities. It is probable that the overall effect of military activity on GDP is also much the same as that of civilian activity, although we have no indication about separate externality effects on nongovernment activity.

Defense Spending and Economic Growth in the LDCs

What can we conclude about the impact of defense spending on economic growth in the LDCs? The evidence remains rather sketchy. Our analysis of the cross-sectional data does not, after all, provide much support for the counterintuitive notion that defense expenditures advance growth in the LDCs. Our analysis implies that the positive effect sometimes observed in the data is the result of the way in which government spending and production are recorded by national statisticians. Once the product of government activity is excluded, government spending does not appear to contribute to growth.

But such a conclusion does not imply the countercorollary that a reduction in government spending, specifically arms reduction, would have little impact on economic development. From the perspective of consumer welfare, the critical issue is whether resources can be reallocated to purposes that will advance consumer well-being, either by increasing private consumption or public services. From the point of view of growth, the critical consideration is whether resources can be reallocated to investment. Externality effects cannot be ignored, however. Not only are they difficult to measure, they also do not appear to be clearly in one direction. The question of whether resource reallocation is possible is not one that can be tested by the statistical analysis of past data. This is, after all, a matter of decision making by the public and by private sectors. Given the availability of appropriate market signals and incentives, resources that have been used for defense purposes can presumably be used in other ways. However, the policies required may be difficult and the cost of implementation may be high.

Notes

This chapter was written prior to Boldin's employment by the Federal Reserve Bank of New York.

    1. Grobar and Porter's (1987) word.

    2. Countries were eliminated if during the 1970s and early 1980s they reported more than 50,000 deaths from war or insurrection (Sivard 1982, 1986). The countries specifically excluded were: (low income) Afghanistan, Ethiopia, and Uganda; (middle income) Angola, El Salvador, Mozambique, Nicaragua, and the Philippines; (industrial) Israel. Other warring countries, such as Iran and Iraq, were not part of the initial data set.

    3. We subdivided the countries in our study into categories that match closely the system used by the World Bank *Development Report* (i.e., low- and middle-income developing countries). In 1974, in per capita terms, ICP GDP (1980 international dollars), the mean income of the low-income countries was $522, and for the middle-income group GDP, it was $2,326. Comparable evaluations, not shown here, were carried out for the industrial countries. They do not reveal positive relationships between growth and military expenditures.?

    4. For an elaborate correlation study, see Landau (1986).

    5. This is consistent with the results of Landau (1983).

    6. There is a similar positive relationship between the growth rate of GDP and the growth rate of exports (Adams, Behrman, and Boldin 1989).

    7. If $\partial=0$ and $N_X=0$ there is no productivity differential and there are no externalities, and equation (6.7) reduces to the traditional "sources of growth" equation. The special contribution of exports drops out so that output growth is determined simply by the growth of capital stock and labor.

    8. We ignore here the possibilities of interaction between the two advanced sectors. These interactions are not likely to be important except in the countries that have taken advantage of their military sector demands to develop an arms export industry.

    9. It is possible to disentangle these terms (Feder 1982). But we have not tried to do so here because the empirical estimates of the disentangled effects would be subject to a great deal of uncertainty.

    10. Again, we assume there are no interactions.

    11. There are, of course, numerous issues of measurement. We deal only with the one immediately relating to the model considered here.

    12. It has not been widely recognized that the effect of investment would otherwise be understated because the available statistics are for investment on a gross rather than net basis, and in the production function I is K, the net increase in capital stock.

13. See, for example, Adams, Behrman, and Boldin (1989).

14. This is consistent with the negative empirical impact of war observed by Landau (1986).

15. Data from the ICP for 1980 allowed us to split government expenditures into wages and purchases. For some countries similar data were available for 1975. It appeared that there was no systematic trend. Consequently, the 1980 split between wages and other government spending was applied to total government spending. A consequence of this assumption is that we cannot distinguish separate growth rates for military and nonmilitary spending.

The GDP/population variable was added to test the possibility that the effects depend on the relative positions of the countries on the income scale. Although there may be some impact, the coefficient of GDP/population is just below the margin of significance.

16. The coefficients reflect the fact that in these equations private GDP (Y_C) has been computed by subtracting our estimate of government real-wage payments, which have been computed as a a fixed share of government spending, from total GNP.

Bibiography

Adams, F. G., J. R. Behrman, and M. Boldin (1989). "Productivity, Competitiveness and Export Growth in Developing Countries". In B. Hickman (1990), *International Productivity and Competitiveness*, New York: Oxford University Press.

Balassa, Bela (1985). "Exports, Policy Choices, and Economic Growth in Developing Countries After the 1973 Oil Shock." *Journal of Development Economics* 18 (1): 23-35.

Benoit, Emile (1972). "Growth and Effects of Defense in Developing Countries." *International Development Review*, Vol. 1: 2-10.

Benoit, Emile (1973). *Defense and Economic Growth in Developing Countries.* Boston: D.C. Heath.

Benoit, Emile (1978). "Growth and Defense in Developing Countries." *Economic Development and Cultural Change* 26 (2), 271-280.

Biswas, B., and R. Ram (1986). "Military Expenditures and Economic Growth in Less Developed Countries: An Augmented Model and Further Evidence." *Economic Development and Cultural Change* 34 (January) 361-372.

Carr, Jack L. (1989). "Government Size and Economic Growth: A New Framework and Some Evidence from Cross-Section and Time-Series Data: Comment." *American Economic Review* 79 (1): 267-271.

Chan, Steve (1985). "The Impact of Defense Spending on Economic Performance: A Survey of Evidence and Problems." *ORBIS* 29 (Summer): 403-434.

Deger, Saadet (1986). "Economic Development and Defense Expenditures." *Economic Development and Cultural Change* 35 (October): 179-196.

Deger, S. and R. Smith (1983). "Military Expenditures and Growth in Less Developed Countries." *Journal of Conflict Resolution* 27 (2): 335-353.

Faini, R., P. Annez, and L. Taylor (1984). "Defense Spending, Economic Structure and Growth: Evidence Among Countries and Over Time." *Economic Development and Cultural Change* 32 (3): 486-498.

Feder, Gershon (1982). "On Exports and Economic Growth." *Journal of Development Economics* 12 (1/2): 59-73.

Frederiksen, P. C., and R. E. Looney (1983). "Defense Expenditures, External Public Debt and Growth in Developing Countries." *Armed Forces and Society* 9 (Summer): 633-45.

Frederiksen, P. C., and C. J. LaCivita (undated). "Defense and Economic Growth: An Alternative Approach to the Causality Issue." Unpublished paper, Naval Postgraduate School, Monterey, Calif.

Grobar, L. M., and R. C. Porter (1987). "Benoit Revisited: Defense Spending and Economic Growth in LDCs." Research Seminar in International Economics, University of Michigan, Discussion Paper No. 205.

Joerding, Wayne (1986). "Economic Growth and Defense Spending: Granger Causality." *Journal of Economic Development* 21 (1): 35-40.

Kravis, I. B., A. Heston and R. Summers (1982). *World Product and Income: International Comparisons of Real Gross Product*, Baltimore: Johns-Hopkins University Press.

Landau, Daniel (1983). "Government Expenditure and Economic Growth: A Cross-Country Study." *Southern Economic Journal* 49: 783-92.

Landau, Daniel (1986). "Government and Economic Growth in the Less Developed Countries: An Empirical Study for 1960-1980." *Economic Development and Cultural Change* 35 (October): 35-75.

Ram, Rati (1986). "Government Size and Economic Growth: A New Framework and Some Evidence from Cross-Section and Time-Series Data." *American Economic Review* 76 (1): 191-203.

Ram, Rati (1987). "Exports and Economic Growth in Developing Countries: Evidence From Time Series and Cross Section Data." *Economic Development and Cultural Change* 36 (1): 51-72.

Ram, Rati (1989). "Government Size and Economic Growth: A New Framework and Some Evidence From Cross Sections and Time Series Data Reply." *American Economic Review* 79 (1): 281-284.

Rao, Vhandji (1989). "Government Size and Economic Growth: A New Framework and Some Evidence from Cross-Section and Time-Series Data: Comment 1989." *American Economic Review* 79 (1): 272-280.

Reich, U.P. (1986). "Treatment of Government Activity on the Production Account." *Review of Income and Wealth*, 32 (1): 69-86.

Rothschild, Kurt W. (1977). "Military Expenditure, Exports and Growth." *Kylos* 26 (December): 804-13.

Scholing, E., and V. Timmermann (1988). "Why LDC Growth Rates Differ: Measuring 'Unmeasurable' Influences." *World Development* 16 (11): 1271-1294.

Sivard, Ruth Leger (1982). "World Military and Social Expenditures." *World*

Military and Social Expenditures, World Priorities (7th edition), Washington, D.C.

Sivard, Ruth Leger (1986). *World Military and Social Expenditures*, World Priorities (11th edition), Washington, D.C.

Summers, R., and A. Heston (1988). "A New Set of International Comparisons of Real Product and Price Levels Estimates for 130 Countries, 1950-1985." *The Review of Income and Wealth* Series 34 (Number 1, March): 1-25.

7

Defense Expenditures and Economic Growth in the Philippines: A Macrosimulation Analysis

F. Gerard Adams, Roberto S. Mariano, and Innwon Park

Introduction

Do defense expenditures enhance or retard growth in developing economies? Since Benoit (1972, 1973), numerous authors have written on this subject—but with no clear answer. Adams, Behrman, and Boldin (Chapter 6 in this volume), address this question through a cross-section study of low-income, middle-income, and industrialized countries. The two-sector model of Feder (1982) is adapted to obtain a "sources of growth" equation, which separately treats defense and nondefense government spending. The estimated equations based on annual data over the period 1974–1986, "show positive relationships between government spending, generally even military spending, and economic growth once the other growth determining factors have been taken into account." Adams, Behrman, and Boldin conclude, however, that the bulk of the positive effect observed is attributable to the direct effect of military spending on government output (value added), which is measured by national accounts statistics as part of the GDP.

This paper reports initial efforts from another angle—a case study of the Philippines through a macroeconometric model estimated from a time series of Philippine data. Such a model forms a basis for quantifying the short-term macroeffects of government and defense spending in the Philippines and the medium-term impact on Philippine production. Such an approach also clarifies the role of such spending in the national accounts.

This chapter quantifies the macroeconomic effects of additional expenditures[1] in the Philippines through a simulation analysis based on a macroeconometric model of the Philippines. This model is a variant of the system the National Economic and Development Authority, the chief economic planning agency in the Philippines, uses for the formulation of the five-year economic program for the country. This model was developed by Mariano and colleagues at the Philippine Institute for Development Studies (Mariano and Constantino 1987; Constantino, Mariano, and Yap 1989). The basic structure of the model and the linkages within it which capture the effects of higher government expenditures are described in the next section. Then the following section summarizes the results of the simulation exercises, showing how effects of higher expenditures differ across budgetary allocation and the manner in which such additional expenditures are financed.

This chapter is written at a particularly interesting time, after the Philippines went through sensitive negotiations with the United States regarding the military base agreement. The Philippines is a developing economy with surplus labor and with scarce financial resources, due, among other things, to a widening trade gap and a heavy foreign debt burden. Just as the economy was poised to take off in late 1989 on the heels of strong investor confidence and a buoyant stock market, the December putsch, followed by a lingering drought and power shortages in Manila, combined with slower world economic activity to dampen the economy. More shocks in the second half of 1990 slowed down the economy further—a high intensity earthquake in July in the Gulf conflict in August.

Military expenditures in the Philippines (per capita or as a percent of GNP) are one of the lowest in the South East Asian region (1 percent of GDP). Government expenditures in total represent 9 percent of GDP, again relatively low compared to other South East Asian economies.[2] There is substantial military aid from the United States in the form of grants and soft loans. The grant portion of military aid is not necessarily limited to defense spending: a major component of it is allocated to a so-called economic stabilization fund. Basic salaries of military personnel, especially at the lower ranks, are rather low, and have been more than doubled since a major coup attempt in 1987. Further substantial adjustments in salaries and benefits are being contemplated but are seriously hampered because of the government budgetary deficit.

An Annual Macroeconometric Model of the Philippines

The model we have used for our simulation analysis consists of about one hundred equations; half of them are identities, and half are statistically estimated. This simultaneous system consists of four major blocks—the real, fiscal, financial, and external sectors. Figure 7.1 illustrates the linkages among the various sectors.

The core of the model is the real sector block, which determines output, its production and expenditure components, prices, employment and wages. Domestic output is determined within the model with simultaneous feedback between the supply and demand sides in the real sector block. Supply and demand equations are estimated for each of the production categories (agriculture, industry, services), and it is assumed that sectoral prices clear the market. (The most recent version of the model, in Constantino et al. [1989], modifies this market clearing assumption for the industrial sector, which is often characterized by excess capacity so that adjustments to increases in demand take place on the quantity side.)

GDP is built up from the production side and GNP is then determined with the addition of net factor income from abroad to GDP. This is reconciled with the expenditure side by taking the statistical discrepancy as a residual component of GNP from the expenditure side[3]

The expenditure side of the real sector is disaggregated into traditional components in the national income accounts. The linkage from the expenditure side to the production sector comes in two major ways. One is in the form of aggregate expenditure categories appearing as arguments in the demand functions in the production sector. Second, appropriate investment expenditure variables also show up as explanatory variables in some of the supply functions in the production sectors. Feedback from production to the expenditure sector is reflected through the use of output as an activity variable in the equations for some of the expenditure components.

In the fiscal sector, government expenditures at the budget level are treated exogenously in the model and are decomposed into operating expenditures and capital outlays. These two variables then feed directly into estimated equations for national income accounts data on government consumption expenditures and government construction, respectively.

Government spending for operating expenses and capital outlays affect the system differently—the former through government and private consumption in the expenditure side of the model, and the latter through the investment equations in the expenditure side and the supply equations in the production sector.

Government operating expenditures can also be directed toward economic activity in the public sector directly, through increases in public sector employment and/or through wage increases to public employees. This would be the case of an increase in military personnel

110

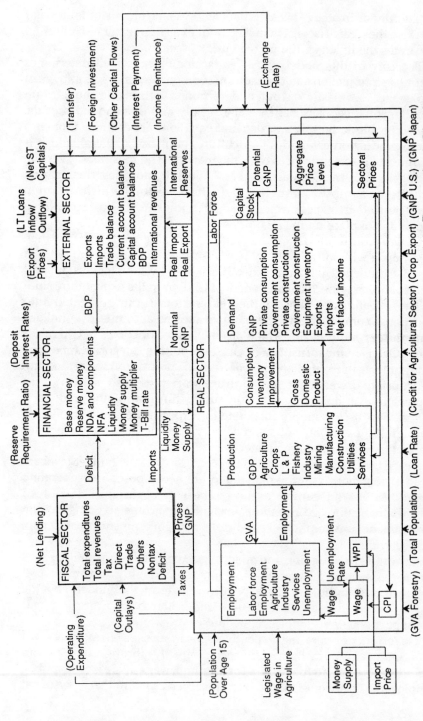

FIGURE 7.1 Flow chart: The macroeconomic model for the Philippines.

Notes: The variables enclosed in boxes are endogenous variables. The variables in parentheses are exogenous variables. The arrows show the linkage between sectors.

in the former case and alternatively an increase in military wage rates in the latter. To deal with these possibilities we have augmented the production side of the model by showing the government sector, which had been part of services output, as an additional production sector, and by recognizing the government wage rate in the government sector deflator. Changes in public sector employment affect value added produced in the government sector. Changes in public sector wage rates affect the government sector deflator.

Government revenues can be held constant or can be endogenously linked to total output. The government budget deficit is thus endogenous; and in turn, it affects the aggregate price level, money supply, and, consequently, interest rates. Figure 7.2 provides more details on the linkages between government expenditures and the various sectors in the model.

Simulation Analysis of Higher Government Expenditures

The model described above was not developed explicitly for the analysis of government expenditures. Nevertheless, it contains enough features to allow a series of simulations for the purpose at hand. The model does not contain defense spending as a separate variable. To estimate the effects of increased defense spending, we proceeded to simulate the model under various scenarios with higher government expenditures. To accommodate variations in the composition of the increase in spending, higher government expenditures in the model are introduced through either operating expenditures alone or capital outlays alone, increases in government employment, or increases in public employee wage rates. Alternative cases are also considered for the effects of the increase in spending on the government budget deficit. This is done through alternative assumptions regarding the manner in which the additional spending is financed.

To accommodate various types of spending, we have standardized the simulations on an expenditure shock amounting to 1 percent of GDP *in nominal terms*. This makes possible simulations that involve only an increase in wages, but, as we discuss further below, it is the source of some problems in interpreting the simulation results. There are four types of alternatives:

- CGNOT, an increase in government consumption above baseline amounting to 1 percent of nominal GDP.
- FTEMPSG, an increase of government employment corresponding to an expenditure increase at current government wages equal to 1 percent of nominal GDP.

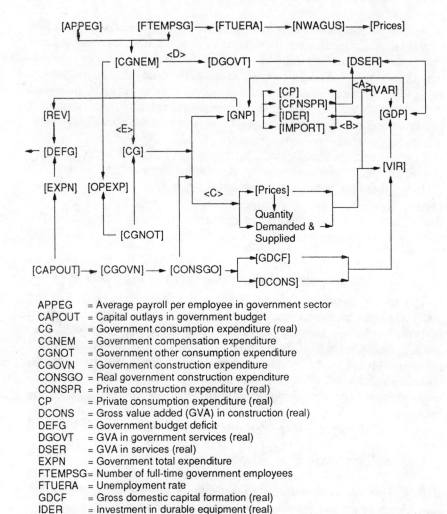

APPEG   = Average payroll per employee in government sector
CAPOUT = Capital outlays in government budget
CG   = Government consumption expenditure (real)
CGNEM   = Government compensation expenditure (real)
CGNOT   = Government other consumption expenditure
CGOVN   = Government construction expenditure
CONSGO = Real government construction expenditure
CONSPR = Private construction expenditure (real)
CP   = Private consumption expenditure (real)
DCONS   = Gross value added (GVA) in construction (real)
DEFG   = Government budget deficit
DGOVT   = GVA in government services (real)
DSER   = GVA in services (real)
EXPN   = Government total expenditure
FTEMPSG = Number of full-time government employees
FTUERA   = Unemployment rate
GDCF   = Gross domestic capital formation (real)
IDER   = Investment in durable equipment (real)
NWAGUS = Nominal weage of unskilled labor (1972 = 100)
OPEXP1 = Government operating expenditure
REV   = Government revenue

Notes:
1. For CGNOT shock, the shock is transmitted to the real sector through real government consumption expenditure.
2. For FTEMPSG shock, routes <A>, <B>, and <C> are adjusted to avoid the double calculation of the effect of GDP through output changes
3. For APPEG shock, the effect through routes <D> and <E> is insignificant because the change in APPEG will also result in increases in the price index for DGOVT and the price index for CG.
4. For CAPOUT shock, the change in CAPOUT results in the change in CGOVN. The effect is directed to the real sector through change in capital stock

FIGURE 7.2   Model linkage: Government expenditure to real sector.

- APPEG, an increase in government wage payments without any change in government employment amounting to 1 percent of nominal GDP.
- CAPOUT, an increase in government capital expenditures amounting to 1 percent of nominal GDP.

Before examining the results, we consider our expectations for these simulations. A number of forces will be operating simultaneously in the entire model; therefore, we consider only the first stage impacts here.

The distinction between the simulations depends on the first stage impact of the additional expenditure on real demand flows in the economy and on the response of output to the demand impacts. The CAPOUT simulation also includes a supply impact through the accumulation of additional public sector capital investment.

CGNOT is intended to represent a demand shock on the private producing sectors of the economy. The increased purchases by the public sector draw on private sector product and feed through the economy through the increased activity of private producing sectors.

In contrast, FTEMPSG represents an increase in government employment. It is treated by national accounts statisticians as an increase in government consumption directly satisfied by increased government output. An increase in government production (GVA) corresponding to the increase in government employment has been introduced. At the same time, there is, of course, no additional direct impact from this government spending increase toward the private sector, although the increase in public employee wage payments represents a secondary-level demand factor to the rest of the economy.

The contrast here is with the increase in public sector wage rates assumed in the APPEG simulation. In this case, there is no first stage increase in real demand at all. An increase in public sector wage rates without any change in the number of employees causes a proportional change in the government sector price index and no change in real public expenditures. However, as above, secondary effects result as government employees now spend their increased wages.

Finally, the increase in government investment (CAPOUT), like CGNOT, represents a real increase in government demand for output of nongovernment sectors of the economy.[4] The result of these differences is that we anticipate normal demand multipliers associated with the CGNOT, FTEMPSG, and CAPOUT simulations. Over time, the CAPOUT simulation might give somewhat higher multiplier results because the increased public sector investment is included in capital stock and should improve the economy's productive capacity. But the

APPEG simulation should have little real impact, at least by way of direct channels, because there is no change in government demand for real product, only an increase in wages and prices.

A problem arises in the comparability of these simulations as a result of the fact that they have been formulated in terms of a common nominal increase in government spending. In each case, the same nominal change has been assumed: an increase of government nominal spending equal to 1 percent of nominal GDP. The difficulty lies in the fact that such a change can translate into different real demand shocks depending on the level of the price deflator applied. This does not pose a serious problem if the deflators are the same because the real impacts would cluster around 1 percent of real GDP. In fact, the real shocks vary somewhat between the simulations.[5] We consider these differences in our discussion of the simulation results below.

The alternative approaches to funding the increased government expenditures are as follows:

- Without tax change: No changes in the tax parameters. Because taxes are endogenous in the model, tax revenues will respond to changes in the economy even though there has been no change in the tax parameters.
- With tax change: The tax equations were adjusted so that added expenditure is financed by tax increases.

We anticipate that the multipliers for the simulations without a change in tax rate could be somewhat more stimulative and inflationary than those in which an effort at maintaining budget balance by increasing tax rates has been attempted.

The results of these simulations are summarized in Tables 7.1 and 7.2. (Detailed results are shown in the appendix to this chapter.)

We compare first the two simulations that represent increases in demand for private sector product, CGNOT and CAPOUT, without adjustment in tax rates. Not surprisingly, these simulations yield very similar results. GDP multipliers rise gradually from 1.3 to 2.1. The critical difference for CAPOUT is the accumulation for capital stock, which is approximately 1.4 percent above the base simulation in year in the CAPOUT simulation. This also translates into a somewhat different composition of output against agriculture and in favor of industry (see Tables 7.A1 and 7.A4 in the appendix). Inflationary impacts are modest, from 0.4 percent to 1.0 percent in CGNOT, and somewhat lower again in line with expectations for CAPOUT. The trade impacts are also close to expectations, with very little change in exports and a 1.5 to 2.0 percent increase in imports, causing the balance of payments to deteriorate. The budget deficit increases about the same amount in both cases.

The simulations dealing with government wage payments, for more personnel (FTEMPSG) and for higher wage rates (APPEG) are considered next. As noted above, the nominal expenditure of these simulations is the same as for the CGNOT and CAPOUT simulations. In FTEMPSG the increase is entirely translated into an increase in government employment and production. Because of differences in the deflator (we note that there is an initial reduction in the GDP deflator), the real impact of a nominal change equal to 1 percent of nominal GDP comes out somewhat larger in this case in real terms than in the CGNOT simulation (1.3 percent in 1985 and approximately 1.1 percent thereafter). The effect on GDP is also somewhat larger in 1985 and 1986, but after that it settles down to multipliers that are very close to those obtained from the CGNOT simulation.[6] Except for the differences in the first two years of the simulation, the impact of government spending on additional public employees is substantially similar to the impact of an increase in government purchases from the private sector. The basic output increase in this case originates in the government sector. The point is that an increase in government employment will have an aggregate economic impact very similar to an increase in government demand from the private sector. We are confident that this applies to military as well as to civilian spending

The APPEG simulation, in contrast, has no direct "real" impact on demand or output. Through indirect channels there is a positive impact on GDP, rising gradually to 0.7 percent. Not surprisingly, there is a significant inflationary effect of approximately 1.1 percent. The budget deficit increases by more than the other simulations. Because there is little change in real economic activity, the effect on trade and the balance of payments is relatively small.

Once we increase taxes, as seen in Table 7.2, the multiplier effects are, of course, much lower. This is not quite a balanced budget multiplier. Indeed, the exogenous change in taxes just equal to the increase of expenditures overcompensates a little because there is some endogenous increase in tax receipts. The GDP multiplier amounts to 0.4–0.5 percent. The price impacts are very small positives in the CGNOT simulation and there are even some very small negatives when expenditures are directed at capital goods (CAPOUT) or government employment (FTEMPSG). The same slightly more favorable impact on manufacturing output, as we noted above, is observed in CAPOUT. If an increase in taxes is used to pay for a government wage increase, there is substantial negative impact on real GDP, up to 0.9 percent negative; the effect on inflation continues

TABLE 7.1 The Effect of Alternative Policies Without Tax Change (percentage deviation from baseline)

	1985	1986	1987	1988	1989
Effect on real GNP (GNP)					
Base GNP (million pesos)	86,612	93,164	97,751	106,367	109,400
Increase in:					
CGNOT of 1% of nominal GDP	1.30	1.39	1.51	1.59	2.00
FTEMPSG/(CGNEM is 1% of nominal GDP)	2.09	1.71	1.62	1.54	2.06
APPEG/(CGNEM is 1% of nominal GDP)	0.34	0.28	0.30	0.42	0.68
CAPOUT/(CGOVN is 1% of nominal GDP)	1.31	1.47	1.67	1.86	2.12
Effect on GNP deflator (PGNP)					
Base PGNP/(1972=100)	697	657	714	744	847
Increase in:					
CGNOT of 1% of nominal GDP	0.37	0.60	0.72	0.85	0.97
FTEMPSG/(CGNEM is 1% of nominal GDP)	0.46	0.59	0.53	0.54	0.66
APPEG/(CGNEM is 1% of nominal GDP)	0.52	0.82	0.95	1.08	1.12
CAPOUT/(CGOVN is 1% of nominal GDP)	0.19	0.28	0.34	0.42	0.49
Effect on government deficit (DEFG)[a]					
Base DEFG/(million pesos)	15,665	39,263	24,109	29,630	42,838
Increase in:					
CGNOT of 1% of nominal GDP	4,714	4,407	4,766	5,1274	6,003
FTEMPSG/(CGNEM is 1% of nominal GDP)	3,925	4,037	4,727	5,531	6,195
APPEG/(CGNEM is 1% of nominal GDP)	5,520	5,426	5,986	6,591	7,674
CAPOUT/(CGOVN is 1% of nominal GDP)	4,820	4,537	4,870	5,291	6,263
Effect on balance of payments (BOP)[a]					
Base BOP/(million dollars)	1,815	1,229	−648	30	739
Increase in:					
CGNOT of 1% of nominal GDP	−90	−102	−138	−162	−209
FTEMPSG/(CGNEM is 1% of nominal GDP)	−138	−124	−143	−148	−200
APPEG/(CGNEM is 1% of nominal GDP)	−33	−34	−46	−59	−82
CAPOUT/(CGOVN is 1% of nominal GDP)	−85	−97	−135	−166	−202
Effect on imports (IMPORT)					
Base IMPORT/(million pesos)	14,840	17,872	22,486	25,106	25,598
Increase in:					
CGNOT of 1% of nominal GDP	1.51	1.58	1.48	1.51	1.91
FTEMPSG/(CGNEM is 1% of nominal GDP)	2.35	2.01	1.65	1.50	1.97
APPEG/(CGNEM is 1% of nominal GDP)	0.50	0.42	0.36	0.43	0.65
CAPOUT/(CGOVN is 1% of nominal GDP)	1.50	1.63	1.60	1.72	2.04

CGNOT   = Government other consumption expenditures (nominal).
FTEMPSG = Number of full-time government employees.
APPEG   = Average payroll for government employees.
CGNEM   = Government compensation expenditure for employees (Nominal).
CAPOUT = Capital outlays (cash basis).
CGOVN   = Government construction expenditures (nominal).

[a]Difference from baseline.

TABLE 7.2 The Effect of Alternative Policies With Tax Change (percentage deviation from baseline)

	1985	1986	1987	1988	1989
Effect on real GNP (GNP)					
Base GNP (million pesos)	86,612	93,164	97,751	106,367	109,400
Increase in:					
CGNOT of 1% of nominal GDP	0.46	0.40	0.39	0.31	0.42
FTEMPSG/(CGNEM is 1% of nominal GDP)	1.24	0.71	0.49	0.26	0.47
APPEG/(CGNEM is 1% of nominal GDP)	−0.51	−0.72	−0.83	−0.87	−0.91
CAPOUT/(CGOVN is 1% of nominal GDP)	0.46	0.47	0.54	0.58	0.53
Effect on GNP deflator (PGNP)					
Base PGNP/(1972=100)	697	657	714	744	847
Increase in:					
CGNOT of 1% of nominal GDP	0.26	0.32	0.29	0.25	0.31
FTEMPSG/(CGNEM is 1% of nominal GDP)	0.36	0.33	0.11	−0.05	0.01
APPEG/(CGNEM is 1% of nominal GDP)	0.41	0.55	0.53	0.49	0.48
CAPOUT/(CGOVN is 1% of nominal GDP)	0.09	0.01	−0.09	−0.18	−0.17
Effect on government deficit (DEFG)[a]					
Base DEFG/(million pesos)	15,665	39,263	24,109	29,630	42,838
Increase in:					
CGNOT of 1% of nominal GDP	−506	−542	−548	−485	−678
FTEMPSG/(CGNEM is 1% of nominal GDP)	−1299	−917	−591	−233	−493
APPEG/(CGNEM is 1% of nominal GDP)	297	472	666	823	980
CAPOUT/(CGOVN is 1% of nominal GDP)	−400	−411	−445	−471	−427
Effect on balance of payments (BOP)[a]					
Base BOP/(million dollars)	1,815	1,229	−648	30	739
Increase in:					
CGNOT of 1% of nominal GDP	−5	9	14	26	19
FTEMPSG/(CGNEM is 1% of nominal GDP)	−52	−14	10	40	28
APPEG/(CGNEM is 1% of nominal GDP)	52	77	106	128	145
CAPOUT/(CGOVN is 1% of nominal GDP)	1	14	18	22	26
Effect on imports (IMPORT)					
Base IMPORT/(million pesos)	14,840	17,872	22,486	25,106	25,598
Increase in:					
CGNOT of 1% of nominal GDP	−0.15	−0.37	−0.37	−0.44	−0.43
FTEMPSG/(CGNEM is 1% of nominal GDP)	0.69	0.06	−0.22	−0.45	−0.38
APPEG/(CGNEM is 1% of nominal GDP)	−1.17	−1.53	−1.50	−1.53	−1.69
CAPOUT/(CGOVN is 1% of nominal GDP)	−0.16	−0.32	−0.26	−0.23	−0.30

CGNOT   = Government other consumption expenditures (nominal).
FTEMPSG = Number of full-time government employees.
APPEG   = Average payroll for government employees.
CGNEM   = Government compensation expenditure for employees (Nominal).
CAPOUT = Capital outlays (cash basis).
CGOVN   = Government construction expenditures (nominal).

[a]Difference from baseline.

positive but a little less than without increased taxes. Unfortunately, the mechanism of the model does not yield a lower interest rate, and the level of capital cumulation is hardly affected.

Conclusions

How can we relate the above results to the impact of military spending on the Philippines? We remind the reader that the simulations have dealt with government spending for all purposes and that the data have not permitted us to single out defense spending. But we also remind the reader that national accounting practice deals with government spending for defense comparably with other government consumption.[7] Military personnel contribute to the GDP, regardless of whether external observers would view their efforts as a positive contribution or as a wasted effort.

Subject to the assumption about the similarity of government spending for defense or for other purposes we find the following conclusions. Increases in spending for products of the private economy have a multiplier effect and tend to increase output in the private sectors of the economy. There are inflationary effects, but the Philippine economy is evidently not far enough up the Phillips curve that real output impacts are apparent. This is also apparent if the expenditures are for capital goods and construction. Note, however, that military spending calls for purchases of goods and services that are entirely different from those purchased for the support of civilian activities. Military purchases may have less perceived value from the perspective of consumer welfare than civilian spending. Contrast, for example, the purchase of guns as compared to the purchase of school supplies.

Similar comments apply to the changes with respect to government payrolls. The increase in the number of government workers affects GDP, whether it is for additional military or civilian employees, assuming that the wage rates are the same for the two groups. But the difference is that the effect on measured GDP has very different welfare content. Of course, that may be considered a matter of judgment! In any case, an increase in the number of military employees has a clear impact on GDP and on activity in other sectors, and even a small positive effect on capital stock. There is some inflationary effect but no clear evidence of crowding out. Increases in government wage rates have effects on real output only indirectly because they do not account for a direct increase in real demand or output. In turn, they have inflationary impacts through their direct representation in the government sector deflator. It is probable that the effects are comparable whether wage increases go to civilian or military employees.

The time series macro model simulation results are thus consistent with other work, which suggests that military spending has direct positive impacts on GDP because additional employees make a direct measured contribution to GDP, whether civilian or military. This is not surprising because the Philippine model is not strictly constrained to capacity limits. Part of the demand increase is translated into additional output, although part also causes an increase in the price level. In contrast to the typical CGE model,[8] the macro model simulations suggest that demand increases, even from nonwelfare producing expenditures, will have at least a temporary effect on measured output.

Notes

1. Due to lack of appropriate data, the model computations deal with alternative approaches to government spending in total rather than just the military component.

2. *World Development Report* (1990).

3. Adjustments are made in the simulations to maintain the same level of the statistical discrepancy in the alternative scenario simulations as in the control solution.

4. In order to pass through the entire increase in CAPOUT on government construction expenditure, we have overruled the functional relation between these variables that operate in the model with a coefficient of less than one.

5. Of course, APPEG should not show a first stage real shock.

6. The differences may also be due to a delayed impact of increased government demand on production in the private sectors in the CGNOT simulation in contrast to FTEMPSG, whose effect on government output is direct and immediate.

7. Government investment expenditures are by definition for civilian purposes. Military spending is treated as government consumption even when it is for hardware or construction.

8. Most CGE models are constrained to be full employment or at a specified level of output (Dervis et al. 1982), although there are exceptions (Levy 1987).

References

Adams, F. Gerard, Jere R. Behrman, and Michael Boldin (1988). "Defense Expenditures and Economic Growth in the LDCs: An Application of the Feder Approach to Military and Non-Military Government Spending," University of Pennsylvania Discussion Paper.

Adams, F. Gerard, Jere R. Behrman, and Roberto Mariano (1988). "Defense

Expenditures and Economic Growth in the LDCs: A Preview of Ongoing Research," University of Pennsylvania Discussion Paper.

Ball, Nicole (1988). *Security and Economy in the Third World*, Princeton: Princeton University Press.

Benoit, Emile (1972). "Growth and Effects of Defense in Developing Countries," *IDR*, 2-10.

Benoit, Emile (1973). *Defense and Economic Growth in Developing Countries*. Boston: D.C. Heath.

Constantino, W.M., Roberto S. Mariano, and Josef T. Yap (1989). "The PIDS-NEDA Annual Macroeconometric Model, Version 1989," Philippine Institute for Development Studies Discussion Paper.

Dervis, K., J. de Melo, S. Robinson, (1982), *General Equilibrium Models for Development Policy*, New York, Cambridge University Press.

Feder, G. (1982), "On Exports and Economic Growth", *Journal of Development Economics*, 12: 1/2, 59-73.

Levy, S. (1987). "A Short-Run General Equilibrium Model for a Small Open Economy," *Journal of Development Economics* 25: 63-88.

Mariano, Roberto S. and W.M. Constantino (1987). "An Annual Econometric Model for Macro-Policy Analysis in the Philippines," Philippine Institute for Development Studies Discussion Paper. Revised

Appendix

TABLE 7A.1 The Effects of CGNOT Shock Without Tax Change
(percentage deviation from baseline)

	1985	1986	1987	1988	1989
Real GNP	1.30	1.39	1.51	1.59	2.00
GNP deflator	0.37	0.60	0.72	0.85	0.97
Nominal GNP	1.67	2.00	2.25	2.46	2.99
Real GDP	1.27	1.35	1.49	1.58	1.90
GDP deflator	0.37	0.60	0.72	0.85	0.97
GVA in agriculture	0.67	1.07	1.47	1.84	2.26
GVA in industry	2.40	2.18	2.19	2.08	2.53
GVA in services	0.78	0.87	0.94	0.99	1.16
GVA in government services	0.00	0.00	0.00	0.00	0.00
PCG	0.07	0.10	0.12	0.14	0.19
PGOVT	0.00	0.00	0.00	0.00	0.00
WPI	0.21	0.39	0.54	0.68	0.79
CPI	0.37	0.61	0.74	0.87	0.99
Nominal wages	0.23	0.45	0.62	0.77	0.92
Unemployment rates[a]	−0.004	−0.008	−0.012	−0.016	−0.022
Total labor force	0.00	0.00	0.00	0.00	0.00
Budget deficit/(million P)[a]	4,714	4,407	4,766	5,274	6,003
Tax revenue	2.35	2.83	2.74	2.83	3.12
Nontax revenue	0.853	0.56	0.61	0.68	0.85
Government expenditure	7.38	5.42	5.86	5.71	5.56
BOP/(million $)[a]	−90	−102	−138	−162	−209
Exports	−0.13	−0.19	−0.29	−0.30	−0.32
Imports	1.51	1.58	1.48	1.51	1.91
Total liquidity	1.30	1.41	2.39	3.44	4.53
Money supply	1.80	1.93	2.14	2.35	2.94
Monetary base	0.09	0.22	1.21	2.21	3.09
Funds	0.38	1.25	1.44	1.56	2.29
Treasury bill rate	0.10	−0.10	0.07	0.13	−0.16
Net foreign assets	1.72	3.07	4.26	5.95	9.24
Capital stock	0.03	0.07	0.11	0.14	0.17
Real private consumption	1.01	1.05	1.17	1.28	1.66
Real government consumption	13.93	12.79	11.88	10.75	10.58
Real government construction	−0.16	−0.31	−0.46	−0.60	−0.72
Real private construction	0.54	1.26	1.43	1.37	1.47

GVA   = Gross value-added.
PCG   = Price index for real government consumption.
PGOVT = Price index for GVA in government services (DGOVT).
[a]Deviation from Baoolino.

TABLE 7A.2   The Effects of FTEMPSG Shock Without Tax Change
(percentage deviation from baseline)

	1985	1986	1987	1988	1989
Real GNP	2.09	1.71	1.62	1.54	2.06
GNP deflator	0.46	0.59	0.53	0.54	0.66
Nominal GNP	2.56	2.31	2.15	2.09	2.74
Real GDP	2.03	1.66	1.60	1.53	1.97
GDP deflator	0.46	0.59	0.53	0.54	0.66
GVA in agriculture	0.06	0.29	0.50	0.83	1.22
GVA in industry	−0.05	−0.09	−0.06	−0.04	0.10
GVA in services	5.20	4.13	3.76	3.32	3.92
GVA in government services	22.82	19.69	18.20	15.63	16.34
PCG	0.09	0.08	0.08	0.08	0.12
PGOVT	0.00	0.00	0.00	0.00	0.00
WPI	0.28	0.33	0.35	0.40	0.49
CPI	0.47	0.60	0.53	0.55	0.67
Nominal wages	0.27	0.43	0.45	0.48	0.59
Unemployment rates[a]	−0.002	−0.003	−0.004	−0.007	−0.010
Total labor force	0.00	0.00	0.00	0.00	0.00
Budget deficit/(million P)[a]	3,925	4,037	4,727	5,531	6,195
Tax revenue	3.63	3.39	2.78	2.56	2.96
Nontax revenue	0.80	0.70	0.65	0.64	0.77
Government expenditure	7.38	5.42	5.86	5.71	5.56
BOP/(million $)[a]	−138	−124	−143	−148	−200
Exports	−0.15	−0.18	−0.20	−0.16	−0.17
Imports	2.35	2.01	1.65	1.50	1.97
Total liquidity	−0.07	0.51	1.97	3.74	5.07
Money supply	2.89	2.17	2.02	1.98	2.71
Monetary base	−1.90	−0.89	0.81	2.70	3.71
Funds	2.47	2.11	1.39	1.04	1.93
Treasury bill rate	−0.33	0.32	0.42	0.29	−0.26
Net foreign assets	2.62	4.09	5.01	6.30	9.38
Capital stock	0.05	0.10	0.14	0.17	0.19
Real private consumption	1.53	1.32	1.27	1.24	1.70
Real government consumption	13.91	12.80	11.93	10.81	10.66
Real government construction	−0.21	−0.29	−0.32	−0.36	−0.45
Real private construction	0.94	1.80	1.79	1.49	1.52

GVA   = Gross value-added.
PCG   = Price index for real government consumption.
PGOVT = Price index for GVA in government services (DGOVT).
[a]Deviation from Baseline.

TABLE 7A.3 The Effects of APPEG Shock Without Tax Change
(percentage deviation from baseline)

	1985	1986	1987	1988	1989
Real GNP	0.34	0.28	0.30	0.42	0.68
GNP deflator	0.52	0.82	0.95	1.08	1.12
Nominal GNP	0.86	1.09	1.25	1.50	1.81
Real GDP	0.32	0.26	0.29	0.41	0.61
GDP deflator	0.52	0.82	0.95	1.08	1.12
GVA in agriculture	0.24	0.45	0.70	1.02	1.34
GVA in industry	0.30	0.01	−0.07	−0.01	0.15
GVA in services	0.39	0.32	0.30	0.32	0.46
GVA in government services	1.57	1.10	0.83	0.53	0.62
PCG	13.29	13.03	12.69	11.60	11.49
PGOVT	20.92	18.38	17.23	15.01	15.62
WPI	0.25	0.49	0.64	0.79	0.87
CPI	0.52	0.83	0.96	1.10	1.14
Nominal wages	0.29	0.58	0.73	0.88	0.98
Unemployment rates[a]	−0.001	−0.002	−0.004	−0.007	−0.011
Total labor force	0.00	0.00	0.00	0.00	0.00
Budget deficit/(million P)[a]	5,520	5,426	5,986	6,591	7,674
Tax revenue	1.04	1.24	1.24	1.42	1.65
Nontax revenue	0.32	0.34	0.39	0.45	0.57
Government expenditure	7.38	5.42	5.86	5.71	5.56
BOP/(million $)[a]	−33	−34	−46	−59	−82
Exports	−0.12	−0.18	−0.27	−0.27	−0.26
Imports	0.50	0.42	0.36	0.43	0.65
Total liquidity	2.63	3.03	5.00	5.45	6.29
Money supply	0.75	1.04	1.21	1.54	1.78
Monetary base	2.16	2.64	4.62	5.02	5.68
Funds	−1.84	−1.27	−0.73	−0.22	0.23
Treasury bill rate	0.67	0.10	−0.13	−0.10	−0.09
Net foreign assets	0.63	1.06	1.45	2.09	3.42
Capital stock	0.00	0.01	0.01	0.02	0.03
Real private consumption	0.36	0.22	0.24	0.35	0.59
Real government consumption	0.63	−0.12	−0.60	−0.62	−0.63
Real government construction	−0.19	−0.39	−0.56	−0.70	−0.80
Real private construction	−0.08	−0.02	0.10	0.20	0.38

GVA   = Gross value-added.
PCG   = Price index for real government consumption.
PGOVT = Price index for GVA in government services (DGOVT).
[a]Deviation from Baseline.

TABLE 7A.4   The Effects of CAPOUT Shock Without Tax Change
(percentage deviation from baseline)

	1985	1986	1987	1988	1989
Real GNP	1.31	1.47	1.67	1.86	2.12
GNP deflator	0.19	0.28	0.34	0.42	0.49
Nominal GNP	1.50	1.75	2.02	2.29	2.62
Real GDP	1.27	1.43	1.66	1.85	2.03
GDP deflator	0.19	0.28	0.34	0.41	0.49
GVA in agriculture	0.37	0.63	0.93	1.27	1.59
GVA in industry	2.68	2.74	3.01	3.16	3.44
GVA in services	0.79	0.93	1.06	1.18	1.25
GVA in government services	0.00	0.00	0.00	0.00	0.00
PCG	0.03	0.05	0.06	0.07	0.09
PGOVT	0.00	0.00	0.00	0.00	0.00
WPI	0.11	0.19	0.26	0.35	0.37
CPI	0.19	0.28	0.34	0.42	0.49
Nominal wages	0.12	0.22	0.29	0.37	0.45
Unemployment rates[a]	−0.003	−0.004	−0.005	−0.007	−0.009
Total labor force	0.00	0.00	0.00	0.00	0.00
Budget deficit/(million P)[a]	4,820	4,537	4,870	5,291	6,263
Tax revenue	2.18	2.64	2.63	2.83	2.91
Nontax revenue	0.46	0.47	0.52	0.59	0.72
Government expenditure	7.38	5.42	5.86	5.71	5.56
BOP/(million $)[a]	−85	−97	−135	−166	−202
Exports	−0.05	−0.07	−0.11	−0.11	−0.10
Imports	1.50	1.63	1.60	1.72	2.04
Total liquidity	1.67	1.76	2.80	3.71	4.83
Money supply	1.62	1.70	1.94	2.20	2.57
Monetary base	0.46	0.58	1.57	2.31	3.35
Funds	0.16	0.87	1.17	1.46	1.84
Treasury bill rate	0.06	−0.19	−0.10	−0.07	−0.08
Net foreign assets	1.62	2.90	4.09	5.89	9.06
Capital stock	0.26	0.54	0.83	1.13	1.41
Real private consumption	1.01	1.10	1.27	1.46	1.74
Real government consumption	−0.03	−0.05	−0.06	−0.07	−0.09
Real government construction	32.88	34.22	33.95	34.61	33.88
Real private construction	0.64	1.46	1.69	1.70	1.75

GVA   = Gross value-added.
PCG   = Price index for real government consumption.
PGOVT – Price index for GVA in government services (DGOVT).
[a]Deviation from Baseline.

TABLE 7A.5 The Effects of CGNOT Shock With Tax Change
(percentage deviation from baseline)

	1985	1986	1987	1988	1989
Real GNP	0.46	0.40	0.39	0.31	0.42
GNP deflator	0.26	0.32	0.29	0.25	0.31
Nominal GNP	0.72	0.72	0.68	0.56	0.72
Real GDP	0.44	0.38	0.38	0.31	0.39
GDP deflator	0.26	0.32	0.29	0.25	0.31
GVA in agriculture	0.10	0.16	0.18	0.14	0.15
GVA in industry	0.78	0.61	0.59	0.44	0.64
GVA in services	0.41	0.36	0.35	0.32	0.37
GVA in government services	0.00	0.00	0.00	0.00	0.00
PCG	0.09	0.10	0.08	0.07	0.10
PGOVT	0.00	0.00	0.00	0.00	0.00
WPI	0.30	0.41	0.36	0.33	0.40
CPI	0.26	0.33	0.30	0.26	0.31
Nominal wages	0.15	0.23	0.25	0.23	0.26
Unemployment rates[a]	−0.001	−0.001	−0.002	−0.002	−0.002
Total labor force	0.00	0.00	0.00	0.00	0.00
Budget deficit/(million P)[a]	−506	−542	−548	−485	−678
Tax revenue	11.08	10.84	9.60	9.32	9.32
Nontax revenue	0.24	0.22	0.22	0.20	0.23
Government expenditure	7.38	5.42	5.86	5.71	5.56
BOP/(million $)[a]	−5	9	14	26	19
Exports	−0.11	−0.12	−0.14	−0.12	−0.14
Imports	−0.15	−0.37	−0.37	−0.44	−0.43
Total liquidity	−0.34	−0.00	−0.01	0.12	−0.11
Money supply	0.84	0.69	0.63	0.52	0.71
Monetary base	−0.73	−0.37	−0.33	−0.09	−0.35
Funds	1.42	1.60	1.24	0.85	1.05
Treasury bill rate	−0.19	0.01	0.22	0.23	−0.02
Net foreign assets	0.09	−0.09	−0.29	−0.65	−0.94
Capital stock	0.01	0.03	0.06	0.09	0.12
Real private consumption	−0.61	−0.63	−0.61	−0.69	−0.68
Real government consumption	13.90	12.78	11.92	10.83	13.69
Real government construction	−0.23	−0.34	−0.34	−0.33	−0.37
Real private construction	0.16	0.53	0.75	0.84	3.94

GVA   = Gross value-added.
PCG   = Price index for real government consumption.
PGOVT = Price index for GVA in government services (DGOVT).
[a]Deviation from Baseline.

TABLE 7A.6   The Effects of FTEMPSG Shock With Tax Change
(percentage deviation from baseline)

	1985	1986	1987	1988	1989
Real GNP	1.24	0.71	0.49	0.26	0.47
GNP deflator	0.36	0.33	0.11	−0.05	0.01
Nominal GNP	1.60	1.04	0.60	0.21	0.49
Real GDP	1.20	0.69	0.49	0.25	0.45
GDP deflator	0.36	0.33	0.11	−0.05	0.01
GVA in agriculture	−0.51	−0.62	−0.79	−0.88	−0.90
GVA in industry	−1.67	−1.67	−1.67	−1.69	−1.81
GVA in services	4.83	3.62	3.16	2.65	3.13
GVA in government services	22.82	19.69	18.20	15.63	16.34
PCG	0.11	0.09	0.04	0.01	0.03
PGOVT	0.00	0.00	0.00	0.00	0.00
WPI	0.36	0.35	0.18	0.05	0.12
CPI	0.37	0.34	0.11	−0.05	0.01
Nominal wages	0.19	0.22	0.09	−0.05	−0.06
Unemployment rates[a]	0.001	0.003	0.006	0.008	0.010
Total labor force	0.00	0.00	0.00	0.00	0.00
Budget deficit/(million P)[a]	−1,299	−917	−591	−233	−493
Tax revenue	12.36	11.41	9.64	9.05	9.16
Nontax revenue	0.51	0.37	0.26	0.15	0.15
Government expenditure	7.38	5.42	5.86	5.71	5.56
BOP/(million $)[a]	−52	−14	10	40	28
Exports	−0.12	−0.11	−0.06	0.02	0.01
Imports	0.69	0.06	−0.22	−0.45	−0.38
Total liquidity	−1.73	−0.91	−0.43	0.41	0.41
Money supply	1.93	0.95	0.52	0.17	0.49
Monetary base	−2.72	−1.49	−0.73	0.40	0.26
Funds	3.51	2.47	1.21	0.34	0.71
Treasury bill rate	−0.61	0.42	0.57	0.39	−0.12
Net foreign assets	1.00	0.93	0.47	−0.30	−0.80
Capital stock	0.03	0.07	0.09	0.11	0.14
Real private consumption	−0.08	−0.36	−0.51	−0.74	−0.65
Real government consumption	13.88	12.80	11.97	10.89	10.76
Real government construction	−0.27	−0.32	−0.21	−0.09	−0.11
Real private construction	0.55	1.06	1.11	0.95	0.99

GVA   = Gross value-added.
PCG   = Price index for real government consumption.
PGOVT = Price index for GVA in government services (DGOVT).
[a]Deviation from Baseline.

TABLE 7A.7 The Effects of APPEG Shock With Tax Change
(percentage deviation from baseline)

	1985	1986	1987	1988	1989
Real GNP	−0.51	−0.72	−0.83	−0.87	−0.91
GNP deflator	0.41	0.55	0.53	0.49	0.48
Nominal GNP	−0.10	−0.17	−0.30	−0.38	−0.44
Real GDP	−0.51	−0.72	−0.82	−0.87	−0.90
GDP deflator	0.41	0.55	0.53	0.49	0.48
GVA in agriculture	−0.33	−0.47	−0.59	−0.68	−0.78
GVA in industry	−1.32	−1.56	−1.67	−1.65	−1.75
GVA in services	0.03	−0.19	−0.29	−0.35	−0.33
GVA in government services	1.57	1.10	0.83	0.53	0.62
PCG	13.32	13.04	12.65	11.53	11.40
PGOVT	20.92	18.38	17.23	15.01	15.62
WPI	0.34	0.51	0.48	0.45	0.50
CPI	0.42	0.56	0.56	0.50	0.48
Nominal wages	0.21	0.34	0.37	0.35	0.33
Unemployment rates[a]	0.002	0.004	0.006	0.007	0.009
Total labor force	0.00	0.00	0.00	0.00	0.00
Budget deficit/(million P)[a]	297	472	666	823	980
Tax revenue	9.77	9.26	8.10	7.92	7.83
Nontax revenue	0.04	0.02	−0.01	−0.03	−0.05
Government expenditure	7.38	5.42	5.86	5.71	5.56
BOP/(million $)[a]	52	77	106	128	145
Exports	−0.09	−0.11	−0.13	−0.09	−0.08
Imports	−1.17	−1.53	−1.50	−1.53	−1.69
Total liquidity	0.97	1.61	2.59	2.13	1.65
Money supply	−0.21	−0.19	−0.29	−0.36	−0.44
Monetary base	1.34	2.04	3.07	2.70	2.22
Funds	−0.79	−0.88	−0.90	−0.89	−0.97
Treasury bill rate	0.38	0.21	0.03	0.01	0.06
Net foreign assets	−0.99	−2.09	−3.09	−4.50	−6.74
Capital stock	−0.01	−0.03	−0.03	−0.03	−0.02
Real private consumption	−1.25	−1.45	−1.53	−1.62	−1.75
Real government consumption	0.60	−0.13	−0.57	−0.56	−0.55
Real government construction	−0.26	−0.42	−0.45	−0.43	−0.47
Real private construction	−0.46	−0.75	−0.58	−0.34	−0.16

GVA — Gross value-added.
PCG = Price index for real government consumption.
PGOVT = Price index for GVA in government services (DGOVT).
[a]Deviation from Baseline.

TABLE 7A.8   The Effects of CAPOUT Shock With Tax Change
(percentage deviation from baseline)

	1985	1986	1987	1988	1989
Real GNP	0.46	0.47	0.54	0.58	0.53
GNP deflator	0.09	0.01	−0.09	−0.18	−0.17
Nominal GNP	0.54	0.48	0.46	0.40	0.36
Real GDP	0.44	0.46	0.54	0.58	0.52
GDP deflator	0.09	0.01	−0.09	−0.18	−0.17
GVA in agriculture	−0.20	−0.28	−0.36	−0.43	−0.53
GVA in industry	1.05	1.16	1.41	1.52	1.54
GVA in services	0.42	0.42	0.47	0.51	0.47
GVA in government services	0.00	0.00	0.00	0.00	0.00
PCG	0.06	0.05	0.02	0.00	−0.00
PGOVT	0.00	0.00	0.00	0.00	0.00
WPI	0.20	0.20	0.08	0.01	−0.01
CPI	0.09	0.01	−0.09	−0.18	−0.17
Nominal wages	0.04	0.00	−0.08	−0.17	−0.21
Unemployment rates[a]	0.001	0.003	0.005	0.008	0.011
Total labor force	0.00	0.00	0.00	0.00	0.00
Budget deficit/(million P)[a]	−400	−411	−445	−471	−427
Tax revenue	10.91	10.65	9.49	9.32	9.11
Nontax revenue	0.17	0.14	0.12	0.11	0.10
Government expenditure	7.38	5.42	5.86	5.71	5.56
BOP/(million $)[a]	1	14	18	22	26
Exports	−0.03	−0.00	0.04	0.08	0.07
Imports	−0.16	−0.32	−0.26	−0.23	−0.30
Total liquidity	0.02	0.35	0.40	0.38	0.18
Money supply	0.66	0.47	0.43	0.38	0.35
Monetary base	−0.35	−0.01	0.04	0.01	−0.10
Funds	1.20	1.23	0.98	0.76	0.62
Treasury bill rate	−0.23	−0.08	0.05	0.03	0.06
Net foreign assets	−0.01	−0.27	−0.46	−0.72	−1.12
Capital stock	0.25	0.51	0.79	1.08	1.36
Real private consumption	−0.61	−0.58	−0.51	−0.51	−0.61
Real government consumption	−0.06	−0.05	−0.02	−0.00	0.00
Real government construction	32.79	34.18	34.10	34.98	34.34
Real private construction	0.25	0.73	1.01	1.17	1.22

GVA   = Gross value-added.
PCG   = Price index for real government consumption.
PGOVT = Price index for GVA in government services (DGOVT).
[a]Deviation from Baseline.

PART THREE

Arms Reduction and the Centrally Planned Economies

For the centrally planned economies, arms reduction played a much greater—some would say overwhelming—economic role than in the industrial market economies. Paradoxically, the shift from guns to butter also posed much more serious—some would say insurmountable—organizational challenges.

In the face of stagnant aggregate output, continued and growing military spending during the late 1970s and 1980s imposed ever larger burdens on the Soviet Union and most other centrally planned economies.[1] These countries had been facing increasing domestic discontent as living standards failed to rise and as the economy proved unable to satisfy consumer demands, often even for basic food and durable products available freely in the West for generations. The Gorbachev strategy of arms reduction had its proximate cause in the desire to reallocate resources from military use toward civilian investment and consumption. This shift came at a time when political and economic life in the centrally planned economies was undergoing radical change. The formerly centrally planned economies do not face simply a problem of reorienting their planning targets, but rather one of economic reform. They must integrate the transfer of resources from military to civilian use with total restructuring of their economies.

The military defense sector has had a favored role, benefiting from priority availability of material inputs, investment, and human capital. A reshuffling of objectives toward civilian production will call for reducing defense in favor of consumer and investment goods production. Organizationally, this can be accomplished by phasing out some military organizations and building new ones or by transforming industries now producing military goods to civilian production. The history of the past few years' failures in civilian industry, suggest that such changes are difficult, if not impossible, to achieve in a command-style economy. It is widely recognized in the former Soviet bloc as well as in the West that a turn toward civilian production requires a reorientation of economic management to enterprises guided by competitively determined market prices and to substantial, if not complete, privatization. The gains from arms reduction—psychological as well as physical—will materialize only if the available resources can be utilized efficiently to produce goods and services sought by consumers and if these products can be distributed broadly to the population.

In Part Three we present chapters that reflect different aspects of the extensive research work dealing with the economics of the military in the centrally planned economies. After many years of serious economic intelligence, the predominant issue in this regard is still one of measurement. As Charles Wolf documents in Chapter 8, in the Soviet Union the burden of defense spending had reached astronomical proportions, as much as 27 percent of GDP, more than twice earlier estimates. It is astonishing that this realization has been so recent, but evidence suggests that economists had somewhat underestimated Soviet expenditures on defense and related activities, while they had vastly overestimated Soviet GDP. Glasnost has revealed some of these realities even in Soviet publications. This makes clear why arms reduction had such a high priority in recent Soviet strategy.

It is difficult to determine with existing models how much a massive downscaling of defense spending will mean for the Russian consumer. The impact of arms reduction will depend not only on the resources available. Standard models of the Soviet economy follow past and existing paradigms of centrally planned economy behavior. Satisfying consumer needs calls for altogether different strategies, and these in turn call for different models. The impact of arms reduction will depend critically on the degree and nature of reform that takes place. Until there are meaningful market price signals, the transformation in the CIS republics will be a good deal more difficult than in the market economies. Arms reduction without reform would produce little *peace product dividend*.

The issues of transformation appear in the newly independent slates of the former Soviet block. Some of them can cut back their own military spending directly, although many of them may need to spend more as they accept a greater role of defending themselves in the face of much less regional stability and great frictions with their neighbors. They are also greatly affected by Russian efforts to pull back from foreign economic and political entanglements, greatly reduced or eliminated foreign economic support, and a need to pay world market prices for fuel and other material supplied by the Soviet economy. There is less for these countries to gain from arms reduction and there are increased burdens for many of them. Their need for economic reform has been recognized everywhere. In Chapter 9, Crane and Yeh describe these processes in three centrally planned economies —Poland, Hungary, and China. All three of these countries have already been involved in the process of economic change for some years.

Yeh and Crane do not paint an optimistic picture. It appears that only in China has reform yielded positive results clearly apparent on the macroeconomic level, a rapid rate of growth like that achieved in the newly industrialized economies (NIEs). But Crane and Yeh suggest that this is largely the result of a successful reform in agriculture, still China's most populous sector, and that the promise of efficient management in the industrial sectors has so far escaped all three countries. The dismantling of bureaucratic management is not yet far enough along, even in Poland, to create a truly competitive market economy. But these are precisely the issues that must be faced if resources taken from the military sector are to be used successfully to improve availability of goods to consumers.

Chapters by Davis and Hildebrandt focus once again on the former Soviet economy. Davis documents in detail the changes in Soviet military spending since the mid-1980s, suggesting that, at least on the surface, it would appear that there were massive reductions, although we cannot be sure whether these are cutbacks from planned—but unachieved—levels or whether they represent outright reductions in military outlays.

A detailed appraisal of military cutbacks is useful to evaluate how resources may be shifted from military to civilian use and how much more potential there is for additional cutbacks. Hildebrandt recognizes the importance of the machine-building industry in Soviet economic development. Using a specialized supply-side model of the growth model of the Soviet economy, Hildebrandt carries out alternative simulation of Soviet economic development assuming various scenarios of arms reduction.

This book closes, appropriately, with a more philosophical perspective. Murrell contrasts the neoclassical paradigm with a Schumpeterian view, finding the latter more relevant to the challenges of economic reform, arms reduction, and conversion in Eastern Europe.

Notes

1. The only exceptions are Hungary and China; Hungary because its military spending was very small, China because it made considerable progress, particularly in agriculture.

8

Defense and the Macroeconomy in the Soviet Union

Charles Wolf, Jr.

Introduction

If it is true that the "end of history" impends, then much of what is addressed in this chapter will become obsolete. All major economies will become more or less market-oriented democratic systems, with resource allocation guided by more or less competitively determined prices. The distinctive characteristics of centrally planned economies (CPEs) and of their prominent defense sectors, which are addressed in this chapter, will become historical curiosities, rather than matters of current policy relevance.

Whether and when this scenario will materialize is not considered here. Instead, this chapter focuses on various aspects of the relationships between the defense sectors and the macroeconomy of the Soviet Union and other CPEs, with primary emphasis on the former.

In the past two decades, the U.S. government has probably devoted more time, effort, and money to analyzing centrally planned economies, principally the Soviet Union and its defense sectors, than to analyzing this subject in any other foreign economy or group of foreign economies.

Notwithstanding the scale of this effort, accurate knowledge and understanding of the subject have been elusive and sometimes spurious. I make this judgment on the basis of two criteria: accuracy of measurement and validation of predictions. On both counts, the returns from this effort have not been commensurate with the resources devoted to it. To explain this outcome would require an essay on the sociology of the field—a subject I do not propose to address here.

However, in support of the general point, I will briefly address two issues—both relating principally to the Soviet Union; *mutatis mutandis*, they apply more generally to the CPEs as a group: first, the performance of the Soviet economy in the late 1970s and the 1980s—in particular, the failure of most Western analysts to predict or anticipate the severity of its crisis predicament or to track it accurately; and second, the still unresolved controversy over the relevant size of the Soviet economy and its defense burden.

These issues are of central concern in the collaborative work in which the Hoover Institution and RAND have engaged, with generous support from the Pew Charitable Trusts as well as the U.S. Department of Defense, over the past three years.1 While the central focus of this work and this chapter is on the Soviet Union, some attention will also be devoted to CPEs in Eastern Europe and China.

The Performance of the Soviet Economy

Throughout much of Soviet history, criticisms of economic methods, and debates over the quality of Soviet statistical calculations were stifled by repressive controls. For many years, an almost private discussion was carried on within the statistical community, with little if any influence on the practices of central organs.

While some daring Soviet economists, including Val'tukh, Khanin, Krasovskii, and Fal'tsman, published technical, albeit less broadly critical, articles at variance with official positions, their debate was for the most part limited to intellectual discussion and did not influence reporting by the Central Statistical Administration (TsSU). Moreover, this underlying doubt and criticism was rarely reflected in Western analysis of the Soviet economy.

As the mandates of glasnost began to take hold and were reinforced within the Soviet statistical establishment by the leadership's concern with the dilapidated state of the economy, more articles appeared in the Soviet press exposing the failures of Soviet statistical methods.

In 1987, the attack by economists on official Soviet statistics was dramatically escalated by an article in *Novy mir* by Seliunin and Khanin. They asserted that Soviet national income statistics since 1928 grossly overstated the economy's actual performance and, in fact, have little relationship to the real state of the economy.[2] Furthermore, they argue that because a false set of statistics was established and continues to provide unreliable information in measuring economic growth and productivity, this falsification was viewed as one of the causes of the continued economic decline over the past 30 years, and the failure to seek earlier remedies. In their article, Seliunin and Khanin call for an overhaul of current statistical methods as well as of the statistics themselves from earlier periods as a necessary component of any meaningful economic reform and for *perestroika's* success.

Richard Ericson has observed that Seliunin's and Khanin's alternative accounting shows that

> much of the claimed achievements of Soviet socialism are fictitious, are the consequence of a "game" of exaggeration played by subordinates and superiors whose outcomes are validated by the faulty methodology of aggregation and measurement of the central statistical authorities. . . . [N]ot only the size but also the structure of the economy are quite different from what the official statistics indicate. . . . Khanin and Seliunin are anywhere near being correct, then we can no longer believe in the "command economy" as an effective mobilizer of resources or instrument for change over any but the shortest period of time.[3]

While the Seliunin and Khanin article received tremendous attention both in the Soviet Union and in the West, the outspoken criticisms by many other critics, including Shmelev, Abalkin, Bogomolov, Zaichenko, Aganbegyan, and Orlov, have combined to exert noticeable pressure on the leadership to address the problem.

Even Gorbachev's own advisors have become involved in the dialogue of criticism. Aganbegyan, probably the most visible Soviet economist in the West, acknowledged in a 1987 article that

> the statistical data concerned with the increase in national income and the gross output do not sufficiently account for the real increase of prices. . . . Therefore, the [official] rates of increase in the national income. . . . of the 10th and 11th Five Year Plans are too high. In reality, for a number of years, particularly 1979–1982, the real growth of the national economy came to a halt and there was stagnation.[4]

In his book, *Economic Challenge of Perestroika*, Aganbegyan confirms that "in the period 1981–85 there was practically no economic growth," and that "during the period 1979–82 . . . production of 40 percent of all industrial goods actually fell" and "agriculture declined."[5]

The picture that emerges of the state of the economy is bleak:

- Official statistics are highly biased upward and generally are unreliable. Moreover, the biases have increased over time, resulting in exaggerated estimates of the economy's growth as well as its size.
- Inflation in the investment sector has been substantial, and much of the growth reported in capital investment in the 1970s and early 1980s did not occur.

- Inflation has been widespread throughout the economy, much of it hidden through the manipulation of fictitious improvements in product quality, or the concealment of quality deterioration. Particularly among manufactured goods, prices have soared as products are re-categorized, allowing for repricing of the virtually identical "new" products, while quality declined for products with unchanged prices.[6] Although there was no recorded inflation in the 1989 Soviet statistical handbook, Bogomolov estimated that prices rose during 1988 by 5 to 9 percent.[7]
- Real growth has been much less than officially reported, and somewhat less than generally estimated in the West, with near-stagnation since the mid-1970s.[8]
- While the 1989 Soviet statistical handbook indicates that there was a 200 million ruble *surplus* in the state budget in 1988, one Soviet academic predicted that the state would run up approximately a 100 billion ruble budget *deficit* during 1989. In an interesting twist, Goskomstat issued a press release in July 1989 after the publication of the handbook, in which for the first time it revealed a more realistic assessment of the size of the deficit, placing it at 90 billion rubles for 1988, or more than 10 percent of the published size of the Soviet GNP (866 billion rubles for 1988).[9]
- Conditions affecting the Soviet standard of living are deplorable: as of the beginning of 1988, the official number of Soviet urban families and individuals entitled to and awaiting improved housing rose to 13 million; and the average infant mortality rate in 1986 was 25.4 deaths per one thousand live births, with a shocking republic average of 58.2 deaths per one thousand live births in Turkmenistan, where infectious disease is responsible for quadrupling the number of deaths for infants under the age of one.
- Finally, the degradation of the environment has led not only to a severe environmental crisis, but also to deterioration in the quality of life and health of the Soviet population. According to the chairman of the USSR State Committee for Environmental Protection, approximately 50 million Soviet citizens living in 102 cities endure pollution levels exceeding by tenfold internationally acceptable standards.[10]

Although the foregoing points relate directly to the performance of the Soviet economy, they apply broadly and generally, if not uniformly, to virtually all of the centrally planned economies in Eastern Europe, China (until its market-oriented reforms got under way at the end of the 1970s), North Korea, Vietnam, and Cuba.

The severity and pervasiveness of the Soviet Union's economic predicament was not accurately described, nor were its manifold contributing causes properly illuminated by most Western analysts. Instead, their estimates continue to show appreciable positive, if declining, rates of real economic growth. Table 8.1 shows the sharp contrast between growth estimates of, respectively, official Soviet statistics, CIA and Western estimates, and those of Khanin.

The Khanin estimates derived by Ericson are more realistic than the CIA/Western estimates. The former may themselves be somewhat on the high side, but they receive general if impressionist corroboration from such diverse sources as Gorbachev, Aganbegyan, and private conversations with a number of other Soviet economists.[11]

The basic errors in the Western estimates arise from their general acceptance of the physical production data in official Soviet statistical sources. Assuming that the Khanin figures are in the right ballpark, the errors reflected by the Western estimates are really quite extraordinary: about 85 percent for the decade of the 1970s, and nearly 240 percent for the first half of the 1980s!

Moreover, since the total Soviet population grew by something over 1 percent per annum during the past two decades, another significant difference emerges between the two estimates. The CIA/Western estimates would represent an appreciable if declining rate of growth in per capita GNP, whereas the more realistic estimates derived from Khanin imply near stagnant per capita GNP in the 1970s, and appreciably negative growth in per capita GNP in the 1980s.

A similar pattern emerges with respect to forecasts by Western analysts. These have over the years generally tended to be pretty close to the subsequent estimates of outcomes and performance—again, arising from the same underlying point noted above concerning Western acceptance of the underlying Soviet physical production data.[12]

As already noted, these observations about economic performance as well as Western analysis have focused predominately on the Soviet Union. However, the general tenor of the comments applies more broadly to the CPEs as a group—including as well Eastern Europe,

TABLE 8.1 Soviet Economic Growth Estimates, 1970–1985
(average annual rate in percent)

Period	Official Soviet	CIA/Western	Khanin/Ericson
1970–1980	5.3	3.7	2.0
1981–1985	3.2	2.0	0.59

Cuba, Vietnam, Ethiopia, Angola, North Korea, and China, prior to the late 1970s and since July 1989. Forecasts and ex post performance estimates for the CPEs typically err on the high side, for reasons relating to the structure of incentives and institutions characteristic of these economies.

It would be worthwhile to do a systematic evaluation of the CPEs individually, considering their official estimates of GNP, composition, and performance, as well as those by Western analysts, and compare these estimates and forecasts with critical ex post evaluations of actual outcomes. Based on one case I have looked at in some detail—North Korea—I would make a guess concerning the performance of CPEs in general compared to the counterfactual case of what their performance would have been as market economies (MEs): their GNPs probably would have been about 40–50 percent below what the same economies would have produced over the past two decades had they been MEs, and their annual rates of real growth have perhaps averaged about 25–30 percent less than what would have prevailed in the counterfactual case. This guess is based on the empirical work at RAND comparing North and South Korea,[13] as well as my impression of what a comparison between East and West Germany would show.

Measurement of GNP and the Defense Burden

These measurement issues bear on the general question of the overall size of the Soviet economy. The relevant estimation method, pioneered by Kravis and his associates and applied to countries at widely different levels of development,[14] measures purchasing-power parity. Although this technique carries with it considerable uncertainty—especially when applied to nonmarket economies—it is a useful device for cross-country comparisons of economic size.

A widely quoted CIA estimate puts Soviet GNP in 1985 at around 55 percent of that of the United States, and about 47 percent the U.S. level per capita.[15] Robert Campbell estimated a much lower ratio, around 37 percent per capita (with a wide range of uncertainty), for 1980.[16] Anders Aslund puts it still lower, at about 30 percent of U.S. per capita GNP for the late 1980s. And even this estimate might be too high.

One might ask what difference it makes if Soviet GNP is a third that of the United States or the European Community, instead of a half; or whether it matters that Soviet aggregate output grew little if any after the late 1970s instead of at a rate of 2 to 3 percent annually. These are not trivial differences: A 2 percent difference in annual growth rates amounts to a 35 percent difference over 15 years and 100 percent over 36 years. Second, no growth per capita over time—if that is indeed the case—together with no realistic prospect for future improvement, provides a plausible explanation for some of the extraordinary events—political as well as economic—that have occurred in recent months in the Soviet Union, as well as a plausible impetus for radical change in the future. Third, given that we have independent evidence on the scale of the Soviet military effort, a substantially smaller Soviet economy implies that the share of resources taken by the military is larger than we had believed. This finding suggests the importance of reassessing the Soviet Union's ability to sustain its military competition with the West; it also provides the most compelling explanation for the evident and remarkable Soviet and post-Soviet motivation recently to reduce military burden and change foreign policy. Gorbachev's "new thinking," both at home and abroad, surely had a substantial, perhaps decisive, economic impetus behind it.

Analyzing the defense sector's role in the Soviet economy entails both specific technical issues and broader security and policy questions relating to the structure of the system. At the narrower, technical level, analysis of the defense sector's role involves measurement of its size, including the militarily relevant activities usually left out of Western estimates, and also the cost of maintaining the Soviet empire. Here we are interested principally in the Soviet national security system broadly defined, the size of the Soviet economy as a whole, and the ratio between them—the so-called "defense burden."

Estimating accurately both the numerator—the cost of the defense sector and the Soviet empire—and the denominator, or Soviet GNP, presents formidable problems that apply to the CPEs generically. Because arbitrary values are set on many major inputs and products of the defense sector, large discrepancies often exist between the cost of an item for the military and the cost of the same item to another buyer. For example, Kuznetsov, deputy director of the U.S. desk at the Soviet Foreign Ministry, in urging adoption of a new accounting system, observed that "under the old system, a truck could cost many times less for the military than for a collective farm," due to the arbitrary nature of pricing and the distribution of goods to priority sectors.[17]

The conclusion that Harry Rowen and I have reached is that the numerator has generally been underestimated and the denominator overestimated in most previous work. Consequently, the burden of the defense sector on the Soviet economy has been and is probably appreciably higher than has been estimated by most Western analysts.[18]

It is both interesting and significant that the CIA's published estimates of the Soviet defense burden have risen almost monotonically over the past two decades: from 6 percent in the early 1970s, to 9 percent in the mid 1970s, to 11–12 percent in the early 1980s, and to 15–17 percent more recently.[19] Although some of these notable changes reflect real relative growth of the numerator, much of the changes are due to improved methodology, and wider although still incomplete data coverage.

At the broader policy level, the defense sector's relatively large share of the economy relates to the fundamental character of the Soviet system, and more generally to a strong and frequent tendency in other CPEs that have emulated it. For example, RAND studies comparing communist and noncommunist systems suggest that the former are characterized by significantly higher levels of military spending, more people in the armed forces, and a higher level of military than civil technology.[20]

Several hypotheses can be advanced as explanations; for example, that these systems have a comparative advantage in producing military rather than nonmilitary output, or that their leaderships have generally placed a higher value or preference on military than on civil output. Whatever the explanation, it seems clear that Marxist-Leninist systems have often shown a marked tendency to accord their military establishments relatively high priority and favored treatment compared with that granted by other political systems.

Spending on the military and on Soviet activities abroad have been the most important sectors of the economy, and only recently has the influence of glasnost begun to be felt in discussions of the military budget and production. The official Soviet response in the past to questions about spending levels has been that the leadership is uncertain about the exact size of the defense budget. Members from the party and military elite, including former Chief of the General Staff Akhromeev and Deputy Minister of Foreign Affairs Petrovskiy, have confirmed this. In part, this relates to the point noted earlier that the ruble's "value" in the defense and nondefense sectors is not the same, and hence accurate financial accounting is nearly impossible.

The influence of glasnost has prompted speculation about military spending levels and has allowed some useful data to surface, particularly regarding the degree of inclusiveness in the published military budget. For example, earlier Soviet confirmation that the budget excluded research and development (R&D) and military procurement is significant and useful to analysts because the bulk of military spending falls within these excluded categories. Recently published data on military spending, to be discussed below, purport to include these categories of outlays. While these data appreciably raise prior Soviet estimates, there are strong reasons for believing that the new figures, too, cover only a part of the total.

There have also been public statements that military spending needs to be curtailed. At the same time, indirect evidence has been supplied by senior military officers' statements on the allegedly disastrous effects of Khrushchev's unilateral cuts in the late 1950s, which are clearly intended as warnings against repetition of that policy by Gorbachev. Opposing articles have also appeared expressing support for a professional and smaller military establishment. Clearly an intense internal debate has been under way.

One outcome of this internal process was the announcement by Gorbachev at the United Nations at the end of 1988 that the Soviet Union would reduce its existing military manpower by approximately 10 percent (500,000 men), including ten tank divisions, half of which would be withdrawn from Eastern Europe. The announcement does not make clear exactly how much of this reduction would be in the form of active military servicemen, and how much would represent a reduction of authorized but unfulfilled manpower slots. Later he stipulated that military spending and weapons production would be cut by 14.2 and 19.5 percent, respectively.

During his speech before the Congress of People's Deputies in May 1989, Gorbachev announced that Soviet defense spending totaled 77.3 billion rubles, equivalent to approximately 9 percent of the Soviet GNP according to Western calculations.[21] This is slightly more than half the 15–17 percent level estimated by U.S. intelligence agencies (in 1982 rubles). Interestingly, on the heels of Gorbachev's remarks, Chief of the General Staff Moiseyev announced that the Soviet Union plans to reduce its defense expenditures by 1995 "by a factor of 1.5–2."[22]

A serious problem for Western leaders is that they do not know the base from which Soviet defense reductions will occur. As noted earlier, there has been continued controversy over the magnitude of Soviet military spending. Suffice it to say that Western governments, especially the United States, can estimate the physical components of Soviet forces, presumably with fair reliability; the difficulty comes in estimating the cost of these forces. Various methods have been applied: the CIA's "direct costing" method; Lee's attribution of the residual from the output of machinery ministries (after the deduction of known civilian goods) to weapons production; and Steinberg's conclusion that value added in the defense production sector is excluded from Soviet national income accounts. Some analysts, most notably Lee and Rosefielde, have concluded that Soviet military spending has been underestimated, whereas others, including Holzman, claim that it has been overestimated.[23]

David Epstein, of the U.S. Defense Department, has taken a different approach, addressing the *scope of coverage* of such estimates to provide estimates for relevant categories omitted from the usual accounting. Specifically, Epstein has assessed the relative drains on and contributions provided to the Soviet economy by military activities that do not fall within traditional estimates. This includes, among other things, expenditures for civilian transportation services (Aeroflot, trucking, the merchant marine, the railroads) that have dual civilian-military use; civil defense programs and military education; the maintenance of stocks of materials and machinery ("mobilization kits") at nonmilitary industrial sites that theoretically allow for the immediate conversion to defense production in the event of war; and related costs of maintaining Soviet influence abroad.[24]

Epstein's analysis has been based on the need for a broader scope of accounting that has been advocated, over the past several years, by Andrew Marshall, Director of Net Assessment of the Defense Department. For example, Marshall argues that Soviet merchant ships also serve as naval auxiliaries, at additional costs in construction and operation; that Aeroflot is a branch of the VTA (Voenno-Transportnaia Abiatsiia), the Soviet military airlift fleet; that civil defense and the heavy costs of the "deep underground" program for leadership protection are omitted from the standard accounts; and much more. In general, the military gets preference in the Soviet shortage economy, while others go short. There are, to be sure, partly offsetting influences in the form of military help with harvests and military work on dual-use projects (the BAM railroad, for example), but the net effect is, according to Epstein's estimates, a heavy burden on the economy.

Another relevant category of defense spending is the cost of maintaining the Soviet empire abroad. The costs of supporting Cuba, Vietnam, Ethiopia, and Angola are borne principally to extend and protect challenges to Soviet power. So too are the costs of the overseas operation of the KGB. These costs have been estimated by RAND at about 3 percent of Soviet GNP in the mid 1980s.[25]

Epstein concludes that the share of Soviet GNP spend on security, using a broad definition, is 22–28 percent, a range that incorporates the 1987 CIA and DIA estimate of military spending, narrowly defined, of 15–17 percent of GNP. Such a high level is extraordinary, and usually observable only in nations at war.

Which definition to use, broad or narrow, depends on the question at issue. If it concerns a comparison of the costs of fielding the U.S. versus the Soviet military using some common metric—say, dollars—then the narrow definition is probably appropriate. If, in contrast, the question is the cost of maintaining the Soviet position of power in the world—that is, what resources are diverted from consumption, investment, education, health, housing, etc., to support the Soviet Army, the four other military services, Cuban troops in Angola, the communist controlled states of Vietnam and Nicaragua, and what Gorbachev refers to as the "old thinking" in Soviet foreign policy—then a broad definition is more pertinent. Given the Soviet Union's economic crisis, the broad definition seems more relevant; the West's focus on the narrow definition has failed to convey the weight of the military-empire burden that the Soviet leadership must recognize and the public must feel.

How does this share of spending compare with that of the United States? For the United States, a broad definition that includes Department of Energy expenditures on nuclear weapons, security assistance, intelligence activities, the U.S. Information Agency, and other international security-related programs in fiscal year 1989 came to around $330 billion, about 6.5 percent of GNP. Similarly, NATO allies and Japan spend between 1.5 and 5 percent of their GNPs on defense activities. The differences between these ratios and that of the Soviet Union are large.

Technical Problems in Analyzing the Defense Burden in CPEs

Most of the basic empirical efforts to estimate the size and growth of the Soviet economy have used the adjusted factor cost (AFC) method developed by Bergson and his followers in the 1950s and 1960s, and further refined since then.[26] The AFC method proceeds by subtracting from each sector's product the sum of enterprise profits and "lump-sum taxes" paid to the state, and then redistributing this sum over all sectors of the economy in accordance with their estimated respective capital stocks. This "adjustment" does not principally affect the size of the aggregate product estimate, but rather its relative distribution across economic sectors. Thus, the AFC method does not account for the substantial differences between the reported costs of the factors of production and their "real" economic or opportunity costs. Nor does it account for the indirect and largely hidden costs imposed by the high priority accorded some sectors, notably the military, and the low priority accorded others, such as health care.

U.S. government estimates of the size of the Soviet defense sector and its conversion into equivalent U.S. dollars have followed the building-block method, whose purpose is to evaluate various Soviet defense activities in dollar terms to facilitate a comparison to similar activities in the U.S. defense sector. With the application of "constant dollar costs chosen for Soviet goods and services. . . . based on average prices and wages prevailing in the United States in the basic year," it is possible to compare, financially, various components of Soviet and U.S. defense programs.[27]

In addition, Soviet activities are measured in "constant rubles," which indicate the impact of various activities on the economy as a whole as well as the influence of changing priorities among Soviet defense activities. While this method is meticulous and valuable as far as it goes, it suffers from serious shortcomings—for example, the questionable assumption that official Soviet statistics on net material product reflect, in the aggregate, the economic cost of factors of production involved in generating the product.[28]

It is easier to criticize existing methods than to design practical improvements. However, one possibility is to use several different, reasonably independent, measures of the Soviet national product as cross-checks. For example, one might begin with physical production estimates from official Soviet sources, since these are presumably more reliable than ruble estimates, which involve the further unreliability of ruble prices. The physical output of both defense and nondefense sectors might be evaluated by relating them to the market prices for these goods—or similar categories of goods—on foreign markets. For example, Soviet cars are sold in Belgium and India; Soviet tractors and earth-moving equipment and machinery appear in other markets (especially in developing countries); and Soviet military hardware trades on foreign markets at prices that can be ascertained by comparing the prices of Soviet and U.S. military equipment in various international arms-market journals. Independent estimates are made for some sectors, such as the production of Soviet weapons and Soviet grain, and extended comparisons of these estimates would facilitate a more accurate overall estimate of not only the defense sector, but of the economy as a whole.

One might use, along these lines, Grossman's and Treml's estimates, in their pioneering work on the Soviet underground economy, of what they call "legitimate state income" to arrive at estimates of real consumption.[29] Those estimates might then be supplemented by an independent estimate of grain production and other measures of per capita diet and caloric intake. Such preliminary measures of the consumption component of the Soviet national product could then be supplemented by estimates of producers' durable-goods output, which might be obtained from such sources as engineers, Western businessmen, and information increasingly available in Soviet publications.

Another approach is to take the existing AFC estimate made by the intelligence community and adjust it with information from published reports of losses and waste, hidden inflation, and quality deterioration—a course followed by Kontorovich in connection with the investment-goods sector of the Soviet economy.

By pursuing several independent methods to estimate the Soviet product—or at least substantial components of it—we may be better able to check the estimates against one another and against official figures. Furthermore, if glasnost proceeds in conjunction with perestroika, data should become increasingly available for pursuing these various lines of inquiry and improving estimates of the role of the defense sector in the Soviet economy.

Our knowledge of the Russian economy and its defense sector, although it has improved modestly, remains inadequate, posing a substantial barrier to improved economic relations on the one hand and to confidence in arms-control agreements on the other. The Russian government needs to make progress on both these fronts, and it is thus in the leadership's own interest to be more forthcoming with information. Moreover, unless and until such information emerges, the United States and the West should be properly skeptical of high-powered Russian rhetoric that stresses "new thinking," intended military cuts, and defensive reconfiguration of military forces without decisive actions and evidence confirming these changes.

Special Data Problems: Reporting Biases, Hidden Inflation, and Waste

The technical problems involved in analyzing CPEs and their defense burdens are compounded by certain characteristic peculiarities of these economies. These peculiarities were especially prevalent in the Soviet Union, but they were more generally characteristic of CPEs.

The first problem is that economic statistics are often unreliable, and tend to be systematically biased upwards. This bias follows from the incentive structure of centrally planned economies that typically focus on quantitative production norms in evaluating the performance of producing units. Moreover, the bias increases as the complexity, and hence the number of reporting nodes in the system, increases.[30] Hence, the bias distorts estimates of growth as well as the size of the centrally planned economies.

A second problem is the extent to which hidden inflation is overlooked or underestimated by the usual procedures for deflating value data in current prices to arrive at estimates in constant prices. In an economic system based on administered prices, rather than market-based ones, hidden inflation can take the form of diminished product quality for output evaluated at constant prices, or the attribution of higher prices to products whose invoiced description involves fictitious rather than actual upgrading of quality. Both types of hidden inflation have occurred frequently and extensively in the Soviet economy and other CPEs in recent years.[31]

A third problem that arises in trying to size the Soviet economy and other CPEs concerns the production of tangible, but valueless, output as a result of incentives faced by enterprises to satisfy quantitative production norms. To meet these norms, enterprises may produce output which is delivered to other user enterprises, but which the latter regard as worthless. Examples of such valueless output abound in accounts by Soviet as well as Western writers: bulldozers delivered to construction and mining enterprises whose managers know from prior experience that it is preferable to let the equipment stand idle than to risk the consequences of fragile blades and underpowered engines; consumer appliances that not only do not work, but are a safety hazard to their users; and so on.[32] In effect, this is the ultimate stage of quality degradation.

These problems are still further aggravated and reinforced by the pervasive tendency in command systems to use data for political and propaganda purposes. It is not an exaggeration to observe that often the data generated in CPEs are intended to further a political purpose—either internal or international—rather than to describe economic reality.

Modeling CPES and their Defense Sectors

As already indicated, some of the salient characteristics of CPEs include repressed inflation, declining product quality, and use of valued input to produce valueless output. Additionally, command economies typically exhibit preferential treatment of military and security-related demands, pervasive disequilibria in both product and factor markets, and patterns of income distribution that are often highly unequal across regions (e.g., the Soviet Muslim republics) and individuals (when appropriate allowance is made for perquisites and privileges), and that reflect position and power rather than productivity. These characteristics have been especially prevalent in the Soviet Union, but they have been evident in the other centrally planned economies, as well.

However, it is precisely these characteristics that were not reflected in the earlier theoretical models of CPEs developed by Lange and Lerner, nor in the large-scale input-output models developed in the past 15 years for the Soviet Union and other CPEs. The principal examples I have in mind, in the Soviet case, include the Wharton SOVMOD model, the CIA's SOVSIM model, DSA's DYNEVAL, and RAND's optimal control model. Although each of them was designed for a different purpose, they share a common feature: a tendency to "mirror-image" standard Western-type market or mixed economies. The inter-industry matrices underlying these models are too much like their Western counterparts to reflect the realities of command economies. Consequently, the models typically ignore the salient characteristics referred to above, thereby concealing more than they reveal about the actual functioning of CPEs.[33] The unrealism of these models has both reflected and contributed to inaccuracies in the measurement of economic size, the evaluation of economic performance, and in forecasts of the prospects of the Soviet economy and other CPEs.

Some, although not all, of the distinguishing characteristics of CPEs are more accurately reflected in smaller-scale, partial, and more transparent models that have been developed more recently. One example is Ericson's model of the dualistic structure of the Soviet economy—a structure with partial interaction and asymmetrical penetration by the military sector into the nonmilitary remainder of the economy. Another is Hildebrandt's model of the military sector in the Soviet economy, focusing on the military's partial lexicographic command over resources available in the rest of the economy. These models, although not invulnerable, approach more closely the reality of the CPEs and their defense sectors.[34]

Other recent RAND work has focused on some of the major reasons why mirror-imaging type models of the CPEs should be drastically revised or discarded. For example, Lee Badgett has pointed out that CPEs "differ fundamentally from market-exchange economies in where [sic] effective decision making is made and, consequently, in the preferences or objectives that characterize the systems and the control mechanisms employed to realize those objectives."[35] Furthermore, Badgett points out that consumption is not an appropriate maximand in models of the Soviet Union or other Soviet-type economies. A more appropriate representation would focus on national power or security, internal stability, the interests of the leadership and bureaucracy, and their international interests. Because of the priority given to these considerations and to the military as their reflection, as well as to internal security forces and the administrative apparatus, "models that assume an integrated flow of resources" without reflecting the "distinguishing advantages of the defense-industrial sector are likely to be misspecified." In sum, the Soviet system, and CPEs in general, probably had "more in common with nonmarket institutions than . . . with the market exchange systems" on which the standard mirror-imaging models are based.[36]

Other recent work at RAND provides some interesting and potentially useful guidance for further efforts to model CPEs based on a critical analysis and comparison between the economy of Sparta and that of the Soviet Union. This work, by a scholar of classical Greek history, Alvin Bernstein, suggests that command economies, like Sparta and the Soviet Union, are characterized by a "sacrosanct defense enclave whose requirements. . . . are satisfied," even if and as the civilian economy is "plundered, as long as that does not cause the general economy to collapse."[37] The result is that demand—in this case the preferences of the leadership for the instruments of advancing state power and endurance—creates its own supply.[38]

Of course, these considerations may be changing dramatically and rapidly, as part of the transformation under way in the political conditions of Eastern Europe and in the former Soviet Union. And it is possible that the new conditions may make the mirror-imaging models of the past more relevant for the future than they were for the period and the economies they were intended to represent. Thus, the economic systems that emerge from these dramatic changes, and the corresponding economic models, may approach the conditions of market economies rather than command systems.

Nevertheless, the Ericson, Hildebrandt, Badgett, and Bernstein contributions contain some possibly valuable guidance for future modeling of CPEs. This is more than simply stipulating what the preferences of the planners or leadership are. The defining characteristics also affect the dynamics, the persistent disequilibria, the nonapplicability of the usual first- and second-order optimality conditions, and the long-term performance of the centrally planned economies. The widespread prevalence of perverse incentives and the pervasiveness of what I have referred to elsewhere as "nonmarket failure" are ingredients that should be given much more attention in future modeling efforts relating specifically to CPEs.[39]

Economic Reform and the Former Military's Role

In addressing this subject in the former Soviet Union, it is important to emphasize that the content, progress, and prospects of economic restructuring (perestroika) confront a crucial dilemma. On the one hand, the cumulative shortcomings of state control, centralized decision making, and administered prices that are characteristic of command economies create a compelling need for a more decentralized, market-oriented system. Indeed, few in the West have been as severe in deploring the existing system's shortcomings, nor as convincing in their advocacy of decentralization, as Gorbachev and some of his top economic advisors.[40]

On the other hand, strong pressures exist to retain or even increase the centralization of decision making and resource allocation to resolve the immediate and sharply conflicting demands for scarce resources: to raise personal consumption as well as quasi-public consumption in health care, education, and housing; to maintain and improve transportation, communications, and distribution; to reverse the deterioration of air and water quality and the damage to the natural environment; to cut military spending while modernizing the armed forces; and to reduce expenditures on the disintegrating former Soviet empire.[41]

The dilemma is not adequately conveyed by the standard "guns versus butter" metaphor. It also involves such questions as to the kinds of weapons to forgo, retain, or enhance, and at what time, and for what contingencies; the kinds of consumption and investment to expand, and for whom, for which republics, and with what delays; and the types of subventions to Eastern Europe, Cuba, Vietnam, Nicaragua, Afghanistan, and elsewhere that should be reduced.

To understand the economic benefits that may ensue from a reduction in defense spending, or retrospectively, the economic retardation caused by the long military buildup under Brezhnev, one needs to consider the extent to which the serious plight of the Soviet economy was due to the large defense share, and the extent to which it was attributable to the shortcomings of the system itself. Clearly, both elements are responsible; the issue is determining their relative influence.

The share directly attributable to the defense sector is complex. At issue is the relationship between the military and the structure of Soviet industry, infrastructure, and R&D, as well as the relationship among them over time. One does not need the explanation of a huge military burden to explain poor economic performance: the latter is sufficiently explained by the debilitating effects of the CPE system on incentives, innovation, competition, and productivity, as illustrated by the sorry condition of the Eastern European and Chinese economies despite their lower shares of military spending in GNP.

To convey a rough idea of these relationships, suppose the share of the Russian military were to be reduced from, say, 25 percent of GNP to 15 percent, with the saved resources reallocated equally between consumption and investment, but *with no other changes in the system.*

What effect would such a major reduction in the defense sector have on consumption and economic growth?

If one assumes, as suggested earlier, that the Soviet GNP was about one-third that of the United States (or about US$1.7 trillion in 1989 dollars), that Soviet consumption was about 55 percent of GNP, and that the Soviet population was 280 million and growing at a rate of about 1 percent per year, the effect of this relatively large resource reallocation would be modest. Soviet consumption per capita was recently about $3,000, or about 25 percent of the U.S. level and about equal to that of Turkey or Mexico. Transferring, for example, 5 percent of Soviet GNP to consumption would represent an increase in consumption of 9 percent. Assuming that the defense spending cuts and ensuing resource reallocations were spread over a four-year period, the resulting annual increase in aggregate consumption would be about 2.25 percent, and in per capita consumption about 1.25 percent. The annual increase in per capita consumption would be about $42 a year, accumulating to $168 over the four-year period.[42] Moreover, this would represent a one-time boost in consumption, which would thereafter remain at the same level. Reallocating the remaining half of the 10 percent cut in military spending to investment and R&D—again assuming that the Soviet system otherwise remained unchanged— might add 1 percent to the annual rate of Soviet real economic growth. If this growth were sustained, further growth in consumer welfare would ensue as well. Although these are only rough approximations, they give an idea of the results of reallocating resources from military to nonmilitary uses *without accompanying changes in the system itself*. Altogether, they would give a small boost to the economy, but would hardly transform it.

On the other hand, what would be the effects of fundamental changes in economic institutions through genuine price reform, enterprise reform, property ownership, monetary reform, and currency convertibility, assuming only minor changes in the size of the defense sector? What would be the economic effects, apart from the political and social strains, that such drastic reform would set in motion? Would the burst of effort and energy released by the new environment propel the economy forward at a high and sustained rate, or would the still-massive size of the defense sector continue to exercise a severe braking effect on productivity and real economic growth? Such systemic changes would transform the economy, but the maintenance of a huge military sector would surely slow the process.

To be sure, the policy options open to the Russian leadership are not this sharply drawn. Some military reductions might be seen as making an early and critical contribution toward motivating cynical workers, while most systemic changes would take several years to be felt. And there are other options, such as importing more goods from the West.

It is likely that the Russian leadership will pursue various combinations of reduced defense, increased imports, and gradual systemic reform, rather than relying on any one of these options alone. The possibilities are numerous and hard to predict. But there are several candidates, and while each seems improbable taken alone, the adoption of a combination seems moderately probable. For the time being, the economic outcome as well as the political consequences are somewhere between uncertain and unfathomable. Yet, potentially, the relations among the options are synergistic: If military reductions and reallocations are wisely combined with pervasive system reform, the effects of each may well be enhanced.

Conversion from Military to Civil Production

The previous calculations relating to the Soviet Union generally assumed that the microeconomics of macroeconomic reallocations will proceed more or less smoothly. In fact, conversion from defense to civil production is much more likely to be impeded in the former CPEs by frictions, bottlenecks in some sectors and surpluses in others, and other errors than is conversion in market economies (MEs).[43] In MEs, the conversion process will be assisted and lubricated by flexible prices in factor and product markets, as well as by factor mobility and entrepreneurial activity in response to price signals. The absence of such signals in the former CPEs, or the miscuing to which substitute mechanisms are prone, will probably significantly impede the conversion process in these systems. The speed and efficiency with which U.S. conversion proceeded after World War II illustrates the allocative strength of market signals. The lethargy of the conversion process in the Soviet Union through the years of Gorbachev's perestroika suggests the handicaps to which conversion is prone in CPEs—perhaps especially those engaged in limited and anemic types of market-oriented reform.

Notes

1. This RAND-Hoover collaboration resulted in the first biennial Symposium on the Defense Sector in the Soviet Economy conducted by the two institutions, held at the Hoover Institution in March 1988. A book covering the symposium papers ad proceedings was published in 1990: *The Impoverished Super Power: The Defense Burden On The Soviet Economy*, Henry S. Rowen and Charles Wolf, Jr. (eds.), ICS Press, San Francisco, with

contributions by the editors as well as Anders Aslund, Arthur Alexander, Derk Swain, Richard Ericson, Boris Rumer, Gregory Hildebrandt, Vladimir Kontorovich, Steven Meyer, and David Epstein. The second symposium in this series was held at RAND on March 29–30, 1990

2. Vasili Seliunin and Grigori Khanin, "Lukavaia tsifa" ["Cunning Figures"], *Novy mir*, February 1987, pp. 181–201.

3. Richard Ericson, "The Soviet Statistical Debate: Khanin vs. TsSU," in Rowen and Wolf, *The Impoverished Superpower*, pp. 33–34.

4. Abel Aganbegyan, "Programma korennoi perestroiki," *EKO* (November 1987) pp. 3–19.

5. Abel Aganbegyan, *The Economic Challenge of Perestroika* (Blooming-ton, Indiana: Indiana University Press, 1988).

6. Also, as the result of severe shortages of food in state stores, the cost of meat and produce sold at collective farm markets has risen approximately 20 percent since 1985. Central Intelligence Agency and Defense Intelligence Agency, *The Soviet Economy in 1988: Gorbachev Changes Course*, report prepared for the U.S. Congress, Joint Economic Committee, April 14, 1989, p. 11.

7. Oleg Bogomolov, "Mogut li byt' den'gi 'lishimi'," *Argumenti i fakty*, Number 3, 1989, pp. 2–4.

8. Richard Ericson, "The Soviet Economic Predicament," in *The Future of the Soviet Empire*, Henry S. Rowen and Charles Wolf, Jr. (eds.), ICS Press, San Francisco, 1987, pp. 98–99.

9. *SSSR v tsifrakh v 1988 godu*, Moscow, 1989, p. 5.

10. See "'Ostatochyi printsip' eshche v ostatke," *Izvestia*, January 30, 1988; "Goskomstat SSSR soobshchaet," *Sotsiologicheskie issledovaniia*, No. 5 (September-October 1987), p. 8; *Pravda*, July 2, 1988, pp. 6–7.

11. Mikhail Gorbachev, *Perestroika: New Thinking for Our Country and the World*, Harper & Row Publishers, New York, 1987; and Abel Aganbegyan, *Inside Perestroika: The Future of the Soviet Economy*, Harper & Row Publishers, New York, 1989.

12. See Ericson, "The Soviet Economic Predicament."

13. See Charles Wolf, Jr., et al., *The Changing Balance: South and North Korean Capabilities for Long Term Military Competition*, RAND, Santa Monica, California, R-2205-NA, October 1985.

14. Irving Kravis, Alan Heston, and Robert Summers, *World Product and Income: International Comparisons of Real Gross Product*, Johns Hopkins University Press, Baltimore, 1982.

15. U.S. Congress, Joint Economic Committee, *Gorbachev's Economic Plans*, Government Printing Office, Washington, DC, 1987, pp. viii, 136.

16. Cited in Paul Marer, *Dollar GNPs of the USSR and Eastern Europe*, Johns Hopkins University Press, Baltimore, 1985.

17. David Epstein, "The Economic Cost of Soviet Security and Empire," in Rowen and Wolf, *The Impoverished Superpower*.

18. See Rowen and Wolf, *The Impoverished Superpower*, pp. 1–12.

19. CIA/DIA, "The Soviet Economy in 1988," p. 40; CIA, Soviet Analysis

Division, "Investment and Operating Expenditures by Service," 1988; Franklyn D. Holtzman, "Politics and Guesswork: CIA and DIA Estimates of Soviet Military Spending," *International Security*, Fall 1989, Vol. 14, No. 2, pp. 101–131.

20. Charles Wolf and Benjamin Zycher, *Military Dimensions of Communist Systems: Findings and Implications*, RAND, Santa Monica, California, R-3629-USDP, January 1989.

21. Soviet Television, May 30, 1989.

22. *Pravda*, June 11, 1989, p. 5.

23. William T. Lee, *The Estimation of Soviet Defense Expenditures, 1955–1975*, Praeger, New York, 1977; Dmitri Steinberg, "The Real Size and Structure of the Soviet Economy: Alternative Estimates of Soviet GNP and Military Expenditures for 1987," paper for the RAND-Hoover symposium on the *Defense Sector in the Soviet Economy*, 1990; Steven Rosefielde, *False Science: Underestimating the Soviet Arms Buildup*, Transaction Press, New Brunswick, New Jersey, 1987; and Holtzman, "Politics and Guesswork."

24. David Epstein, "The Economic Cost of Soviet Security and Empire."

25. Charles Wolf, et al., *The Costs and Benefits of the Soviet Empire, 1981–1983*, RAND, Santa Monica, California, R-3419-NA, August 1986.

26. Abram Bergson, *The Real National Income of Soviet Russia Since 1928*, Harvard Press, Cambridge, Massachusetts, 1961. See also Rowen and Wolf, "Introduction," *The Impoverished Superpower*.

27. Derk Swain, "The Soviet Military Sector: How It Is Defined and Measured," in Rowen and Wolf, *The Impoverished Superpower*.

28. Swain, "The Soviet Military Sector."

29. Gregory Grossman and Vladimir Treml, "Measuring Hidden Incomes in the USSR," in Sergio Alessandrini and Bruno Dallago (eds.), *The Unofficial Economy: Consequences and Perspectives in Different Economic Systems*, Gower Publishers, Gower, England, 1986.

30. See Ericson, "The Soviet Economic Predicament," especially pp. 105–110; and Aslund, *Gorbachev's Struggle*, pp. 8–9 ff. The upward bias and unreliability of Soviet statistics have been documented and elaborated by a number of other Soviet economists. See, for example, Selyunin and Khanin, "Cunning Figures"; and Anders Aslund, "How Small Is the Soviet National Income?" in Rowen and Wolf, *The Impoverished Superpower*.

31. See Philip Hanson, *USSR: Puzzles in the 1985 Statistics*, Radio Liberty Research, RL 439/86, November 1986; Aslund, *Gorbachev's Struggle*, p. 15; and Aganbegyan, *Inside Perestroika*.

32. See Aganbegyan, *Inside Perestroika*, pp. 33–36 ff.

33. For a critical exposition and analysis of these models, see Gregory G. Hildebrandt (ed.), *RAND Conference on Models of the Soviet Economy*, RAND, Santa Monica, California, R-3322, October 1955.

34. See Richard E. Ericson, *Priority, Duality, and Penetration in the Soviet Command Economy*, RAND, Santa Monica, California, N-2643-NA, December 1988; Gregory E. Hildebrandt, "Models of the Military Sector in the Soviet Economy," in Rowen and Wolf, *The Impoverished Superpower*; and J. M. van

Brabant, "Socialist Economics: The Disequilibrium School and the Shortage Economy," *Journal of Economic Literature*, Spring 1990.

35. See Lee D. Badgett, *Defeated by a Maze: The Soviet Economy and Its Defense Industrial Sector*, RAND, Santa Monica, California, N-2644-NA, October 1988, p. vi.

36. Badgett, *Defeated by a Maze*, pp. vi-vii.

37. See Alvin H. Bernstein, *Soviet Defense Spending: The Spartan Analogy*, RAND, Santa Monica, California, N-2817-NA, October 1989, p. 4.

38. Bernstein, *Soviet Defense Spending*, p. 5.

39. See Charles Wolf, Jr., *Markets or Governments: Choosing Between Imperfect Alternatives*, MIT Press, Cambridge, Massachusetts, 1988.

40. See, for example, Gorbachev, *Perestroika*; and Aganbegyan, *Inside Perestroika*. Aganbegyan notes the following: "Clearly the system of centralized supply ties an enterprise up with directives and leaves no room to manoeuvre. . . . It is virtually impossible to live and work under such an inflexible administrative system" (p. 32). See also Ericson, "The Soviet Economic Predicament," especially pp. 117–120, on the need (and poor prospects) for radical decentralization.

41. Aganbegyan inadvertently highlights this part of the dilemma by associating *perestroika* with "...new spending in the social sphere, a breakaway in the provision of housing and socially necessary buildings, much greater expenditures on health and education, redoubled growth of food production, triple growth in the service sector, and vast capital and currency investments in the development of light industry" (*Inside Perestroika*, p. 113).

42. These calculations are based on the following simple model:

$$C_t = S_c / Y_c / t = .091 / t = .0227;$$

$$c_t = C_t - p = .0227 - .010 = .0127.$$

where S_C = share of GNP reallocated from military to consumption uses (= 5%); S_i = share of GNP reallocated from military to investment (= 5%); Y_C = consumption share of GNP (=55%); t = number of years over which resource reallocations are equally spaced (= 4 years); C_t = annual rate of increase in consumption resulting from transfers from military to consumption uses over t–period; p = annual rate of growth of population (= 1%); c_t = annual rate of increase in per capita consumption over t–period

43. For a recent RAND study of the conversion process in the Soviet Union, see Arthur J. Alexander, *Perestroika and Change in Soviet Weapons Acquisition*, RAND, Santa Monica, California, R-3821-USDP, June 1990.

References

Abel Aganbegyan, *Inside Perestroika: The Future of the Soviet Economy*, Harper & Row Publishers, New York, 1989.

———, *The Economic Challenge of Perestroika*, Indiana University Press, Bloomington, 1988.

————, "Programma korennoi perestroiki," *EKO*, November 1987, pp. 3–19.

Alexander, Arthur J., *Perestroika and Change in Soviet Weapons Acquisition*, RAND, Santa Monica, California, R-3821-USDP, June 1990.

Aslund, Anders, "How Small Is the Soviet National Income?" in Henry Rowen and Charles Wolf, Jr. (eds.), *The Impoverished Superpower: Perestroika and the Soviet Military Burden*, ICS Press, San Francisco, 1990.

————, *Gorbachev's Struggle for Economic Reform*, Cornell University Press, Ithaca, New York, 1989.

Badgett, Lee D., *Defeated by a Maze: The Soviet Economy and Its Defense-Industrial Sector*, RAND, Santa Monica, California, N-2644-NA, October 1988, p. vi.

Bergson, Abram, *The Real National Income of Soviet Russia Since 1928*, Harvard Press, Cambridge, Massachusetts, 1961.

Bernstein, Alvin H., *Soviet Defense Spending: The Spartan Analogy*, RAND, Santa Monica, California, N-2817-NA, October 1989, p. 4.

Bogomolov, Oleg, "Mogut li byt' den'gi 'lishimi'," *Argumenti i fakty*, No. 3, 1989, pp. 2–4.

CIA, Soviet Analysis Division, "Investment and Operating Expenditures by Service," 1988.

CIA and DIA (Defense Intelligence Agency), *The Soviet Economy in 1988: Gorbachev Changes Course*, report prepared for the U.S. Congress, Joint Economic Committee, April 14, 1989, p. 11.

Epstein, David, "The Economic Cost of Soviet Security and Empire," in Henry Rowen and Charles Wolf, Jr. (eds.), *The Impoverished Superpower: Perestroika and the Soviet Military Burden*, ICS Press, San Francisco, 1990.

Ericson, Richard E., "The Soviet Statistical Debate: Khanin vs. TsSU," in Henry Rowen and Charles Wolf, Jr. (eds.), *The Impoverished Superpower: Perestroika and the Soviet Military Burden*, ICS Press, San Francisco, 1990.

————, *Priority, Duality, and Penetration in the Soviet Command Economy*, RAND, Santa Monica, California, N-2643-NA, December 1988.

————, "The Soviet Economic Predicament," in Henry S. Rowen and Charles Wolf, Jr. (eds.), *The Future of the Soviet Empire*, ICS Press, San Francisco, 1987, pp. 98–99.

Gorbachev, Mikhail, *Perestroika: New Thinking for Our Country and the World*, Harper & Row Publishers, New York, 1987.

Grossman, Gregory, and Vladimir Treml, "Measuring Hidden Incomes in the USSR," in Sergio Alessandrini and Bruno Dallago (eds.), *The Unofficial Economy: Consequences and Perspectives in Different Economic Systems*, Gower Publishers, Gower, England, 1986.

Hanson, Philip, *USSR: Puzzles in the 1985 Statistics*, Radio Liberty Research, RL 439/86, November 1986.

Hildebrandt, Gregory E., "Models of the Military Sector in the Soviet Economy," in Henry Rowen and Charles Wolf, Jr. (eds.), *The Impoverished Superpower: Perestroika and the Soviet Military Burden*, ICS Press, San Francisco, 1990.

———— (ed.), *RAND Conference on Models of the Soviet Economy, October 11–12, 1984*, RAND, Santa Monica, California, R-3322, October 1985.

Holtzman, Franklyn D. "Politics and Guesswork: CIA and DIA Estimates of Soviet Military Spending," *International Security*, Fall 1989, Vol. 14, No. 2, pp. 101–131.

Kravis, Irving, Alan Heston, and Robert Summers, *World Product and Income: International Comparisons of Real Gross Product*, Johns Hopkins Press, Baltimore, 1982.

Lee, William T., *The Estimation of Soviet Defense Expenditures, 1955–1975*, Praeger, New York, 1977.

Marer, Paul, *Dollar GNPs of the USSR and Eastern Europe*, Johns Hopkins University, Baltimore, 1985.

"'Ostatochyi printsip' eshche v ostatke," *Izvestia*, January 30, 1988; "Goskomstat SSSR soobshchaet," *Sotsiologicheskie issledovaniia*, No. 5 (September–October 1987), p. 8; *Pravda*, July 2, 1988, pp. 6–7.

Pravda, June 11, 1989, p. 5.

Rosefielde, Steven, *False Science: Underestimating the Soviet Arms Buildup*, Transaction Press, New Brunswick, New Jersey, 1987.

Rowen, Henry, and Charles Wolf, Jr. (eds.), *The Impoverished Superpower: Perestroika and the Soviet Military Burden*, ICS Press, San Francisco, 1990.

Selyunin, Vasili, and Grigori Khanin, "Cunning Figures," *Novy Mir*, February 1987, pp. 181–201.

Soviet Television, May 30, 1989.

SSSR v tsifrakh v 1988 godu, Moscow, 1989, p. 5.

Steinberg, Dmitri, "The Real Size and Structure of the Soviet Economy: Alternative Estimates of Soviet GNP and Military Expenditures for 1987," paper for the RAND-Hoover symposium on the *Defense Sector in the Soviet Economy*, 1990.

Swain, Derk, "The Soviet Military Sector: How It Is Defined and Measured," in Henry Rowen and Charles Wolf, Jr. (eds.), *The Impoverished Superpower: Perestroika and the Soviet Military Burden*, ICS Press, San Francisco, 1990.

U.S. Congress, Joint Economic Committee, *Gorbachev's Economic Plans*, Government Printing Office, Washington, D.C., 1987, pp. viii, 136.

van Brabant, J. M., "Socialist Economics: The Disequilibrium School and the Shortage Economy," *Journal of Economic Literature*, Spring 1990.

Wolf, Charles, Jr., *Markets or Governments: Choosing Between Imperfect Alternatives*, MIT Press, Cambridge, Massachusetts, 1988.

Wolf, Charles, Jr., and Benjamin Zycher, *Military Dimensions of Communist Systems: Findings and Implications*, RAND, Santa Monica, California, R-3629-USDP, January 1989.

Wolf, Charles, Jr., et al., *The Costs and Benefits of the Soviet Empire, 1981–1983*, RAND, Santa Monica, California, R-3419-NA, August 1986.

————, *The Changing Balance: South and North Korean Capabilities for Long Term Military Competition*, RAND, Santa Monica, California, R-2205-NA, October 1985.

9

The Military and Economic Reform in Poland, Hungary, and China

Keith Crane and K. C. Yeh

Introduction

This chapter provides an empirical assessment of the economic reforms of three centrally planned economies: Poland, Hungary and China. It is intended to contribute to the empirical foundations of the debate on the effects of economic reforms in these systems. A related aim is to examine the interactions between these changes and the military.

This chapter is a guide to the pitfalls of moving from central planning to systems that no longer use compulsory plan targets but maintain state-ownership and one-party rule. As such, the study is now irrelevant for two of the three protagonists, the economies of Poland and Hungary. These countries have abandoned socialism for market economics. However, the study should remain of interest for countries such as China and Vietnam, and possibly some parts of the former Soviet Union, that continue to struggle to maintain remnants of the old system while adopting some aspects of market economies.

The traditional centrally planned system can be characterized by the following principles:

1. The domination of the preferences of the political elite over those of the populace.
2. The imposition of those preferences through direct allocation of goods and services.
3. The use of an annual plan composed of physical plan targets to impose the center's preferred pattern of resource allocation.
4. The use of a bonus system tied to plan fulfillment to induce producers to increase output and conserve inputs.

   5. Central allocation of primary inputs.

   6. A monopoly on foreign trade designed to prevent arbitrage and preserve the center's power to determine the allocation of goods and services.

We define changes in the economic system that transgress some of these basic principles as *economic reform*. This terminology is used to differentiate changes that devolve decisions on resource allocation to markets and enterprise managers from administrative changes that move the locus of decision making in the bureaucratic hierarchy or alter performance indicators. It also serves to differentiate changes designed to change, but preserve socialism, to wholesale abandonment of the system such as currently transpiring in Poland, Hungary, Czechoslovakia and Germany.

Before the revolutions of 1989 in Eastern Europe, Poland, Hungary and China had implemented economic reforms. None of these governments agreed to let consumer preferences dominate their own. However, in all three systems, the center attempted to replace direct allocation of goods and services through the use of obligatory plan targets with allocation through direct sales between buyers and sellers mediated by indirect instruments such as taxes, subsidies and the exchange rate. In these new systems, managers of state-owned enterprises were rewarded in part on their success in increasing profits or value-added, not output. Because of the increased importance of net rather than gross measures, prices became of more importance and the center gave markets a greater role in determining prices and allocating resources.

Our purpose of this study is to determine whether the changes had the desired effects: Did changes in incentives and prices lead to significant improvements in productivity and international competitiveness?

A second objective is to determine the effect of the military on the implementation and operation of economic reforms. With the advent of a reformed system, the military sector faces problems and promises. On the one hand, the old system of priorities and commands which ensured its primary position in the economy would be destroyed in a market-oriented system. On the other, the new system should lead to higher output levels, some of which could be spent on the military.

The military sectors in these three economies provide a useful spectrum for illuminating the implications of the military for economic reform and vice versa. China is a major, regional military power. It has the largest armed forces in the world, possesses nuclear weapons and has its own indigenous military technology. On the other extreme, Hungary had one of the smallest armies of the Warsaw Pact and spends a very small share of output on the military (about 2 percent of GNP). It imports all its heavy weapons. Poland occupies the middle ground. It has the second largest army in the Warsaw Pact, produces heavy weapons, and is a significant arms exporter. The experiences of these three countries with integrating their military sectors into a reformed economic system should illuminate the potential benefits and pitfalls awaiting newcomers to reform.

Poland

The System

In 1982 Poland's leaders introduced an economic reform to reverse the severe declines in economic output and living standards experienced in the early 1980s and in response to the accompanying popular pressure for an economic system more responsive to consumers and that would provide a higher standard of living. (We do not consider here the more radical economic changes introduced in Poland in 1990.) On paper, the reform significantly altered the operation of the Polish economy. Although Poland had previous reforms (e.g., in 1956 and 1972), Polish state-owned and cooperative industry has generally been run according to the principles of the traditional Soviet-type model. The 1982 reform purported to change some of the central tenets of this system.

The core of the Polish economic reform in state-owned industry centered on the three S's: *samofinansowanie* (enterprise self-financing), *samorzadnosc* (self-management), and *samodzielnosc* (independence).[1] According to these principles, Polish enterprises were to be independent, self-financing entities managed by directors chosen by workers' councils (but approved by the government). The idea was to force managers to improve efficiency by making them accountable for enterprise performance and by making financial results the primary criterion for enterprise success. Meddling by government authorities in enterprise decision making was to be limited by making the workers' council the locus of ultimate authority in each enterprise. Financial discipline was to be imposed by making markets a major means of allocating resources.

Despite this original design, the Polish reform should not be viewed as an attempt to establish market socialism. Even under the reformed system, enterprises were not to operate like independent, profit-maximizing units, because the central authorities were to continue to play an important role in the hiring, firing, and remuneration of managers, and in the allocation of investments and intermediate goods. It was still appropriate to think of state-owned enterprises as part of a gigantic state-owned corporation, Poland, Inc., a paradigm used to describe the traditional Soviet-type system,[2] in which the head management (the center) sought to improve the efficiency of the operation through decentralization. Managers, like line managers in the West, remained dependent on the center for their incomes and jobs. Their actions were therefore determined to a great extent by their perceptions of what the center wanted them to do.

The major goal of the reform was to improve economic efficiency. However, the center also attempted to lower the rate of inflation, prevent factory closures and unemployment, and preserve real wage levels for sensitive political groups—workers in heavy industry and mining. Economic policy and reform measures were often dictated by immediate concerns about the popularity of particular decisions. This led to the introduction of ad hoc, often contradictory decrees, making economic policy instruments inconsistent with the principles of the reform. This welter of macro economic policy goals heavily influenced the decisions of enterprise managers.

In this system the primary goal of the manager was to stay in the good graces of the branch ministries, and, to a lesser extent, of the workers' councils, both of which influenced his tenure and renumeration. Because of the government's emphasis on preserving labor peace, the ministry's primary goal often boiled down to keeping the work force content. For the enterprise manager, this meant increasing workers' wages.

One of the most effective ways to raise wages was to increase after-tax, after-subsidy profits. To some extent, managers also followed the path of reducing costs and innovation. Because of the many obstacles they faced in adapting production, however, managers found that lobbying the center for tax relief, investment grants, and subsidies could be of greater importance in determining the financial health of their enterprises. Enterprise managers devoted a great deal of their energy to lobbying, partly because the rate of return was high, but also because of the multiplicity of constraints that limited their managerial freedom. In 1986, income tax reliefs were given on 21.3 percent of the gross taxes of the 500 largest Polish enterprises. Arbitrary grants of individual reliefs comprised an important fraction of these reliefs. Only 28 of the 500 largest Polish enterprises were not granted some form of tax relief.[3]

Price controls had a debilitating effect on profitability and on more rapid enterprise response to changes in demand and input costs. In general, the larger the share of fixed-price goods in total sales, the lower the profitability of the enterprise.[4] Neither subsidies, tax relief, nor annual increases in fixed prices compensated enterprises for the greater profitability possible from selling goods with contract prices.

"Shortage," a consequence of the failure to liberalize prices, characterized the reform. For example, the lack of workers was considered the primary constraint on output levels according to 70 percent of one group of enterprise managers.[5] Because of the lack of workers, capacity utilization averaged 72.5 percent and was especially low in the machine-building sector (62.4 percent), where the average number of shifts was 1.44, as compared with more than 2 in other industries.[5] The reasons for excess demand for labor are easily traced to Polish monetary policy and wage controls, which preserved a condition of excess demand or "shortage".

Problems with supplies constituted another important, binding constraint on production. Most enterprises received almost all their inputs through obligatory deliveries ordered through the center. These deliveries were often obtained under central government programs or through government orders. For example, in metallurgy an average of only 14.5 percent of supplies were contracted for on a free basis; the rest came from obligatory deliveries by suppliers.

Assessing the Reform

By most measures the 1982 Polish reform was a failure. In one small survey of enterprise managers 14 of 56 evaluated the reform positively; the rest were critical. The critics argued that the reform had not been implemented as planned. The sharpest criticism was directed toward the center for its unwillingness to trust decisions made by enterprise managers. One manager criticized the center for constantly changing regulations and for being too soft—for not making enterprises suffer the consequences of the decisions taken by their directors. He argued that there was a lack of freedom to make decisions and a lack of responsibility for those that were made.[7]

By some measures, productivity growth improved after the reform. Capital productivity growth and improvements in the efficiency with which electric power was used increased more rapidly in the 1983–1985 period than in the pre reform 1976–1979 period. The figures mask, however, the tremendous declines experienced in factor productivity in Poland. The ratio of net material product (NMP) produced by socialized industry to capital was 65 percent lower in 1985 than in 1975, implying an enormous decline in capital productivity. The ratio of NMP produced in socialized industry to electrical consumption by socialized industry was 20 percent lower in 1985 than in 1977. On the other hand, the ratio of NMP produced in socialized industry to hours worked was 3 percent higher in 1985 than in 1979, showing an absolute rise in the productivity of labor. In sum, socialized industry had not become notably more efficient since the introduction of the economic reform.

A second indicator of the success of the reform is whether resources have been reallocated to more efficient sectors. We found capital and labor flows have been the *reverse* of what one would have expected, based on profitability considerations. The coal and food industries have had the worst profitability performance, yet these two industries and electricity generation registered the largest gains in the shares of investment in the post-reform period. Both industries also registered strong increases in their shares of employment at the expense of apparently more profitable industries. These figures may merely reflect the irrational Polish price system, in which goods facing high excess demand, such as meat and coal, have relatively lower fixed prices and therefore are not profitable. However, they indicate the very limited role of profits in determining the allocation of investments and labor.

A major problem with the reform was the frequency with which regulations were changed and the poor flow of information between the center and enterprise managers. Even the managers of large enterprises frequently did not understand or were not aware of new directives. There was also very little coordination between the central plan and enterprise plans. Because the state allocated such a large share of inputs directly, this lack of knowledge led to large efficiency losses and poor planning.[8]

The major problem faced by enterprise managers was that of supply uncertainties. Production was frequently constrained by shortages of labor and intermediate goods, especially imports. These shortages reflected the excess demand endemic to the system and the absence of a price system that reflected relative scarcities and permitted the highest bidder to purchase scarce goods and services. This excess demand stemmed from the central authorities' unwillingness to impose hard budget constraints on enterprises. The ad hoc grants of subsidies and tax reliefs that increased the budget deficit (and excess demand) served to reward poorly performing enterprises and provided substantial incentives for enterprises to lobby for these reliefs rather than focus on changing internal operations.

Interviews reveal the quick responses of enterprise managers to changes in incentives and the close attention they paid to trade-offs. For example, the authorities provided tax relief for products that were deemed deserving of "quality symbols." Enterprise managers claimed that the costs of producing higher-quality products were greater than the benefits of the tax reliefs or the increases in prices permitted for products that were given the quality sign.[9] In other words, managers calculated the relative costs and benefits of the program and decided against participation.

In general, we found the argument to be false that the mentality of consumers, producers, and especially managers must be changed before the reform can function. The argument, somewhat akin to the argument that the Soviet-type system will work well when people have developed a "socialist" mentality, is used to mask the real problems with the reform: the many constraints on production and investment imposed on enterprise managers by the center. Whether state-owned enterprises would still function poorly in a market system is open to question. However, the argument that they failed under the reforms reflects the inability of the center to introduce market conditions in the economy, rather than attitudinal problems of managers and consumers.

Why did the center fail to introduce these conditions? Macroeconomic policy concerns other than efficiency led to the introduction of a plethora of policy instruments (individual subsidies, tax reliefs, etc.) that sharply reduced the effectiveness of measures to improve efficiency. If monetary and fiscal policy had been less accommodating, there might have been less pressure to introduce these efficiency-reducing measures. However, the Polish central authorities appear to have been unwilling to bear the political costs of some loss of power and of antagonizing certain interest groups by implementing sterner measures. This unwillingness was the primary reason for the failure of the reform to markedly improve economic efficiency.

The Military and Economic Reform

The reform may have encouraged cost consciousness in the military. The Polish army has found that production and development costs in the defense industry have been rising. It has responded by pushing for better utilization of capacity and more effective cost accounting. Army officers argue that measures taken to improve management have led to reduced costs and better utilization of military assets.[10] The Polish deputy quartermaster general, the individual in charge of securing supplies for the Polish army, has argued that the reform has had a notable impact on supply operations.[11] The Military Trade Administration, a system of army stores, earned a profit and became more cost conscious and has covered its investments from its own profits. On the other hand, the quartermaster's performance was still evaluated in terms of exceeding plan targets, and military supply groups were still geared toward plan targets.

Cost minimization in the military was not however a new phenomenon. A system to induce quartermasters and commanders to minimize waste was introduced in the mid-1970s.[12] Bonuses had been introduced for drivers to conserve fuel and quartermasters received training on efficiency and conservation.

Because the military has been a priority client, it fared better than others during the reform. However, excess demand in so many markets affected as well. Because of shortages, many units began to grow their own food. In the Warsaw Military District, for example, soldiers grew half their annual pork consumption; they also bred cattle, sheep and poultry.[13] Fifty-four percent of all pork consumed in the military was raised by the military units themselves; soldiers produced office and barracks furniture. These measures were aimed at self-sufficiency, not necessarily economic efficiency. Quartermasters also started to produce clothing by hiring soldiers' wives to sew garments. In short, economic stringencies forced military commanders to become more economically autarchic.

The military suffered from labor shortages during the reform. As more attractive possibilities opened up in the private sector, the military experienced a decline in applicants to military academies.[14] This may be due to political disenchantment with the military, but is more likely to be the consequence of differences in renumeration; Polish opinion polls indicate that the army continued to have a great deal of respect despite its role under martial law.

The Polish reform and the military appear to have been, even if unintentionally, at cross purposes since the initiation of the reform. The reform was introduced immediately after the declaration of martial law, a period when both political and economic power was being centralized within defense committees. At a time when managers could be summarily fired and enterprise assets such as trucks, cranes and other machines redeployed at a word from the Defense Committee commander, enterprise directors were supposed to begin operating much more independently than in the past, making decisions on inputs, prices, wages, new products and internal organization. The two were incompatible. Even long after the repeal of martial law, the military sector fitted uneasily into the reformed system. Membership in the military producers' association was compulsory for enterprises producing military goods. These enterprises received priority in receiving inputs, and suppliers were legally compelled to fulfill orders from them.

The military did not do well out of the reform. The economic stringencies preceding the reform did not disappear; the military still appeared to be operating on a very tight budget.[15] Because of supply shortages the military tried to produce more of its own food, consumer goods and parts. Excess demand on the labor market and the high salaries available in the private sector made recruitment more difficult. The army had to construct more of its own housing because of the failure of civilian construction enterprises to fulfill contracts.[16] In short, the military sector in Poland appears to have been an island operating much as it did under the old system, uneasily sitting in the new economic environment in Poland.

Hungary

The System

The purpose of the 1968 Hungarian reform was to improve economic efficiency. The large economic losses suffered by Hungary under the old centrally planned system because of development policies focusing on import substitution and rapid development of heavy industry provided an impetus for creating a more open, rational economic system that would serve to indicate areas of comparative advantage to Hungarian producers. By the same token, Hungary's enduring hard-currency balance-of-payments problems provided a renewed impetus for the changes in the economic system in the late 1970's. As in Poland, deteriorating economic performance spurred change. This appears to have been a precondition for reform in centrally planned economies.

Like their Polish counterparts, the Hungarian authorities sought to improve economic efficiency by decentralizing authority and changing the ways in which resources are allocated. Under the outlines of the reform, enterprises were to be independent, self-financing entities. Generating profits was to become a major goal of enterprise management. As in Poland, the state remained the principal owner of industrial enterprises.

Goods and services were to be distributed through markets, although the center was to continue to play a preeminent role in allocating investments and regulating prices of politically sensitive goods. Enterprises were to be free to decide what and how much to produce and to whom to sell on the domestic and hard currency export markets, making their choices on the basis of profitability. Exports to CMEA countries falling under bilateral trade accords remained compulsory. Enterprise managers were also to decide from whom to purchase inputs. However, CMEA trade agreements and the stipulation that hard currency imports must be accompanied by permits issued by the Ministry of Foreign Trade significantly limited this freedom. As in Poland, enterprises had to fulfill orders for goods deemed necessary for defense.

In contrast to the Polish reform, enterprises in Hungary have been, for all intents and purposes, under the complete control of the manager, although the Party committee also had an important voice. Managers have continued to be beholden to their branch ministry and other party and governmental organs. The branch ministry and party have been able to nominate management candidates, and the ministry could still veto the appointment of a manager and dismiss him once appointed. The central authorities could withold or grant tax reliefs, subsidies and import permits.

In 1985 Hungary set up enterprise councils in state-owned industry. In small state-owned enterprises (enterprises with about one hundred employees), the manager was elected directly by the employees at a general assembly held at least once a year. These enterprises functioned much like cooperatives, although the workers had no direct property rights in the enterprise. In larger enterprises, the director was chosen by an enterprise council composed of employee representatives and representatives of management. The councils make decisions about the issue of bonds, transfer of assets, mergers and important employment problems, besides choosing and evaluating the director.[17] The ministry maintained the right to dismiss enterprise directors and approve the council's choice however. Managers have had an important influence on the council; they may choose up to 50 percent of the members. The important role of the manager in determining the composition of the council imparted a more managerial cast to the Hungarian reform than to the Polish. Since the mid-1980s, enterprises have had the right to issue stock. Stockholder rights were limited by the rights of enterprise councils de jure and ministries de facto.

The Hungarian central authorities have pursued a variety of often contradictory policy goals: full employment, low inflation, regional development, maintenance of the current pattern of income distribution, increases in real wages, foreign creditworthiness, and, of course, economic growth. A multitude of often incompatible policy instruments was used to pursue these policy goals. As a consequence, managers have been fed with a set of distorted signals and incentives.

Because of multiple constraints on obtaining inputs and output decisions, manager responses to changes in markets tended to be much slower than their Western counterparts. They faced an unstable regulatory environment: new taxes were frequently applied retroactively. Consequently, like their Polish counterparts, Hungarian managers received a high payoff through successful lobbying efforts.

Assessing the Reform

Managerial Assessment. The most telling criticism of the reform was voiced by a frustrated manager of Chinoin, a drug company, who had turned his enterprise around:

> It is unfortunate that professional arguments and the play of market forces, are not sufficient to settle matters. Personal connections occasionally prove to be more effective. When I see such two-faced behavior on the part of a central agency, I ask, "How long can enterprise independence last?"[18]

Another of the most common criticisms of the reform voiced by enterprise managers has been regulatory instability.[19] Managers have complained about the ex post imposition of taxes and regulations. In effect, they argued that they played the game by the rules and then the rules were retroactively changed. Managers of well-performing companies found there was no way they could win.

Economic Performance. The primary purpose of the reform in socialist industry has been to increase productivity, or in CMEA parlance, to move from extensive to intensive sources of growth. Consequently, the success of the reform must be partially measured by the relative performance of the Hungarian economy in terms of productivity.

Despite the relatively slow growth of the Hungarian economy in recent years, the country compares very favorably with Czechoslovakia and, less surprisingly, Poland in terms of total factor productivity growth. Using both Hungarian and East German weights, Hungary outperformed both countries. Hungary also outperformed the GDR using East German weights (see Table 9.1). The key to this performance appears to be the more efficient use of Hungarian labor. The disturbing trends are for capital productivity. Hungarian industry appears to have employed capital more poorly than Czechoslovakia and much more poorly than the GDR.

Hungary has also done somewhat better in hard currency foreign trade than these countries. We have measured foreign trade performance using changes in the shares of OECD markets for manufactured goods taken by exports from these four countries and China.

We found all four Eastern European countries lost market share

TABLE 9.1 Comparative Productivity Growth in Eastern Europe: 1968–1985 (average annual figures in percent)

	Czechoslovakia	GDR	Poland	Hungary
Decreases in energy usage[a]	−1.73	−2.44	−0.29	−0.26
Changes in capital productivity	−1.43	−0.30	−2.16	−1.72
Changes in labor productivity	3.54	4.54	3.26	5.35
Changes in total factor productivity (East German weights)	2.23	3.26	2.01	3.47
Changes in total factor productivity (Hungarian weights)	1.23	2.28	0.80	2.04

[a]Vanous (1986). The figures for energy usage are per unitl of total NMP, not per unitl of NMP produced by industry.

TABLE 9.2 European CMEA and Chinese Shares in OECD Imports from Non-OECD Areas (in percentages)

	CMEA	GDR[a]	Hungary	Czechoslovakia	Poland	China
Total						
1965 only	11.65	1.65	0.79	1.21	1.84	1.65
1970–1975	11.30	1.55	0.91	1.15	1.87	1.50
1976–1980	9.76	1.13	0.65	0.73	1.41	1.49
1981–1985	10.03	1.20	0.59	0.64	0.86	2.89
Difference						
1970–1975 and 1981–1985	−1.27	−0.35	−0.32	−0.51	−1.01	1.39
Chemicals (SITC 5)						
1970–1975	32.73	9.15	2.83	3.62	4.54	6.02
1976–1980	38.89	7.90	3.42	3.21	3.50	5.32
1981–1985	31.06	7.78	3.09	3.17	1.88	8.14
Difference						
1970–1975 and 1981–1985	−1.67	−1.37	0.26	−0.45	−2.66	2.11
Machinery (SITC 7)						
1970–1975	27.12	7.57	1.70	5.68	4.44	0.12
1976–1980	18.44	4.09	1.61	2.50	4.64	0.18
1981–1985	8.16	2.17	0.98	1.16	1.44	0.44
Difference						
1970–1975 and 1981–1985	−18.96	−5.41	−0.72	−4.52	−3.01	0.32
Consumer Goods (SITC 8)						
1970–1975	16.19	6.04	2.17	2.37	2.15	2.68
1976–1980	11.46	3.56	1.63	1.36	1.86	3.02
1981–1985	6.91	2.24	0.97	0.83	0.86	6.12
Difference						
1970–1975 and 1981–1985	−9.28	−3.79	−1.20	−1.55	−1.28	3.44

[a]Includes trade with West Germany.

between 1970–1975 and 1981–1983 (see Table 9.2). The major reason for the decline in East European shares has been due to competition from other non-OECD suppliers, especially the newly industrialized countries (NICs). The share of CMEA exports to the OECD in total exports to the OECD from outside the region fell from 11.3 to 10 percentage points. Declines in consumer goods (SITC 8) and machinery and transport goods (SITC 7) were even more marked. The European CMEA share of the OECD import market for consumer goods fell from 16 to 7 percent and 27 to 8 percent of the machinery market between 1970–1975 and 1981–1985.

Notwithstanding the poor performance of the region as a whole, the four countries examined performed markedly differently during this period. Hungary increased its market share in chemicals by almost half, more in relative and absolute terms than the GDR or Czechoslovakia (Poland lost market share). Hungary was also the only one of the four to increase its share of OECD machinery import markets, by 30 percent. The GDR lost one-third and Czechoslovakia one-half of their shares over this period. All four countries lost shares of OECD consumer goods markets to the NICs, although Hungary's losses were smaller than its CMEA competitors. In short, over the life of its reform, Hungary has had substantially greater success than Czechoslovakia, the GDR or Poland in retaining OECD market share. Considering that the GDR and Czechoslovakia started the period with a more sophisticated industrial base and, in the case of the GDR, better market access, these figures provide strong evidence that in this area the reformed Hungarian economy has outperformed the traditional centrally planned economies.

Overall Assessment. Both the qualitative and quantitative analyses above show that Hungary had some success with its reform. Hungary increased total factor productivity more rapidly than Czechoslovakia and Poland, and by some measures, the GDR over the life of the reform. This relatively good performance was due to increases in labor productivity; capital productivity declined. Hungarian industry did a much better job of retaining market share in OECD markets for manufactured goods than the others.

This being the case, why is the Hungarian economy close to a crisis? The most immediate problem, Hungary's difficulty in controlling its hard currency balance of payments, was the consequence of poor policy decisions and the economic system. Between 1974–1978 and 1985–1987 the Hungarian government failed to control aggregate demand. Consumption and investment were allowed to rise, even though output did not keep pace. The government did too little too slowly to control imports.

Part of this reluctance to act stemmed from the sluggish reaction of the economy to the reform instruments. Devaluations have frequently spilled over into price increases and were not followed by major export expansion. Campaigns, ministerial pressure, and bonuses tied directly to hard-currency export increases worked better than changes in relative profitability to induce enterprises to export. This in turn is due to protectionism. Enterprises faced little or no import competition; domestic competition was weak because of the small size of the home market. Consequently, enterprises were able to hide behind Hungary's borders, focusing on the CMEA or domestic market, and failed to produce the hard-currency exports needed to service Hungary's foreign debt.

The Military and Economic Reform

Hungary's military goods production has been relatively and absolutely much smaller than Poland's possibly one-third to one-half percent of gross industrial output versus 4 to 8 percent. Evidence of the effects of the economic reform on the military goods–producing industry are hard to find because the industry itself is so small. However, certain conclusions can be drawn concerning the effect of the reform on the military

First, as in Poland, military goods producers continued to be subject to commands from the center concerning what to produce. Prices were also controlled by the center.

Second, the reform significantly curtailed the army's ability to attract high-quality personnel. The growth of cooperatives and the private sector made it more difficult for the military to compete for labor. As moonlighting became the norm for many Hungarian workers, regulations prohibiting military personnel from supplementing their incomes through second jobs led to a decline in interest in military carriers. This problem was compounded by the retirement of commissioned and non commissioned officers who joined in the 1950s, a period in which it was easy to recruit, as they reached the 55-year age limit.[20] The military responded by trying to make military life less strict, opening up new military high schools to widen the pool of applicants, and recruiting more aggressively. These efforts did not produce significant results.

Third, the military was unable to protect its budget during times of economic stringencies. Whether this would have occurred without the reform is an open question, but the sharp debates concerning the size of the military budget and the lack of information on its composition, which was initiated in 1987, continued in 1988.[21] One parliamentarian,

Ferenc Kiraly, vociferously argued that during times of austerity the military budget ought to be reduced rather than increased.[22] This attack came after a decade in which the reported military budgets increased by less than 1 percent annually in real terms and shrunk as a percentage of GDP.

The military contributed in a minor way to easing labor market shortages. As in Poland, many Hungarian draftees worked in construction and heavy industry.[23] Although not a popular move with the officer corps, these draftees provided unskilled labor in occupations that had been difficult to fill at prevailing wage rates.

Although the linkages between reform and the military appear less clear in Hungary than in Poland, the military was not protected from austerity under the reform. More interestingly, political liberalization appears to have progressed as economic reforms have been expanded. Increased political liberalization, especially the expanded role of the Hungarian Parliament, led to declines in the share of economic resources going to the military.

Economic Reform in China, 1979–1989

Since 1978 the Chinese economy has been undergoing a series of drastic policy and institutional reforms. At this juncture the reform movement is far from complete. In fact, in the wake of the political upheaval in mid-1989, economic restructuring has virtually slowed to a halt, repeated official statements to the contrary notwithstanding. Nonetheless, a decade of reform has brought significant changes in both the economy and the military system.

This section takes stock of the progress and the economic consequences of economic reform and assesses its impact on China's military modernization. Specifically it addresses the following questions: Why did the Chinese leadership decide to restructure the economic system and what is the model system that they aim to develop? What specific progress has been made so far? What are the results of, problems of, and prospects for economic reform? How have economic reforms affected the military?

China's Economic Reform: Background and Objectives

At the Third Plenum of the Chinese Communist Party's Eleventh Central Committee in December 1978 the Chinese leadership under Deng Xiaoping made the momentous decision to reform the economic system that had been operating in China for the previous three decades. What drove the leadership to take such a drastic step was apparently the grim reality that the system had failed to bring China out of poverty. As of 1980, China's per capita GNP ranked low even among the developing countries.[24] To be sure, there had been moderate economic growth since 1949, but GNP growth was achieved mainly through large increases in capital and labor inputs rather than productivity, as shown by the rather low growth of total factor productivity in the state-owned industry, the fastest growing sector during the period 1952–1978.[25]

The Chinese leaders in the late 1970s were divided in their assessment of the existing economic system.[26] Some believed that there was nothing wrong. Problems were the legacies of the Cultural Revolution. With the leftists removed from power, China's economic difficulties could be readily resolved. Reforms were therefore unnecessary. A second group recognized the many shortcomings of the existing system but insisted that the system needed only some modifications, not major reforms. A third group, including Deng Xiaoping, believed that institutional reforms were absolutely necessary. Correspondingly, the three policy options were: no reform, minor modifications, and major changes of the economic system. In late 1978, the Party decided to adopt the third option. Having done so, the leadership now faced another set of questions: what economic system should the existing one be transformed into and how should China proceed to bring about these changes?

The model system to be developed has not been clearly defined, but only loosely referred to as a "planned commodity economy" in which the state, the enterprises and the market all have their roles to play.[27] The state regulates the market largely through economic and legal means, the market guides the enterprises and farm households through the price system, and the enterprises and farm households compete in the market and support the state.

The new system is to be drastically different from the existing command economy in that entirely new elements and operating mechanisms will appear, such as undistorted prices and markets, independently managed enterprises, and active participation in the world economy. But it will also differ from a free market economy in that planning will remain an important allocative and coordinating mechanism. Indeed, Chen Yun, one of the aging but influential leaders, compared the model system to birds in a cage.[28] The birds, representing enterprises and farms, are free to fly, but only within the confines of the cage, which represents the state plan. Moreover, mainly for ideological reasons, public ownership will be predominant so that the size of the private sector will be limited.

Economic Reforms, 1978-89

There have been three milestones in China's reform in the period 1978–1989, separating the reform movement into three distinct phases of development The first major turning point was the party's decision to restructure the economic system in December 1978. The second was the Third Plenum of the Party's Twelfth Central Committee in October 1984, which adopted a broad program for urban reform. The third was the Third Plenum of the Thirteenth Central Committee in September 1988 when the party reoriented its effort toward "improving the economic environment and rectifying the economic order." In each phase, the focus of reform, its progress and effect on the economy and the military sector were markedly different.

Rural Reform, 1978–1984. During the first stage, the main thrust of reform was the restructuring of the farming system. In the early 1980s the party replaced the commune system with household farming.[29] Farm households now "lease" land from the state and the means of production (farm tools, equipment and draft animals) from the collectives. They are responsible for a fixed amount of payments to the state and the collective, but keep the rest of the output for their own use or sale at rural free markets. This greatly enhances the peasant's incentive to work because his marginal income is now directly linked to his marginal effort. At the same time, the state raised procurement prices and opened rural markets. The liberalization of state control over factor mobility led to the development of farm households specializing in producing certain products for the market, and more significantly to a rapid increase in employment in nonfarm activities, particularly small industries in villages and towns.

A second major reform during this period was the decentralization of financial power to local governments and state-owned enterprises. Beginning in 1980 any revenue collected in excess of set quotas would be shared by the central and provincial governments. With increased revenues a provincial government could now increase its expenditures.[30] At the same time, the amount of profits retained by enterprises was permitted to increase rapidly. The purpose was to revitalize the local governments and enterprises by providing them with some financial resources for their own disposal.

A third major change during this period was the opening of the hitherto semiclosed economy to the outside world. In addition to institutional changes to increase foreign trade, various measures were introduced to attract foreign capital on a large scale. In 1979 two coastal provinces, Quangdong and Fujian, were designated areas opened to foreign capital. In 1980, four special economic zones (Shenzhen,

Zhuhai, Shantou and Xiamen) were established to facilitate the movement of offshore manufacturing facilities from abroad. In 1984, 14 more coastal cities were opened up.[31]

Reforming the Enterprise System, 1984–1988. The second stage of the reform began in late 1984, when the party shifted attention from rural to urban areas. The urban reform program had three main tasks: (1) to transform state-owned enterprises from administrative subsidiaries of the state into independent business firms, (2) to develop a competitive market system, and (3) to institute macroeconomic controls to replace the mandatory planning system.[32]

The goal of enterprise reform was to revitalize the enterprises by granting the managers decision-making powers so as to provide them incentives, responsibility and authority to operate efficiently. In principle, the manager has the power to work out his own production and sales plans within the framework of the state's mandatory plans, to hire and dismiss workers, to decide on the size of bonuses, to set prices within limits, and to merge with other enterprises for economic reasons. The enterprise can keep a portion of its profits in proportion to those turned over to the state for use in investment or in the workers' welfare programs. In short, the manager is expected to play the role of an entrepreneur, independent of the control by the party or government.

Outwardly, much progress in enterprise reform has been made. By the first half of 1988, more than 80 percent of the state-owned enterprises had adopted the director responsibility system designed to reduce party and administrative intervention in enterprises. Furthermore, 90 percent of the large and medium-sized state-owned enterprises were now under contract with the state under the new system.[33]

However, the reform has failed to revitalize enterprises. First, the new system itself has many shortcomings. The contract period was relatively short (usually three to four years) and the evaluation of enterprise performance was based solely on achieving the profit objective. There was therefore a tendency for the managers to maximize short-term profits at the expense of the enterprise's long-term interests by wearing down equipment, boosting workers' bonuses and avoiding investments with no immediate payoffs. Most enterprise managers were appointed by the government departments, making the management vulnerable to intervention by government officials. Moreover, the contracted amount to be delivered to the state was based on actual profits prior to the introduction the contract system. As a result, enterprises that were making good profits were penalized with heavier obligations to the state than were poorly run enterprises.[34]

The most fundamental reason for the sluggish progress in enterprise reform was the lack of price reform. The enterprises could not really operate independently and efficiently until the price system was also free of government control and a competitive market system established. Prices in China prior to 1978 were administratively set and rigidly controlled so that they remained fixed for decades. They did not reflect relative scarcities. Given a set of distorted prices there could not be any meaningful measures of efficiency and the managers were not motivated to become efficient.

Up to the mid-1980s, price reform consisted mainly of adjustments to prices. Subsequently, the emphasis shifted to decontrol. The outcome was a mixed price system. By 1988, prices of farm products (except grain, cotton and oilseeds) and minor daily-use manufactured goods had been decontrolled. Those of some manufactured goods (textiles and machinery) were allowed to fluctuate within a certain range. Prices of others (coal and raw materials) had a dual-track system: that portion of output under mandatory planning was priced at fixed planned prices; prices of extra-plan output could vary according to market conditions. However, the prices of certain products, factor prices and exchange rates were still under strict government control.

Whatever rationale the leaders might have for the gradual approach to price reform, the piecemeal process created problems of economic disorder and corruption. The dual-price system has motivated the enterprises to bargain for lower output quotas so that they could produce more for sale at higher market prices, to substitute poor-quality products for high-quality ones in their deliveries to the state, and to hoard raw materials supplied by the state at planned prices. More seriously the system also created opportunities for people with connections to reap high profits. For example, the state is supposed to buy a planned quota of chemical fertilizer from the producer at controlled prices, which are lower than the market prices, and sell the fertilizer to farmers at about the same low prices to compensate farmers who sell their grain to the state at below-market prices. In reality, the factory sells at government set prices, while farmers pay market prices. The state subsidy goes to the middlemen, mainly officials who are able to get fertilizers at low official prices.

Slowdown of the Reform Movement, 1989–1990. In October 1988, Li Peng, the new premier, announced that in the next two years reform movements would be slowed down as the overriding task was to control inflation.[35] By February 1989, the official year-on-year inflation rate reached 30 percent, the highest since 1949.

By mid-1989, disputes over reform policy had developed into a power struggle. The Tianenmen Incident led to the political downfall of the pro-reform group. At the same time it strengthened the belief of the conservative group that the free-market solution to China's economic problems not only created economic instability but also undermined the socialist state and threatened the very legitimacy of the party. Accordingly the new leadership tightened state control of the economy, apparently not merely as a temporary measure but as a permanent feature of the system.

Assessing the Reform

Productivity has clearly improved much more rapidly in the reform than before. Output per worker in agriculture has been growing at a respectable rate of 4 percent per year, in sharp contrast to stagnant growth under the commune system. On the other hand, total factor productivity growth in the state-owned industrial sector has been only 0.4 percent per year. The foreign trade ratio in 1978 was 9.9 percent, about the same as that in 1957, but it rose sharply to 27 percent by 1988.[36] Opening of the economy to external trade apparently generated some benefits from economies of scale and specialization. The presumption is strong that economic reform contributed significantly to this economic improvement and growth.

Differences in productivity growth in the agricultural and industrial sectors probably reflect the different degrees of successful reform in these two sectors. In agriculture, the peasants' lack of motivation to produce was the key bottleneck in the communes. The return to household farming broke the bottleneck and productivity increased. In the industrial sector, enterprise reform never released the factory directors from government and Party control. Unlike the rural markets, markets for industrial products, services and factors never really developed in the urban sector. Hence the urban economy operates far below its production frontier.

The Military and Economic Reform

Impact of Economic Reform on the Military. Economic reform affected the military sector most profoundly in the following areas: the restructuring of the military system, the reform of the military R&D and defense industries, the relationship between the military sector and the outside world, and competition between civilians and the military sector for educated manpower.

The most important development has been the parallel reform of the military system itself. As economic reform progressed, the military was under pressure to reform its own system.[37] In part, this is because poor performance and low productivity, the very factors that prompted the leaders to reform the economic system, also plagued the military sector. The need to improve efficiency was immediate because the growth of defense spending had been slowed down in order to divert more resources to economic modernization. Defense spending as reported in the state budget has increased only moderately in the decade 1978–1988, at an average annual rate of 2.6 percent, far below the growth rates of state budget revenues or GNP.[38] In real terms, defense spending actually declined because of much higher inflation rates.[39] As explained by Chi Haotian, the Chief of General Staff, the tight defense budget was necessary to support economic reform.[40]

The restructuring and modernizing of the PLA had been planned for some time but the process began in earnest only in 1985. The number of China's regional commands was cut from eleven to seven. The change was intended, in part, to streamline the command structure by reducing its size and centralizing the operational command, in part, to conform more logically to the needs of China's land defense, but more importantly, to replace the aging leaders of the PLA with younger, better educated and professionally more competent commanders. By the end of 1985, the number of commanding officers in the seven regional commands had been cut by more than half, and the number of officers at the headquarters of the General Staff, the Political and the Logistic Departments by 23.8 percent. The plan was to raise the ratio between officers and servicemen from 1:2.45 to 1:3.3. At the same time, the average age of the new commanding officers at the seven regional commands fell from 64.9 to 56.7 years, and that at the three headquarters, by 10.6 years. More than 50 percent of the officers at the regional commands and about 80 percent of those at the headquarters are now college graduates, and more than 65 percent of the officers in the combat units have been replaced by others who have had formal training in military institutes.

Notable progress has been made in the development of new weapons, although slowly and selectively. In 1985, the former Minister of Defense, Xu Xiangqian, expressed the hope that China would approach the level of the advanced countries in terms of military equipment and technology within 15 years.[41] The ambitious goal may not be realistic, but it clearly indicated the strong desire of the military leaders to modernize the PLA's weaponry.

A second reason for the continued development of new weapons is that, quite apart from political considerations, improved military equipment may be needed for national security reasons during the transitional period. The likelihood of regional military conflicts cannot be ruled out.

A third reason for maintaining an ongoing development program is that there are technological advantages in maintaining an active, if small, defense industry. One distinct benefit is that of learning by doing. As a result of continual effort, future development programs would start from a higher technological level than if the industry had been standing still. Moreover, to make effective use of the foreign military technology currently acquired by China, there has to be an indigenous R&D effort as well as production facilities to absorb the imported technology.

Prior to 1978 the R&D units were neither motivated nor obligated to be cost-effective.[42] To remedy these shortcomings, the State Council in January 1987 established a contract system for research and the production of military equipment. Under the new system, funds for military R&D are allocated to the armed services according to their needs, and the latter enter into contractual arrangements either through open bidding or negotiations with the R&D units and defense industries that will perform specific tasks at specified costs, quality and delivery schedules.[43]

In the defense industry, reorganization along the lines of civilian industrial reform also took place. Many centrally controlled enterprises were turned over to the local administration in an attempt to revitalize these enterprises through decentralization.[44] At the same time some enterprises in the defense sector were consolidated in order to improve economic efficiency through functional specialization.[45] One notable example is that 2000 enterprises in the third-line areas (interior China) were closed, merged or moved to other locations in line with the reform.[46]

Table 9.3 shows China's arms imports as a percentage of defense expenditures reported in the state budget. The figures are rough estimates because of uncertainties in exchange rate conversion and the extent of undercoverage of reported defense spending. Nonetheless, they are useful to show the increasing importance of arms imports. Arms imports rose from around 1 percent during 1978–1983 to about 8 percent of the reported defense budget since 1983. Of the total, imports from noncommunist countries accounted for about 70 percent, which probably could not have been feasible without the open trade policy.[47] This is because, on the one hand, economic reform in China has led to progressive liberalization of the Western countries' measures restricting high technology transfers to China under the Coordinating Committee for Multilateral Export Controls. On the other hand, the sharp rise in China's exports under the open policy and, until 1989,

TABLE 9.3 China's Arms Trade and Reported Expenditures, 1978–1987

	Arms Imports (Billion Yuan)	Defense Spending (Billion Yuan)	Import Spending (%)	Arms Exports (Million US$)	Total Exports (%)
1975				1.2	
1978	0.15	16.78	0.9		
1979	0.28	22.27	1.2		
1980	0.28	19.38	1.4	0.4	
1981	0.20	16.80	1.2	3.7	
1982	0.15	17.63	0.9	1,288.0	5.5
1983	0.20	17.71	1.1	1,540.7	6.4
1984	0.99	18.08	5.5	1,625.9	5.9
1985	1.79	19.15	9.3	1,057.1	3.4
1986	1.74	20.08	8.7	1,554.4	4.4
1987	0.42	20.98	6.8	2,388.8	5.0

Source: World Military Expenditures and Arms Transfers 1989, U.S. Arms Control and Disarmament Agency, 1989, p. 80; *1988 Abstract*, pp. 74–85; SY86, p. 602.

booming tourism generated substantial foreign exchange earnings to finance imports.

Not all the effects of economic reform have been positive for the military. In at least one area, recruiting new servicemen, economic reforms created problems. China has compulsory military service in principle. However, throughout the years China's soldiers have always been volunteers, attracted by prestige, job security and the opportunity to move up the social and economic ladders. Today, the lure of the army remains as strong as ever in the poor agricultural regions. In prosperous rural areas, however, fewer people want to join the PLA because economic reforms have opened up new, more lucrative employment opportunities.[48]

The Role of the Military in Economic Reform. In its effort to adapt itself to the rapidly changing economic and political environment, the military has adopted policies that in turn affect the reform movement profoundly. Several developments in this respect are particularly significant: the civilization of the defense industry, the sharp increase in arms exports, and changes in the political role of the military.

As defense budgets were cut, the defense industry became the victim of economic reform. More than half of the military factories stopped or drastically reduced production as a result of cuts in military procurement.[49] To survive, the defense industry was forced to participate in the movement toward marketization by producing civilian goods to compete in domestic and international markets. By 1989, 90 percent of the enterprises in the defense industry were producing civilian goods, and one-sixth of them thrived on civilian production alone. Civilian products accounted for more than 60 percent of the total value of output.[50]

Another major development in the military sector that has had a significant impact on the Chinese economy is arms exports. Arms exports are by no means new. Long before Deng took over the leadership in 1978, China supplied arms to Albania, North Korea, Vietnam and some African countries. But recent arms exports differ from those of the past in several respects. First, the volume of arms exports in recent years has been much larger (Table 9.3). In the period 1980–1987, arms exports increased sharply, from US$0.4 million in 1980 to US$2.4 billion in 1987.

Another notable feature of China's arms exports is the variety of products offered for sale. The list includes anti-aircraft missiles, attack aircraft, interceptors, helicopters, tanks, self-propelled howitzers, and armored personnel carriers. Technologically, the Chinese weapons are less advanced than those supplied by Western countries, but they are simple, sturdy and cheap.

Prior to the 1980s China's arms deals were highly political. Now the objective is primarily economic. Through arms exports, Chinese defense industries hope to earn the foreign exchange needed to upgrade their tchnologies. Because of the change in motivation, the list of buyers also changed. China would sell to whomever had the hard currency to pay for the weapons.

In China, as in virtually all communist systems, the military plays a major political role. Its importance, however, has changed over time. In the 1980s the political status of the military in China apparently reached a low point, as the military was asked to take a back seat while the party concentrated its effort on economic reform. At least outwardly, most military leaders were supportive of economic reform, possibly because they realized that in the long run economic reform might well be the most effective way to military modernization. Toward the end of the 1980s, some military leaders were already becoming impatient.[51] The use of the military in the June 4 crackdown of the student movement probably increased the political power of the military leaders just as the Cultural Revolution did in the late 1960s. Meanwhile, the Western countries sanctions that halted all transfers of military technology to China might have reopened the issue whether China should from now on rely more on indigenous R&D than on foreign technology.

Comparison and Conclusion

Assessing the Reforms

The primary goal of economic reform has been to improve economic efficiency, especially in state-owned industry. Although all the reforms have improved efficiency to some extent, in general the results of the reforms in industry have been disappointing. Many of the successes of the reforms have been in the private sector and, in the case of China, agriculture.

Productivity growth in state-owned industry was disappointing in comparison with agriculture or the private sector in China. Since the introduction of the NEM in 1968, Hungary outperformed Poland, Czechoslovakia, and, by some measures, the GDR, in factor productivity growth. In Poland the rate of increase in the efficiency with which capital and energy were used accelerated after the adoption of the reform. However, in general the improvements have been marginal. There was no qualitative jump to much more rapid rates of factor productivity growth in either Poland or Hungary.

The reforms failed to improve allocation of capital. The share of investment of the least profitable sectors in Poland and Hungary increased in the 1980s, precisely when rate of return was to be a much more important determinant of investment. Capital efficiency in Chinese industry has also remained low. The state continued to play the dominant role in allocating capital in all three countries. In no case did the reform appear to contribute to the ability of the state to allocate capital better.

If economic reform was to succeed, economic decision-making authority had to be devolved from the ministries to the institutions that possessed the information needed to make better choices of technologies, inputs and fixed products: the enterprises. However, the independence of enterprise managers had to be preserved from encroachment on the part of the branch ministries or central authorities, if the system was to function. Poland established workers' councils, which nominally served to counterbalance the broad ministry. The rights of Hungarian managers were codified in law and part of their bonuses were tied to profits, thereby leaving them less at the mercy of a critical evaluation from their superiors in the branch ministries. In China the principle of one-man management was stressed and the role of the party secretary downgraded.

None of the reforms successfully established the independence of state-owned firms. In each case the state, through the ministries, the Planning Commission and its control of the distribution system, abrogated decision-making authority formally ascribed to the enterprise. To some extent this failure to transfer control can be traced to the continued existence of a one-party state. However, other characteristics of these systems were more immediate hindrances.

All the governments pursued policies (e.g., low inflation, limited unemployment, increasing exports) other than improving economic efficiency. In many cases these goals ran counter to the consequences of the greater use of markets. To achieve these other goals the governments fell back on the use of the old economic instruments or new economic instruments similar to those used in the past. Moreover, managers often failed to respond to market signals in the manner assumed in the reform. They had quickly discovered the real incentive system was geared toward rewarding managers who fulfilled the desires of their superiors.

All three reforms were marked by the proliferation of controls on prices and the allocation of goods and of taxes and subsidies, many of which became enterprise specific. These controls served to confiscate the profits of profitable enterprises and to distort the domestic price system. They were the primary barrier to the efficient reallocation of resources.

In all three countries the reform increased the role of importance of foreign trade for state-owned industry. In general, the efficiency of trade appeared to improve. The most striking change was the dramatic increase in Chinese exports and its emergence as a major trading country. Hungary did much better in maintaining Western market shares than its competitors in the CMEA. Even Poland, despite its poor economic performance in the 1980s, was able to improve the efficiency of imports and accelerate export growth after the implementation of its foreign trade reform.

The Military and Reform

Effect of Reform on the Military. After the introduction of reforms in Poland and China and the expansion of the Hungarian reform, the militaries faced strong new pressures to cut costs and become more efficient. In the case of Poland and Hungary, cost-cutting pressures may be traced in part to poor macroeconomic performance in the 1980s. Chinese economic performance, however, has been exceptional during much of this period, yet the military still saw its budget shrink. Officers in all three armies have faced incentives to run their units and equipment more efficiently.

In the face of rising cost pressures, all the militaries increased income-generating activities. Polish and Hungarian units raised some of their own food and manufactured some simple products as well as provided soldiers for civilian construction projects (for whom the army was then paid). The Chinese, however, took this process the furthest. In contrast to Poland and Hungary, where almost all military equipment is produced in the civilian sector, the Chinese armed forces owned and operated a large number of plants producing equipment and supplies for the armed forces. These plants have used the reform to become major arms exporters; the Ministry of Defense pockets the profits. Others have profitably invaded the civilian markets with products like television and motorcycles. These activities have fostered competition and generated substantial resources for the defense industry.

All of the militaries have found it more difficult to attract personnel. Recruitment difficulties were primarily due to opportunities in the private sector to generate secondary sources of income. Overtime work, second jobs in cooperatives, and the creation of small businesses became more attractive than a military career.

Effects of the Military on the Reform. The size of the military production sector may have a dampening effect on reform. In the case of Poland the military goods sector was placed in a special industrial union in which enterprises operated much as before the reform. Military goods producers also had priority for obtaining imports. These measures weakened the reform. In Hungary, where the military goods sector is much smaller, similar measures had much less impact on the reform.

The primary effect of the military on reform has been political. In the case of Poland, reform was introduced almost concurrently with martial law. Martial law and the powers that were given the local military commanders effectively nullified the reform for the first year. This false start may have permanently maimed the reform so that it was never implemented in full. In the case of China the involvement of the military in the June 4, 1989, crackdown weakened the position of the reform group in the leadership. Unwittingly or consciously, the army has managed to derail the Chinese economic reform.

Notes

1. *Kierunki reformy gospodarczej*, Ksiazka i Wiedza, Warsaw, 1981.

2. Robert Campbell, *The Soviet-Type Economies: Performance and Evolution*, Houghton-Mifflin, Boston, 1974.

3. Marek Dabrowski, "Changes for the Better?" *Zarzadzanie*, No. 6, June 1987, p. 44, as translated in Joint Publications Research Service, *JPRS Report: East Europe*, JPRS-EER-87-138, September 10, 1987, p. 117.

4. Wojciechowska, Urszula, Grazyna Pasznik, and Andrzej Szeworski, "Sytuacja ekonomiczna przedsiebiorstw przemyslowych w 1985 rodu," Raporty, Instytut Gospodarki Narodowej, Warsaw, 1987, p. 35.

5. Ibid., p. 76.

6. Ibid., p. 35.

7. Wojciechowska, Urszla, Grayzyna Pasznick, and Andrzej Szeworski, "Sytuacja ekonomiczna przedsiebiorstw przemyslowych w 1985 roku," Raporty, Instytut Gospodarki Narodowej, Warsaw, 1987.

8. Wojciechowska, Urszula, and Jan Lipinski, "Funkcjonowanie Prezedsieborstw w 1985 roku," Raporty, Instytut Gospodarki Narodowej, Warsaw, 1986, p. 265.

9. Ibid., p. 21.

10. Major S. Lukaszewski, "Rationally and Thriftily: Council for Economic and Defense Affairs, Ministry of National Defense," Zolnierz Wolnosci, July 1, 1987, pp. 1, 5, as translated Joint Publications Research Service, JPRS Report: East Europe, JPRS-EER-87-135, September 4, 1987, p. 68.

11. Interview with General Division Stanislaw Fryn, Chief of Staff, Deputy Quartermaster General of the Polish Armed Forces," Zolnierz Polski, July 1987, p. 5, as cited Joint Publications Research Service, JPRS Report: East Europe, JPRS-EER-87-132, September 1, 1987, pp. 106–108.

12. JPRS-EER-86-056 April 11, 1986, p. 50; Colonel Waldemar Makowiecki, "Interview with Chief of Staff, Deputy Chief Quartermaster of the Armed Forces, General Division Stanaislaw Fryn, 'Practical School of Economics'" Zolnierz Wolnosci, January 4–5, 1986, p. 3.

13. Reperowicz, Stanislaw, "Food for the Common Table; Army Farms," Trybuna Ludu, July 19, 1984, p. 4 as translated in JPRS-EPS-84-123, pp. 90–93.

14. "Military Academy Recruitment Affairs," Zolnierz Wolnosci, January 28, 1986, p. 1, as translated in JPRS-EER-86-042, March 21, 1986, p. 49.

15. Soroka, Marek, "We Do Not Squander State Money: Interview with General Brigadier Magister Engineer Stanislaw Switalski, Head of Tank Motor Services," Zolnierz Wolnosci, No. 28, July 8, 1984, pp. 5, 9, as translated in JPRS-EPS-84-127, pp. 98–101.

16. Pieklo, Tadeusz, Second Lieutenant, "Aggressiveness, Initiative, Resourcefulness: The Military Economy Under New Conditions," Zolnierz Wolnosci, February 3, 1982, p. 5, as translated in JPRS-80707, pp. 58-59.

17. Adam, Jan "The Hungarian Economic Reform of the 1980s," Soviet Studies, vol. 39, No. 4, October 1987, p. 612.

18. Bossanyi, Katalin, "Demokratizalodo gazdasag: Atallas a kollektiv vezetesre az iparban," Gazdasag, No. 2, 1986.

19. "'A jo fokonyvelo annyi nyereseget hozhat mint ezer munkas': Valaszol egy Vallatati Kozgazdasz," Heti Vilaggazdasag June 25, 1983, p. 46.

20. Exclusive Interview with Comrade Brigadier General Dezso, Director of the Hungarian People's Army Career Guidance Department," Igaz Szo, March 1986, pp. 4–5.

21. "Vekonyodo tarcak," Heti Vilaggazdasag, December 19, 1987, pp. 50–52; "Nyari dieta," Heti Vilaggazdasag, July 9, 1988, p. 7.

22. Ibid.

23. "Interview with Ferenc Karpati, Minister of Defense", *Magyar Hirlap*, September 18, 1987, p. 6, as translated in JPRS-EER-87-161, December 16, 1987, p. 24.

24. According to estimates by the World Bank, China's per capita GNP in 1980 was U.S.$290 compared to the average of U.S.$680 for the developing countries (World Bank, World Tables, 1988–1989 Edition, Johns Hopkins University Press, Baltimore, 1989, pp. 15, 17). A rough estimate based on purchasing power parity for China in 1980 was U.S.$573, again far below the average of U.S.$846 for developing countries (Herbert Block, *The Planetary Product in 1980: A Creative Pause?* U.S. Department of State, Washington, D.C., 1981, pp. 61–73).

25. Net output in constant prices grew at 11.7 percent per year during 1952–1978, to which the growth of total factor productivity contributed 0.96 percentage points, or only 8 percent of total output growth. World Bank, *China: Long-Term Issues and Options*, The Main Report, World Bank, 1985, p. 157.

26. *Jingji ribao* (Economic Daily), April 4, 1987, p. 1.

27. The general principles and tasks of reform have been outlined in "Decision of the Central Committee of the Communist Party of China on Reform of the Economic Structure," *Beijing Review*, 27:44 (October 29, 1984), pp. i-xvi. See also Liu Guonguang, *Zhongguo jingji tizhi gaige de moshi yanjiu* (Studies in Models of China's Economic Reform), China Social Sciences Publishing House, Beijing, 1988.

28. Wang Jiye and Zhu Yuanzhen, *Jingji tizhi gaige xouzhe* (Handbook of Economic System Reform), Economic Daily Publishing House, Beijing, 1987, p. 618.

29. The decision was made only after several years of experimentation. See Wange Jiye and Zhu Yuanzhen, ibid. pp. 823–826. For discussions of rural reform, see China's Rural Development Problems Study Group, *Nongcun jingji biange de xitong kaocha* (A Systematic Survey of Rural Economic Changes), China Social Sciences Publishing House, Beijing, 1984, and Research Institute of the Center for Rural Development, State Council, *Gaige maianlin zhidu Chuangxin* (Reforms Embarking on Institutional Innovations), Sanlian Book Store, Shanghai, 1988.

30. For a brief description of fiscal reform, see Wang Jiye and Zhu Yuanzhen, op. cit, pp. 844–846; Gao Shanquan, Jiunianlai de zhongguo jingji tizhi gaige (Reform of China's Economic System in the Past Nine Years), People's Press, Beijing, 1987, pp. 37–41; Tian Yinong, Zhu Fulin and Xian Huizheng, Lun zhongguo Caizheng guanli tizhi de gaige (On Reform of China's Fiscal Management System), Economic Science Publishing House, Beijing, 1985.

31. See Wang and Zhu, op. cit., pp. 868–874. There were also other reforms besides the three major ones noted here. See Gao, op. cit., pp. 17–69.

32. *Beijing Review*, 27:44 (October 29, 1984), pp. i-Xvi; "Proposal of the Central Committee of the Chinese Communist Party for the Seventh Five-

Year Plan for National and Social Development," Beijing Review, 28:40 (October 7, 1985), pp. Xviii–Xxii.

33. *Guangming ribao* (Guangming Daily), August 17, 1988., p. 2. See also Gao Shanguan, op. cit., pp. 30–33.

34. Zhen Furui and Xie Yuanhai, "Some Thoughts on Improving the Contract Responsibility System," *Jingji yu guanli yanjiu* (Research on Economics and Management), No. 4, August 1989, pp. 59–61, translated in JPRS-CAR-89-119, December 19, 1989, pp. 12–14; *China Daily*, January 10, 1989, p. 4.

35. *Wen hui pao* (Wen hui daily), October 14, 1988, p. 2.

36. The ratios are based on total GNP and total exports and imports in 1989 prices. For source of data, see Statistical Yearbook 1989, pp. 28–30, 633.

37. In the words of Chi Haotian, the Chief of the General Staff, "The reform of the army should conform with the reform situation of the reform situation of the whole country, and should catch up with the pace of reform of the whole country," *Jie fangjun Bao* (Liberation Army Daily), May 8, 1988, p. 1.

38. For defense spending and budget revenues in 1978 and 1988, see SY87, pp. 617, 626; and *RMRB*, April 7, 1989, p. 3. For GNP in 1978 and 1988, see Li Chengrui, "Only Socialism Can Develop China," *Beijing Review*, October 2–8, 1989, pp. 20, 29. The reported defense spending does not include weapons procurement. The latter apparently has declined during this period, as suggested by reports of reduction of sales to the military by the defense industry and the military leaders' complaint of the slow pace of weapons modernization.

39. The official retail price index shows an annual increase of 5.6 percent. See *1988 Abstract*, p. 91; and *RMRB*, March 1, 1989, p. 2.

40. *Jiefangjuin Bao* (Liberation Army Daily), October 12, 1988, p. 1.

41. *China Daily*, September 5, 1985, p. 1.

42. Chen Zhiqiang and Zheng He, "Reforming the System of Placing Production Orders for Arms and Equipment in Our Country," *Liaowang*, No. 13, March 30, 1987, p. 22.

43. *WHP*, February 9, 1987, p. 3; RMRB, May 9, 1987, p. 1; *CD*, March 4, 1988, p. 3. By 1988, contracts were signed for 80 percent of all the projects. *RMRB*, Decemer 11, 1988, p. 3.

44. For example, more than 100 enterprises under the Ministry of the Ordnance Industry were to be transferred to local authorities in 1986 (*JJRB*, July 12, 1986, p. 1). The transfer was intended to facilitate the shift to produce civilian goods by these enterprises.

45. Liu Xingyi, "Preliminary Discussion of Reform Measures to Revitalize the National Defense and Technology Industry," *Kexuexue yu Kexue jishu guanli* (Study of Science and Science and Technology Management), No. 10, October 12, 1986,. pp. 33–35, translated in JPRS- CST-87-001, January 8, 1987, pp. 1–6.

46. JPRS-CEA-86-111, October 17, 1986, p. 53.

47. *World Military Expenditures and Arms Transfers 1988*, U.S. Arms Control and Disarmament Agency, 1989, p. 112.

48. *China Daily*, April 29, 1989, p. 4, RMRB, February 20, 1989, p. 5.

49. *China Daily–Business Weekly*, October 30, 1989, p. 4.

50. *Ibid*. Civilian products include trucks and buses, textile machinery, medical instruments, household electrical appliances and communication satellites.

51. See, for example, the complaint by Zhao Nanqi, General Logistics Department Chief of the PLA, reported in *Ming pao*, April 24, 1988, p. 9.

10

The Defense Sector in the Soviet Economy During Perestroika: From Expansion to Disarmament to Disintegration

Christopher Davis

Introduction

The defense sector in the Soviet Union had substantial macroeconomic significance because of its influence on the choice of economic system, policies, and performance. Throughout most of the history of that nation, the communist party elite was committed to achieving ambitious national security objectives through the development of military and economic power. The other main macroeconomic targets were full employment, low rates of open inflation, and balance of the state budget and foreign trade. The Soviet government allocated exceptionally high shares of national income to defense and investment. Consumption was treated as a residual claimant on national resources.

In order to achieve its goals, despite the backwardness of the economy by international standards, the Soviet leadership adopted and maintained a politico-economic system with dictatorial collective choice mechanisms, state ownership of productive assets, central planning and rationing of supplies, administratively fixed prices, severe restrictions on market forces and competition, and autarky in foreign trade. The primary instrument used to attain them was the quantity-oriented economic plan. Monetary and fiscal policies played only secondary, passive roles.

During 1965–1985, the macroeconomic and national security policies of the Soviet elite enabled the USSR to develop into a military superpower and to exert growing influence in the global political system. However, by the end of the 1970s the Soviet Union was obtaining diminishing security returns from this strategy. Furthermore, the heavy defense burden imposed severe strains on the economy and society, which, together with the systemic problems engendered by central planning and state ownership, undermined macroeconomic performance and caused a growing gap between the economic power, productivity, and competitiveness of the USSR and that of Western nations.

In the years of perestroika (1985–1991), the Gorbachev regime attempted to correct the obvious deficiencies in economic performance while preserving the communist political system and planned economy through a set of reforms imposed from above. It adopted a new strategy to enhance national security that was based on the "new thinking" in foreign policy and emphasized threat reduction measures instead of the expansion of military power. The reform program did not achieve its original objectives; rather, it contributed to the systemic collapse of the Soviet Union by the end of 1991. This paper reviews developments in macroeconomics and defense in three periods since 1985 and assesses their influence on the demise of the USSR.

The first period covers the years 1985–1988, as discussed in the third section of this chapter, when various timid reforms were introduced, the defense burden increased, little progress was made in disarmament, and macroeconomic processes remained under control. During the second period, from January 1989 to August 1991, discussed in the following section, the unanticipated impacts of the reforms undermined the ability of the center to control political processes and contributed to growing macroeconomic instability. Although the Soviet leadership became more committed to disarmament, key aspects of the military-industrial complex remained unchanged, and substantial systemic obstacles to arms reductions existed.

The start of the third period, discussed next, is marked by the failure of the August 1991 coup, which resulted in the decisive political defeat of conservative forces and the rapid elimination of the Communist party as a political force. Over the next several months, the central government was disestablished, the nation fragmented into independent states loosely bound in a commonwealth, and the military-industrial complex started to disintegrate into national components. The new governments of the commonwealth states committed themselves to making transitions from command to a capitalist market economies and to policies of radical disarmament and demilitarization. But these changes were made during a worsening of the economic crisis. It remains to be seen whether the transition process will continue to be conducive to disarmament, or whether economic tensions and political conflicts will impel the newly independent commonwealth states to carry heavy defense burdens that will be detrimental to macroeconomic performance.

The Defense Sector in the Traditional
Soviet Shortage Economy: 1965–1985

For at least 70 years after the 1917 revolution the Soviet leadership had as its primary objectives the maintenance of Communist party rule and the protection of the nation from any real or perceived threat. It therefore awarded the activity of national security production a relatively high weight in the social welfare function. A feature of the traditional Soviet national security strategy was that it placed relatively more emphasis on military power than on threat reduction.[1] Soviet leaders believed that military capabilities were determined by economic power in the long run, so they invested substantial shares of national income to promote growth, especially in crucial sectors such as machine building and fuels.[2]

The Soviet leadership decided that to achieve its challenging goals in a backward nation, it was necessary to make use of centralized planning and rationing systems.[3] The government established priority rankings of sectors, institutions, and programs that expressed its varying degrees of commitment to ensuring that problems were solved or goals were attained. In conjunction with this, a system of resource-rationing procedures and enforcement mechanisms was developed that both protected privileged sectors and penalized less important ones.[4]

The combination of central planning, overambitious output targets, and tight resource constraints generated chronic disequilibrium in producer and consumer goods markets and spawned a socialist shortage economy that was characterized by non–price-control mechanisms, paternalistic relations between superiors and subordinates, independent (and often illegal) behavior by lower-level economic units, sellers' markets, and soft budget constraints.[5] In the "resource constrained" economic system the primary cause of disequilibrium was the quantity-driven behavior of economic institutions, especially in the industrial sector. Prices and money played only secondary roles.

The communist leadership recognized that its plans for the development of military power could be jeopardized by the adverse effects of the socialist shortage economy. They therefore assigned the defense sector a high priority.[6] In the case of the defense industry, its privileged status was reflected in its above-average wage levels and benefits (e.g., housing and medical care), rapid remedial responses by central authorities to production problems, soft budget constraints, high levels of input inventories, low intensity of shortages, and special access to covertly acquired Western military technology. There were, of course, recurrent conflicts between the disruptive forces of the shortage economy and the attempts to protect high-priority institutions.

The Brezhnev-Andropov-Chernenko regimes (1964–1985) hoped to expand their nation's economic power by accelerating technological innovation and shifting economic development from an extensive to an intensive basis. The attainment of these goals was undermined, however, by the reintroduction and maintenance of Stalinist organizational forms (e.g., ministries), mechanisms (e.g., central planning and rationing of supplies), and priorities (e.g., defense as the most favored sector). The various tinkering reforms in 1965, 1973, and 1979 neither corrected the major problems nor reversed the unfavorable trends evident in the Soviet economy.

The severity of the challenge confronting the Soviet Union in its attempt to keep up in the Cold War power competition using its traditional national security strategy can be appreciated by considering the dynamics of Soviet national income relative to that of the other major nations. According to official Soviet statistics, the average growth of produced national income in five-year periods declined as follows: 7.4 percent in 1966–1970; 6.3 percent in 1971–1975; 4.2 percent in 1976–1980; and 3.3 percent in 1981–1985 (Table 10.1).

CIA estimates of GNP growth in constant (1982) prices for the same periods also exhibit a downward trend but are consistently lower: 5.0 percent, 3.2 percent, 2.2 percent, and 1.9 percent. It should be noted, however, that several Soviet and Western economists argue that if Soviet growth is properly adjusted for hidden inflation, then it averaged 2.2 percent per annum during 1966–1985 instead of the CIA estimate of 3.0 percent and the official claim of 5.4 percent.[7] These critics also assert that real national income growth was 0.6 percent during 1981–1985 in contrast to the official Soviet growth rate of 3.3 percent and the CIA estimate of 1.9 percent.

In assessing trends in global power balances, it is appropriate to compare in the first instance Soviet GNP growth rates with those of the United States, which were 3.0 percent in 1966–1970; 2.2 percent in 1971–1975; 3.4 percent in 1976–1980; and 2.4 percent in 1981–1985.[8] This indicates that the Soviet economy grew more rapidly during 1966-75 but relatively slowly during 1976-85. Taking into account these rates and estimates of national income, the ratio of Soviet-to-U.S. GNP (both expressed in U.S. dollars) rose from 50 percent in 1965 to a peak of 58 percent in the mid-1970s, but then dropped back to 53 percent in

TABLE 10.1 Macroeconomic and Defense Trends, 1966–1985

Indicator	8th FYP 1966–1970	9th FYP 1971–1975	10th FYP 1976–1980	11th FYP 1981–1985
GNP (billion1982 rubles)	5.0	3.2	2.2	1.9
National income produced (% growth)	7.4	6.3	4.2	3.3
Industrial output (% growth)	6.0	5.6	2.4	2.0
Capital investment (% growth)	5.5	4.3	4.3	3.4
Consumption per capita (% growth)	5.0	3.0	2.0	0.8
Expenditure ondefense (% growth)	3.7	3.7	2.5	3.2
Defense burden (% GNP)	11-13	12-14	13-15	15-17

Sources: GNP: CIA/DIA (1989, table B-4). National income: Narodnoe (1989, pp. 8–9). Industrial output: CIA/DIA (1989, table B-4). Capital investment: Kurtzweg (1987, p. 151). Consumption: CIA/DIA (1989, table B-3). Defense expenditure: Calculated from estimates of annual spending in 1982 rubles presented in Steinberg (1990). Defense burden: The ranges are from the series of CIA/DIA reports on the Soviet economy.

1985. Over the same period, the ratio of Japanese to Soviet GNP increased from 37 to 65 percent and the USSR share of world GNP declined from 15.3 percent to 13.8 percent.

The critics of the official Soviet and CIA national income statistics mentioned above believe that the size of the Soviet economy is smaller than conventional estimates because of the poor quality of Soviet products, hidden inflation, and falsified reports of output. According to their adjusted calculations the actual ratio of Soviet-to-U.S. GNP (expressed in U.S. dollars) should be in the 28–38 percent range for the mid-1980s, not 53 percent as estimated by the CIA or 66 percent according to official Soviet calculations in rubles.[9] If this ratio was in fact 34 percent or lower, then by 1985 Japan, not the USSR, would have had the second largest economy in the world.[10]

Another determinant of trends in the influence of nations in the global economic system is technological innovation. In the USSR many features of the command economy inhibited technological change, and its minimal links with the outside world prevented it from sharing and assimilating international technological advances. As a result, the technical level of Soviet industrial products, whether military or civilian, remained low relative to world standards, and in many important areas, especially electronics, the gap widened.[11]

In this period the defense sector received generous, increasing allocations of resources. The CIA estimates that defense spending in constant (1982) rubles went up from 60 billion rubles in 1965 to about 110 billion rubles in 1985. This sustained commitment to the buildup of the military power of the USSR resulted in the expansion of all defense institutions and improvements in their capabilities.[12] The defense industry expanded significantly its productive capacity, increased its output of military goods, and upgraded the technological standards of deployed weapons systems. The size of the armed forces and the numbers of deployed conventional weapons in most categories grew. The expanded military R&D establishment upgraded the technical capabilities of all weapons systems. In the military foreign trade area the USSR boosted its exports of arms to socialist countries and the value of its hard currency sales of military equipment to the Third World rose from $240 million in 1970 to a peak of $7.2 billion in 1982.[13] With respect to imports, the Soviet Union obtained significant volumes of noncritical military supplies (e.g., trainer aircraft, armored personnel carriers) from its East European Warsaw Pact allies. It also formalized and expanded the *spetsinformatsiya* (special information) system run by the Military-Industrial Commission, which gathered large quantities of Western defense-related technology.[14]

Despite the many achievements of defense sector institutions, it became clear by the early 1980s that the gap was widening between the demands of the Soviet military for technological innovation and the supply capabilities of the defense industry and military R&D. Furthermore, the growing complexity of weapons production and reliance of defense industry on numerous branches of the malfunctioning civilian economy made it increasingly difficult to protect defense institutions. In consequence, the armed forces and defense industry became afflicted by many of the same problems that existed in other spheres of the economy and society.

The growing defense burden associated with the military buildup was an additional impediment to the balanced development of the Soviet economy. In Western and Eastern Europe defense burdens fell in the 2–5 percent ranges whereas that of the United States was 6–7 percent. For the USSR, according to the CIA, the defense burden rose from 11–13 percent of GNP in 1965 to 15–17 percent in 1985 (see Table 10.1). It should be recalled, though, that there is a dispute concerning the size of Soviet GNP. If Birman and Aslund are correct that the national income of the USSR expressed in dollar terms was around 33 percent of US GNP, rather than 50 percent in 1965 and 53 percent in

1985, and one accepts the CIA defense spending estimates, then the narrowly defined burden actually grew from about 20 percent in 1965 to 26 percent in 1985.[15]

In sum, during the period 1964–1985 there was a growing imbalance between the military and economic capabilities of the USSR. The Soviet economy fell ever further behind those of its major competitors both in terms of size and technological sophistication. Its degree of involvement in the world economy remained disproportionately small and its share of hard currency markets for industrial goods fell. The defense burden of the USSR grew exceptionally heavy and exerted negative feedback on the performance of civilian branches. These developments contributed to the decline of the Soviet Union as a global power.

Reforms in an Expanding Defense Sector During Early Perestroika: 1985–1988

When Mikhail Gorbachev became CPSU General Secretary in March 1985 he strongly criticized past political practices and economic performance in the USSR and introduced many of the themes that were to provide the foundation for the regime's remedial program. But he initially had neither the political power nor the vision necessary to develop radical reforms.

During the next several years, the Gorbachev faction consolidated its power in the party apparatus, which facilitated the introduction of new economic and security policies. Over time glasnost and *demokratizatsiya* contributed to a diminution of the role of the CPSU in the political system.

In 1985 the Gorbachev regime adopted the ambitious goals of *uskorenie* (acceleration) of economic growth and technological progress and the raising the quality of industrial goods up to world standards. These were to be attained on the basis of an economic strategy and set of policies consistent with the inherited system-preserving Andropov program: purging unsuitable high-level personnel, tightening of labor discipline, combating corruption and second economy activity, marginally improving living standards, and experimenting with new forms of management and planning in selected branches of industry.[16] It adopted the 12th Five Year Plan for 1986–1990, which reflected a conservative medium-term strategy.

During 1987, Gorbachev demanded an intensification of the reform effort, and in June of that year the Central Committee Plenum approved a radical-looking program of reforms designed to establish a new, improved economic system in the USSR by 1991.[17] It called for significant changes in enterprise operations, wage setting, planning, supply, banking, wholesale and retail price formation, and the status of central ministries. But over the next eighteen months there was only limited progress in introducing reform legislation and implementing remedial policies.

The Soviet economy initially appeared to respond well to the plans and reform policies of the Gorbachev regime. The growth rate of GNP went up from 0.7 percent in 1985 to 3.9 percent in 1986. However, as Table 10.2 shows, its growth fell back to "stagnation" era standards: 1.3 percent in 1987 and 1.5 percent in 1988. Most of the old problems remained in evidence.

The mediocre performance of the Soviet economy during 1985–1988 was due in part to unpropitious circumstances and obstacles in the political and economic systems. But the inappropriate policies of the Soviet government, the conceptual incoherence of the reform program, and the inconsistent timing of remedial measures also contributed to the growing microeconomic performance deficiencies and macro-economic imbalances. For example, enterprises were supposed to operate on a market-oriented, self-financing basis well before prices were reformed to reflect scarcity values. The government allowed tax revenues to fall while maintaining expenditure. So the budget deficit increased from 18.0 billion rubles in 1985 (2.3 percent of GNP) to 90.1

TABLE 10.2   Macroeconomic and Defense Trends, 1985–1988

	1985	1986	1987	1988
GNP (billion 1982 rubles)	682.6	710.3	719.5	735.2
GNP (% growth)	0.7	4.1	1.3	2.2
State budget deficit (% GNP)	2.3	6.0	6.9	10.3
Currency in circulation (% growth)	NA	6.1	7.8	13.6
Net debt to West (billion US$)	15.7	20.9	26.4	26.8
Defense spending (billion 1982 rubles)	111.0	115.3	120.5	124.0
Defense burden (% GNP)	16.2	16.2	16.7	16.8

Sources: GNP: CIA/DIA (1990, table C-1). GNP growth: 1985, CIA (1986b); 1986–1988 CIA/DIA (1990, table C-4). Budget deficit: Aslund (1991b, p. 24). Currency: Aslund (1991b, p. 21). Debt: CIA/DIA (1991, table B-3). Defense spending: Steinberg (1990, p. 687). Defense burden (%): Divide entries in defense spending row by those in GNP row.

billion rubles in 1988 (10.3 percent). This was covered by printing money, which resulted in an increasing monetary overhang.[18] The government failed as well in its attempt to keep external balance. The trade deficit grew and the net hard-currency debt of the USSR rose from $15.7 billion to $26.8 billion.

In its early years the Gorbachev regime committed itself in public to the "new thinking" about national security, which called for less reliance on military power and progress in disarmament. Its actual reform policies slightly shifted the emphasis within the national security production process in favor of the threat reduction programs of the revitalized diplomatic, propaganda, espionage, and arms control institutions. But on the whole, the policies governing defense sector development during 1985–1988 were conservative and consistent with the 12th Plan, which called for an expansion of the military-industrial complex.

The early defense policies of the Gorbachev regime can be grouped into the categories of leadership, personnel policy, organization, economic mechanisms, and resource allocation. In the case of leadership, many of the older members of the national security elite were replaced by men closer to the Gorbachev faction, and top managers in the defense sector were appointed to key positions in the civilian economy. With respect to personnel policy, serious efforts were made to change the attitudes and behavior of members of the labor force in the defense sector through the antialcohol campaign, tightening of labor discipline, the crackdown on the second economy and corruption, democratization, improvements in living standards, wage reforms, and the *attestatsiya* (attestation) program.

Apparently successful organizational forms in the defense sector were transferred to the civilian sphere. New civilian "super-ministries" were established that were similar in many respects to the Military-Industrial Commission. A civilian quality control organization, *Gospriemka*, was introduced that was modeled on the *voenpredy* (military representative) system of the defense industry. There were, however, some modifications of defense organizations that reflected civilian economic reform policies, such as the campaigns to reduce the size and power of the central ministries and state committees.

The general economic reform process exerted an influence on the development of economic mechanisms in the defense sector. As a result of new legislation on enterprise rights, production establishments of the armed forces and the defense industry gradually shifted over to self-financing and full *khozraschet*.[19] State budget institutions, such as units of the armed forces and military R&D establishments, adopted a variety of new policies and procedures designed to make them more market oriented and financially self-supporting. The reform of planning reduced the importance of Gosplan and its ability to assist the defense sector. Although the introduction of state orders (*goszakazy*) offered defense industry enterprises short-term guarantees of orders for output, this protection was to be withdrawn from civilian production lines within defense establishments in the future.

The public statements of the Gorbachev regime during 1985–1988 suggested that it had raised the importance of civilian economic activities in the social welfare function relative to those of defense. But in 1989 Soviet leaders revealed that the 12th Five Year Plan actually called for rates of growth of defense spending and military production by the defense industry that were higher than those for the economy as a whole.[20] For example, the planned annual increase in defense industry military output during 1986–1990 was 5.5 percent.[21] Table 10.2 indicates that resources allocated to defense grew faster than gross national product, so the defense burden rose slightly from 16.2 percent in 1985 to 16.8 percent in 1988.

Little progress was made in disarmament in this period. The most significant development was the signing of the INF treaty and the subsequent withdrawal and destruction of SS-4 and SS-20 missiles. A number of missile factory production lines were converted to civilian purposes.[22]

Gradual Disarmament in a Collapsing Economy: 1989–1991

In autumn 1988 the reformist faction of the Soviet elite gained an important victory in its struggle with the conservatives. This enabled it to purge a number of influential opponents to perestroika and to accelerate the pace of change. The freer elections in Spring 1989 produced results that discredited the CPSU and encouraged more open debates in parliamentary bodies of outstanding issues, such as uses of national income and sectoral priorities. Not surprisingly, the public wanted more resources to be devoted to consumption and fewer to defense. The democratization of the political system also facilitated the rise of nationalism in republics, which eventually spawned open hostility toward central powers and drives for independence that proved difficult to control.

The Soviet government responded to the changing political forces and continuing problems with the economy by proposing more radical reforms, which eventually included self-financing in industry, leasing of land in agriculture, reduction of state orders, expansion of wholesale trade, price reform, encouragement of cooperatives, macroeconomic stabilization, greater freedom in foreign trade, and an increase in private ownership of property.[23] Annual plans in 1989, 1990 and 1991 called for modest rates of growth of the economy, a decisive shift in the end-uses of national income in favor of consumption at the expense of investment and defense, and much higher growth of consumer goods industries.[24] From late 1989 the central government was publicly committed to shifting the economic system from one characterized by collective ownership and central planning to a market economy with significant holdings of private property.[25] However, in October 1990 Gorbachev missed an opportunity to launch a radical transition when he rejected the "500 days" program in favor of the cautious reform package outlined in his "Main Guidelines on Economic Stabilization and Transition to a Market Economy."

During these years the long-standing problems of the Soviet economy were compounded by new ones. For example, the reform process undermined the command-administrative system but did not develop market mechanisms to replace it. In consequence, confusion increased among decision makers at macro and micro levels. Economic performance was disrupted as well by falling labor discipline, mass strikes of workers, and conflicts between national groups.

The deteriorating conditions caused significant underfulfillment of plan targets in crucial industries (e.g., fuels, metal production, and machine-building).[26] This generated supply deficits and production bottlenecks in industry. Indicators of technological progress, efficiency and productivity all deteriorated. Policy errors allowed wages to grow faster than labor productivity and state budget expenditure to exceed revenue. The deficit remained at about 10 percent of GNP, although its nominal magnitude grew from 90 to 100 billion rubles between 1988 and 1990 (Table 10.3). This was financed by printing money, as indicated by the acceleration in the annual growth of circulation of currency from 13.6 percent in 1988 to 21.5 percent in 1990. Compounding the situation was the fact that output targets for consumer goods and agricultural production were not achieved and imports were cut back. These factors intensified excess demand in retail markets and related phenomena such as pervasive shortages, queueing, and forced saving.

As a result of the worsening microeconomic record, GNP growth decelerated to 1.4 percent in 1989, according to the CIA/DIA.[27] Aggregate output then declined by 5.0 percent in 1990 and by 15.0 in 1991. Furthermore, little actual progress was made in opening up the economy, and the Soviet Union developed trade deficits with both socialist and market economies. By 1990, exports in current prices were

TABLE 10.3 Macroeconomic and Defense Trends, 1988–1991

	1988	*1989*	*1990*	*1991*
GNP				
(billion 1982 rubles)	735.2	745.8	708.5	602.2
GNP				
(% growth)	2.2	4	– 5.0	–15.0
State budget deficit				
(% GNP)	10.3	.9	0.5	NA
Currency in circulation				
(% growth)	13.6	19.5	21.5	NA
Net debt to West				
(billion US$)	26.8	36.1	45.4	NA
Defense spending				
(billion 1982 rubles)	124.0	116.6	109.6	103.0
Defense burden				
(% GNP)	16.8	15.6	15.5	17.1

Sources: GNP: 1989, CIA/DIA (1990, table C-1); 1990, 5% less than 1989; 1991, 15% less than 1990. GNP Growth: 1988 and 1989, CIA/DIA (1990, table C-4); 1990, CIA/DIA (1991, p. 33); 1991, estimated on basis of "nine-month" (1991). Budget deficit: Aslund (1991b, p. 24). Currency: Aslund (1991b, p. 21). Net debt: CIA/DIA (1991, table B-3). Defense spending: 1988 and 1989, Steinberg (1990, p. 687); 1990, 6% less than 1989; 1991, 6% less than 1990. Defense burden (%): Divide entries in defense spending row by those in GNP row.

lower than in 1985, imports were at about the same level, and net hard-currency debt was three times greater.[28]

The change in the political power balance in favor of the reformers enabled Gorbachev to introduce demilitarization policies based on the "new thinking" in his speech at the UN in December 1988:

> After all, it is now quite clear that building up military power makes no country omnipotent. What is more, one-sided reliance on military power ultimately weakens other components of national security. . . . W e are witnessing the emergence of a new historic reality—a turning away from the principle of superarmament to the principle of reasonable defense sufficiency. We are present at the birth of a new model of ensuring security—not through the buildup of arms, as was almost always the case in the past, but on the contrary, through their reduction on the basis of compromise.[29]

In this and subsequent statements he committed the USSR to reducing on a unilateral basis the size of the armed forces, military output of defense industry, and defense spending. Efforts were intensified to reach multilateral arms control agreements and implement reforms in the military.[30]

The new disarmament policies affected the armed forces in several ways. The number of combat and support troops was reduced from 4.6 million in 1988 to 3.1 million in 1990.[31] In addition, about 12,000 heavy/medium tanks, 1,400 artillery pieces and 1,600 fighter/attack aircraft were taken out of service. Significant quantities of military personnel and equipment were withdrawn to the USSR from Eastern Europe and Mongolia. The military supply network of the Ministry of Defense sold substantial quantities of surplus stocks of military commodities (e.g. 20,000 motor vehicles) to the civilian economy.[32] Finally, the conscription system was severely disrupted, first by the exemption of university students and then by the mass refusals of call-ups by young men in the non-Slavic republics.

At this time there were important changes in the public standing, goals, priority, and microeconomic mechanisms of the defense industry. Glasnost resulted in the release of previously secret information on the shortcomings of the industry and its excessive absorption of resources that stimulated public criticism of past and current policies and practices. This shifted public opinion such that defense industry came to be viewed not as the source of solutions to economic problems, as in the early phase of perestroika, but rather a main cause of them.[33]

A major policy development in 1989 was the initiation of a large-scale defense-industry conversion (*konversiya*) program, which had goals of increasing the production of civilian commodities by defense firms and transferring advanced defense industry technology to the civilian sphere.[34] According to the Chairman of the Military-Industrial Commission at that time, the targets of the new conversion program included a 4.5 percent reduction in the output of "military technology" by the defense complex during 1989 from the 1988 level; a cumulative 19.5 percent reduction in the defense industry's output of arms and military equipment by 1991 from the 1988 level; and the increase in the civilian goods' share of defense industry output from 40 percent in 1988 to 60 percent in 1995.[35]

Although there was progress in disarmament during 1989–1991, several obstacles impeded this process both in the military and the defense industry. One major difficulty concerning the armed forces was the absorption by the civilian economy of the personnel released from military service. For example, it was not possible to provide adequate housing for the families of a substantial share of the officers being discharged or returning from abroad. By 1991 the Ministry of Defense was using almost all its construction funds to build flats for these men, capability of local civilian authorities to help resolve these problems diminished over time as housing plans were underfulfilled by growing margins.

In the case of the defense industry there was considerable low-level confusion about the conversion program, which was unexpectedly introduced in the middle of a five year plan. Given the inconsistencies in the general reform process and the growing disequilibrium in the economy, defense industry firms were reluctant to shift from military production in accordance with state orders and supported by central rationing to the provision of civilian goods within an economy in which sales revenue could not be used to obtain inputs needed in the production process. Furthermore, defense industry enterprises continued to operate in sellers' markets for their outputs, especially those that were civilian in nature, and therefore they paid little attention to the quality of their products and technological innovation. On the input side of the defense firm, the erosion of priority protection resulted in an increase in the intensity of shortages. This is especially true for sections of the defense industry that converted to civilian production.

Despite all the changes mentioned above, by the summer of 1991 the structures of the defense sector remained intact. In the case of the central management, the Military Industrial Commission, special military departments in Gosplan and Gossnab, the ministries, and the general staff continued to exist. The Defense Industry Department of the Central Committee was abolished, supposedly in an attempt to reduce party interference with enterprise behavior. But a new Commission on Military Policy continued to provide some Communist party oversight. The armed forces remained unified across the territory of the USSR under a single command. Both the defense industry and the military R&D establishment operated in accordance with all-union plans and budgets.

Radical Disarmament During the Transition from a Command to a Market Economy

Throughout the perestroika period conservative officials within the Communist party apparatus, defense industry, and other security institutions formed an apparently powerful group that tried to constrain Gorbachev's reform program so that it did not threaten the politico-economic system or the territorial integrity of the nation. Until Spring 1991 they probably believed that, in reality, they controlled political processes in the USSR and could force the President to do their bidding. The "nine plus one" agreement in April between Gorbachev and republican leaders to sign a Union Treaty that promised substantial devolution of powers therefore was an unpleasant surprise. After that, the conservative elite developed contingency plans to intervene to prevent the breakup of the USSR and destruction of the communist system.

Their efforts were reflected in the coup launched on 19 August 1991. However, the members of this elite group did not appreciate the irrevocable nature of political change in the Soviet Union at lower levels and the strength of nationalism, particularly that in Russia. As is now clear, the coup failed catastrophically for the conservative forces.

One immediate consequence was that the Communist party was eradicated as a political force. The central government leaders and organizations were further discredited and their powers were undermined. It also catalyzed all the republics into declaring their independence and taking steps to realize this status. Throughout the early autumn, President Gorbachev attempted to create a union of equals on the basis of a new treaty, but his efforts were rejected by republican leaders. Instead they signed an agreement to form a Commonwealth of Independent States (CIS) in early December. By the end of the year President Gorbachev had resigned and the USSR had ceased to exist as a nation.

The economic situation of the disintegrating USSR continued to worsen.[36] During the initial nine months of 1991 industrial output fell by about 8 percent. The grain harvest of 156 million tons was substantially down from the 1990 level of 218 million tons. These developments caused an acceleration of the negative growth of GNP to 15 percent. In contrast, the growth of the population's income rose from 26 percent in the first quarter to 220 percent in the third. Retail sales fell by 12 percent and the excess of income over expenditure rose to a factor of 3.7. Shortages of consumer goods intensified and the rate of open inflation went up to 71 percent for the reporting period. The government was unable to keep its budget under control, with the result that the projected center-republic deficit for 1991 was 240 billion rubles instead of the planned 27 billion rubles. Foreign trade turnover fell by 38 percent relative to the first nine months of 1990, largely as a result of a 60 percent drop in trade with East European countries following the abolition of the CMEA and the shift to world market prices. Exports fell more than imports, and hard-currency debt increased.

The new republican governments did not immediately introduce comprehensive measures to correct the growing economic crisis. It was not until the end of October that Yeltsin unveiled a shock therapy transition program for Russia at the 5th Congress of People's Deputies

RSFSR.[37] It called for price liberalization, rapid privatization and creation of strong private sector, use of world market prices in trade with other republics, severe cuts in the state budget expenditure and tax reform, demonopolization and stimulation of competition, reform of the banking system and monetary policy, development of a social safety net, and opening up of foreign trade. During the remainder of autumn 1991, this package was criticized, debated and revised. After some hesitation and arguments with other republics, Russia embarked on the transition from a command to a market economy in early January 1992 by freeing prices and introducing various decrees to promote privatization and marketization.

Following the defeat of the coup attempt, Minister of Defense Yazov and other leading security officials were arrested. But on the whole, the army emerged from this crisis with some credit due to the resistance put up by key officers and military units to the orders of the emergency committee. The new Minster of Defense, Yevgenii Shaposhnikov, devised a program for accelerated reform in the armed forces and a phased reduction in its size. But these policies were based on the assumption that a union treaty would be signed and the center under President Gorbachev would retain powers in the security field. The formation of the CIS threw these plans into disarray. The original commonwealth agreements provided little guidance concerning the future development of the armed forces. While follow-on negotiations were in progress, several member states, notably Ukraine, asserted their rights to form independent armies and to seize control of military assets on their territories. This sparked off heated arguments between Russia and Ukraine and stimulated the officers in the still unified military to strongly criticize the commonwealth leaders. By early 1992 few changes actually had been made in the armed forces, but it seemed likely that the status quo could not be maintained for long.

In contrast, the defense industry and military R&D network were reorganized in a revolutionary manner in autumn 1991. The various republics seized control of production and research facilities on their territory and developed new management structures to direct their work. There appeared to be no surviving central coordination of defense industry work in the CIS. At the micro level defense establishments were profoundly affected by the reduction of military orders for weapons and equipment, deteriorating supply conditions, and their loss of high priority status. The various republics introduced their own conversion programs to guide and assist defense firms during their transition to the market system and shift to civilian production.[38]

The forecasting of developments in the disarmament process in the CIS during 1992 and beyond is a task of considerable importance, but one that is difficult to fulfill because of several difficulties. The revolution in the USSR and the subsequent transition programs changed key features of the economic systems functioning in the commonwealth states. It therefore is difficult to employ traditional projection methodologies that are based on the use of econometric models that are specified for an economy with a known structure and estimated using data from past periods. Furthermore, there is considerable uncertainty about crucial factors. Will the CIS survive as a political and economic alliance? How will the hybrid economies in the commonwealth react to market forces? What are the prospects for commonwealth state leaders, such as Yeltsin, and the democratization process if falling living standards provoke popular unrest? Will armed conflicts develop between major nationality groups within exrepublics (e.g., Kazakhs versus Russians in Kazakhstan) and between the new states (e.g., Armenia versus Azerbaijan).

In this section three scenarios concerning disarmament in the CIS during the 1990s are presented: an optimistic one based on the successful transition to market economies and the survival of the Commonwealth; a peaceful breakup of the commonwealth leading to more severe economic difficulties; and an acrimonious breakup resulting in economic tensions and wars between commonwealth states.

Successful Transition and Survival of the Commonwealth

In the first scenario the commonwealth states continue to support the radical transition programs that were introduced in early 1992. The budget deficits of the states are reduced through restraints on spending and more efficient tax gathering. A central bank is established that pursues a coherent, prudent monetary policy that prevents the development of hyperinflation. Outstanding economic disputes between the states over responsibility for hard-currency debt, ownership of resources, and interstate trade are resolved in an equitable manner. The Western powers provide the commonwealth with substantial economic assistance.

The basic macroeconomic developments in this optimistic scenario are shown in Table 10.4. It is assumed that industrial production falls by 10 percent in 1992, agricultural output remains stable, and the volume of foreign trade (including that between commonwealth states) declines by 10 percent. Aggregate economic output on CIS territory falls by about 7 percent in 1992 and unemployment grows to 4 million. The budget deficit as a share of GNP is reduced to 7 percent.

TABLE 10.4   Macroeconomic and Defense Trends, 1991–1992

	1991	*Scenarios for 1992*		
		Transition in CIS	*Peaceful Breakup*	*Hostile Breakup*
GNP				
(billion 1982 rubles)	602.2	560.1	529.9	499.8
GNP				
(% growth)	−15.0	− 7.0	−12.0	−17.0
Industrial output				
(% growth)	−10.0	−10.0	−15.0	−20.0
Defense spending				
(billion 1982 rubles)	103.0	87.6	77.3	97.9
Defense spending				
(% growth)	− 6.0	−15.0	−25.0	− 5.0
Defense burden				
(% GNP)	17.1	15.6	14.6	19.6

Sources: 1991, Table 10.3; 1992, projected using assumptions stated in text.

In subsequent years the newly marketized economies recover at a moderate pace.

In this scenario the CFE and START treaties are implemented but they become largely irrelevant documents because domestic pressures generate a radical disarmament in the commonwealth. The defense budget is severely cut and the size of the central military falls from three million in 1991 to one million in 1995. Most commonwealth states develop their own armed forces, but these are primarily national guards without nuclear weapons or offensive strategic missions. The conditions and pay of the regular officers and volunteer soldiers are improved and an attempt is made to raise the quality of their equipment to world levels. As a result of these actions, the commonwealth defense burden falls from 17 percent in 1991 to 9 percent in 1995. But even with a 15 percent cut in real military expenditure in 1992 the defense burden in that year remains a high 15.6 percent.

The defense industries in the commonwealth states continue to provide weapons and equipment to the central and local armed forces. But military procurement is cut sharply as a result of the low levels of international tension and macroeconomic stabilization programs. The CIS governments introduce conversion programs, but over time the scale of state intervention is reduced as market forces dictate the pace and nature of demilitarization. The average size of defense enterprises falls as units producing civilian goods split off and high-tech teams

form small private or cooperative firms. The surviving weapons producers operate on an independent, self-financing basis in competitive
markets. In the new market economies there is a reduction in the
differentials in the technological standards and quality between
civilian and defense firms. With respect to foreign economic relations,
there is a dramatic opening up to the West. The number of defense-
related joint ventures rises rapidly, and Western firms begin to invest
directly in weapons-producing subsidiaries. By 1995 defense enterprises in the CIS are closely integrated with the world economy.

Peaceful Breakup of the Commonwealth

The commonwealth agreements left many crucial economic issues
unresolved. In this scenario it is assumed that it proves impossible for
the main states, Russia and Ukraine, to reach comprise solutions
concerning national currencies, coordination of transition programs,
monetary policy, and ownership of assets of the former USSR. Other
irreconcilable disputes arise over political and foreign policy issues.
As a result, the states mutually agree to dissolve the existing
commonwealth. A new political alliance and economic union is formed
by Russia, Byelorussia, and states in Central Asia and the Caucasus. It
has a common currency and monetary policy, largely determined by
Russia. Ukraine and Moldova establish their own currencies and
monetary systems. The basis of trade between the new union and the
other two states shifts to world market prices. Western governments
and businesses are unhappy about these developments and hold back
on assistance.

In October 1991, the USSR First Deputy Minister of the Economy,
Aleksandr Troshin, presented alternative forecasts of the Soviet
economy to the now defunct Committee for Operational Management of
the National Economy.[39] His pessimistic scenario posited a radical
transition program with poor coordination between the republics. This
generated a drop in GNP of 14 percent in 1992, a large budget deficit,
and unemployment of up to 25 million. This appears somewhat
inconsistent. What is more likely is that trade between the smaller
union and Ukraine collapses in a manner similar to what happened
between Eastern Europe and the USSR in 1991 when world market
prices were introduced. Given the close integration of industry,
transportation and supplies in the former USSR, such a precipitous
fall in trade would disrupt industrial and agricultural production. For
example, assume the former falls by 15 percent, the latter by 5 percent,
and GNP by 12 percent. Political constraints force the governments to
maintain some price subsidies for consumer goods and to help large

unprofitable firms avoid bankruptcy, thereby holding down unemployment. In consequence, the budget defict remains high (8 percent of GNP in 1992), the money supply grows rapidly, and the rate of inflation accelerates. By 1994, however, the macroeconomic situation is stabilized and there is a resumption of growth.

The poor economic performance and absence of major conflicts in this scenario result in more drastic reductions in defense spending. The size of the predominantly Russian armed forces of the smaller union falls to about 800,000 by 1995. A modified START treaty results in the elimination of all strategic missiles in Ukraine, Kazakhstan and Byelorussia. Ukraine builds up an army of 250,000, which possesses some tactical nuclear weapons. All these military units are made up of professionals. The defense industries in these states develop as in the first scenario. As a result of these radical actions, real military spending by commonwealth states is cut by 25 percent in 1992. The defense burden falls to 14.6 percent in that year and to 5 percent in 1995.

Hostile Breakup of the Commonwealth

This scenario begins in a manner similar to the previous one. But it is assumed that no replacement union is formed and that the economies of the independent states respond poorly to the transition programs and the shock caused by the collapse of trade between states of the former USSR. The governments squabble over outstanding economic issues in an increasingly acrimonious fashion. They default on the repayment of hard-currency debts and the West holds back substantial economic assistance.

An April 1991 scenario analysis of the Cabinet of Ministers of the USSR forecast a 30 percent drop of GNP and 30 million unemployed in a similar situation.[40] Western experts have predicted declines in industrial production of up to 50 percent in the event that all the republics of the former USSR split away. A more cautious assessment would be that in 1992 industrial output declines by 20 percent, agriculture by 10 percent, and trade by 40 percent. Aggregate output on the territory of the current commonwealth falls by about 17 percent. Most states tolerate large budget deficits and allow the money supply to grow rapidly. As a result, open inflation rises to exceptionally high levels.

By the end of 1992 most governments introduce increasingly authoritarian stabilization programs. Firms are forced into bankruptcy, social services collapse, and real living standards for the majority of the population fall below the poverty line. Eventually this deterioration generates mass strikes and political demonstrations. In Russia, Yeltsin and his allies are forced to resign. The new government is led by Russian nationalists with support from the military industrial complex and workers in large industries. Most transition policies are frozen or reversed as attempts are made to impose order in the economy using command methods. Similar economic and political developments occur in Ukraine. The more nationalist government there blames the state's difficulties on Russia and on foreign influences. Meanwhile violent conflicts develop between dominant and minority nationality groups in several states and a war erupts between Armenia and Azerbaijan.

These circumstances impel all states to maintain or build up their defense establishments. Russia obtains most of the equipment and men of the former Soviet armed forces and supports a military of 2 million men. Ukraine seizes weapons and facilities on its territory, actions which result in some localized armed confrontations and increased tension with Russia. The size of the Ukrainian army grows to 500,000, despite the protests of Poland, Germany and other Western nations. All states suspend conversion programs and either order more weapons from their defense industries or purchase them from abroad. One consequence of these militarist policies is that real military expenditure is cut by only 5 percent in 1992. The defense burden on the economies of the current commonwealth states rises to 19.6 percent in 1992, but then declines to about 14 percent by 1995. The excessively high defense spending undermines efforts to introduce market systems and ensures that most of the economies remain depressed well into the 1990s.

Conclusions

The traditional Soviet Union possessed an economic structure, coordination mechanism and set of policies that were designed to enable a backward economy to rapidly build up and maintain the large military-industrial establishment that the communist elite considered vital to the survival of that state in a hostile international environment. By 1985, however, the heavy defense burden was undermining the economic power of the USSR while not contributing to greater national security.

During 1985–1991 the Gorbachev regime gradually altered its national security strategy while attempting to introduce political and economic reforms that would preserve the main features of the old system. Perestroika did not generate a consistent process of disarmament. There were, in fact, several subperiods in which military trends and policies often were inconsistent with those in the economic and political spheres. While the center was still in control of the economy in 1985–1988, a military buildup continued and the defense burden increased. During 1989–1991 a cautious disarmament commenced, but by then the growing instability in the economy and political system meant that few benefits were obtained from it. Indeed, it now appears that the USSR was so systematically militarized and mobilized that the reformist objectives of Gorbachev never were realizable and his policies were fatally destabilizing for the old order.

The states in the successor commonwealth now have adopted programs of economic transition and radical arms reductions. It is to be hoped that these will be successful and enable them to evolve into dynamic nations that will become fully integrated into Western political, economic and security institutions. Historical precedents suggest, though, that the transition from centralized to market systems in large countries not benefiting from massive foreign aid is a long process with advances and reverses.[41] Furthermore, considerable political and economic tensions already exist within and between commonwealth states, which are likely to be exacerbated in the future. It therefore is not certain that the key issue in the defense economics of this region will be the interaction of macroeconomics and disarmament.

Notes

Research for this chapter was supported by grants from: the PEW Charitable Trusts through the Hoover Institution project on "Economics and National Security: The Case of the Soviet Union"; the British Economic and Social Research Council through the project "Central Control, Disequilibrium and Private Activity in Socialist Economies"; and the Ford Foundation through the project on "Soviet Conventional Defense and Arms Control Policies: 1985-2000". I would like to thank F. Gerard Adams, Roy Allison, Mirek Gronicki, Michael Kaser, Jim Leitzel, Thierry Malleret, and Jacques Sapir for their helpful comments on early drafts. I also would like to express my appreciation to Anthony Rimmington and Edwin Bacon for their capable research assistance.

1. An analysis of the Soviet national security strategy in the Brezhnev and Gorbachev periods can be found in Davis (Forthcoming).

2. The interconnections between economic power and military capabilities are discussed in Pozharov (1981).

3. The features of the Soviet economic planning system are analyzed in Zaleski (1985). Sapir (1990) provides an insightful assessment of the mobilization effort in the USSR.

4. Discussions of priority can be found in the chapter on "Centralized Allocation of Resources and Planning of Priorities" in Zaleski (1980) and Ericson (1988). According to Davis (1989, 1990a), sectoral priorities can be measured using at least ten indicators: (1) weight given to sectoral output in a planner's welfare function; (2) responsiveness of planners in allocating resources to a sector in which a performance indicator exceeds an established tolerance limit; (3) wage rates and work conditions; (4) adequacy of centrally determined financial norms; (5) degree to which output plans are fulfilled; (6) "hardness" of budget constraints; (7) degree of fulfillment of supply plans for intermediate goods; (8) investment plan fulfilment; (9) magnitude of inventories and reserve production capacity tolerated by the authorities; and (10) intensity of shortage in a sector.

5. The basic shortage model of the socialist economy is presented in Kornai (1980).

6. According to Davis (1990a), the Soviet defense sector consists of six types of economic institutions: armed forces (production of military services); military supply network (distribution of domestic military commodities), defense industry (production of military commodities), military research and development (R&D) (production of military technology), military foreign trade (export and import of military commodities), and the central defense bureaucracy (production of administrative services).

7. The growth rate debate is critically reviewed in Ericson (1990). The growth rates presented in the text were calculated as the averages for the five-year intervals during 1966–1985 given in Aslund (1990) and CIA (1988, pg. 11).

8. Davis (1990b).

9. Davis (1990b).

10. According to the CIA, in 1985 the Japanese GNP of $1,290 billion was 34.4 percent of the U.S. GNP of $3,748 billion. If Soviet GNP was 34 percent of that of the United States, or $1,274 billion, it would have been lower than that of Japan.

11. Gustafson (1990).

12. CIA (1986a), Almquist (1990), Sapir (1991) and the annual U.S. Defense Department reports on *Soviet Military Power*.

13. McIntyre (1987) and Kramer (1987) .

14. CIA (1985) and Gustafson (1990).

15. For the purposes of this calculation the following CIA estimates in billions of 1982 rubles were accepted: 1965 (defense spending 60, GNP 462) and 1985 (defense spending 110, GNP 685). So the defense burdens were 13 percent in 1965 and 16 percent in 1985. If Soviet GNP was 33 percent of that of the Unites States in 1965 (instead of 50 percent) and in 1985 (instead of 53 percent), and there was a stable relationship between Soviet dollar and ruble GNP, then the respective ruble GNP figures for the USSR would be 66 percent of that given above for 1965 (or 305 billion rubles) and 62 percent for 1985 (or 423 billion rubles). With the same defense spending estimates, the respective burdens would have been 20 percent and 26 percent. See Davis (1990b).

16. Hewett (1988).

17. Aslund (1991a).

18. Nordhaus (1991).

19. Yudin (1989).

20. Ryzhkov (1989) stated that the 12th Five Year Plan incorporated "growth of expenditures on defense at a tempo higher than the growth of national income."

21. Belousov (1989).

22. Ritter (1991).

23. Aslund (1991a), CIA/DIA (1990, 1991).

24. Voronin (1989), "O gosudarstvennom plane" (1990), Bezrukov (1991).

25. At least eight different transition programs were considered or adopted by the central government in this period: Abalkin (October 1989); Ryzhkov (December 1989); Yavlinskii (400 days) (February 1990); Ryzhkov (May 1990); Shatalin (500 days) (September 1990); Ryzhkov/Abalkin (September 1990); the compromise Presidental Program (October 1990); and Pavlov's anticrisis package (April 1991). None of them were successfully implemented. Surveys of their features can be found in IMF (1991) and Aslund (1991b).

26. Gaidar (1990), IMF (1991), Economic Commission (1991), and "Ekonomika" (1991).

27. Other analysts, such as Khanin (1990), believed that U.S. government estimates were too high and that the Soviet economy contracted by 4–5 percent in 1989.

28. Davis (1991), CIA/DIA (1991).

29. Gorbachev (1988).

30. Allison (1990).

31. Collins and Rennack (1991, tables 5 and 39)

32. "Arkhipov "(1989).

33. A striking example of this critical reevaluation can be found in Izyumov and Kortunov (1991).

34. Kincade and Thomson (1990), Cooper (1991).

35. Belousov (1989). An updated statement on the "State Program of Conversion of the Defense Industry" that was approved by the Soviet government on 15 December 1990 can be found in an article by the Head of the Gosplan military department in Smyslov (1991).

36. "Nine-month" (1991).

37. Yeltsin (1991).

38. Rutskoi (1991).

39. "Union" (1991).

40. "Government" (1991).

41. Feinstein (1990).

References

Allison, R. (1990) "Gorbachev's arms control offensive: Unilateral, bilateral and multilateral initiatives" in Jacobson, C.G. (Ed.) *Soviet Foreign Policy at the Cross-Roads*, London, Macmillan.

Almquist, P. (1990) *Red Forge: Soviet Military Industry Since 1965*, New York, Columbia University Press.

"Arkhipov on disposal of surplus military equipment", *Summary of World Broadcasts*, SU/0426 C1/1, 5 April 1989.

Aslund, A. (1990) "How small is Soviet national income?" in Rowen, H. and Wolf, C. Jr. *The Impoverished Superpower: Perestroika and the Burden of Soviet Military Spending*, San Francisco, Institute for Contemporary Studies.

Aslund, A. (1991a) *Gorbachev's Struggle for Economic Reform (Second Edition)*, London, Pinter Publishers.

Aslund, A. (1991b) "Gorbachev, perestroyka, and economic crisis", *Problems of Communism*, vol. XL, nos. 1-2.

Belousov, I.S. (1989) "Konversiya. Chto eto znachit".

(Interview with A. Pokrovskii), *Pravda*, 28 August 1989.

Bezrukov, V.B. (1991) "1991 god: prognoz i plan", *Ekonomika i Zhizn*, no. 1 (January 1991).

CIA - See U.S. Central Intelligence Agency.

CIA/DIA - See U.S. Central Intelligence Agency/Defense Intelligence Agency.

Collins, J.M. and Rennack, D.E. (1991) *Soviet Armed Forces Statistical Trends, 1985-1990*, Washington D.C., Congressional Research Service Report, 91-636 RCO.

Cooper, J. (1991) *The Soviet Defense Industry: Conversion and Reform*, London, Royal Institute for International Affairs/Francis Pinter.

Davis, C. (1989) "Priority and the shortage model: The medical system in the socialist economy" in Davis, C. and Charemza, W. (eds.) *Models of Disequilibrium and Shortage in Centrally Planned Economies*, London, Chapman and Hall.

Davis, C. (1990a) "The high priority military sector in a shortage economy" in Rowen, H. and Wolf, C. Jr. *The Impoverished Superpower: Perestroika and the Burden of Soviet Military Spending*, San Francisco, Institute for Contemporary Studies.

Davis, C. (1990b) "Economic influences on the decline of the Soviet Union as a great power: Continuity despite change", *Diplomacy and Statecraft*, vol. 1, no. 3.

Davis, C. (1991) "The exceptional Soviet case: Defense in an autarkic system, *Daedalus*, vol. 120, no. 4.

Davis, C. (forthcoming) "The changing priority status of the Soviet defense sector: 1985-90" in C. Wolf Jr. (ed.) *The Defense Sector in the Soviet Economy*, San Francisco, ICS Press.

Economic Commission for Europe (1991) *Economic Survey of Europe in 1990-1991*, New York, United Nations.

"Ekonomika SSSR v 1990 godu" *Ekonomika i Zhizn*, 1991, no. 5.

Ericson, R.E. (1988) "Priority, duality, and penetration in the Soviet command economy", Santa Monica, *RAND Note: N-2643-NA*, December 1988.

Ericson, R. (1990) "The Soviet statistical debate: Khanin vs. TsSU" in Rowen,

H. and Wolf, C. Jr. *The Impoverished Superpower: Perestroika and the Burden of Soviet Military Spending*, San Francisco, Institute for Contemporary Studies.

Feinstein, C. (1990) *Historical Precedents for Economic Change in Central Europe and the USSR*, Oxford, Credit Suisse First Boston Ltd./Oxford Analytica.

Gaidar, E. (1990) "Trudnyy vybor: Ekonomicheskoe obozrenie po itogam 1989 goda", *Kommunist*, No. 2.

Gorbachev, M.S. (1988) "Vystuplenie M.S. Gorbacheva v Organizatsii Ob'edinennykh Natsii", *Pravda*, 8 December 1988.

"Government research shows three economic options for future", *Summary of World Broadcasts*, SU/1065 C1/1-2, 7 May 1991.

Gustafson, T. (1990) "The response to technological challenge" in Colton, T.J. and Gustafson, T. (Eds.) (1990) *Soldiers and the Soviet State: Civil-Military Relations from Brezhnev to Gorbachev*, Princeton, Princeton University Press.

Hewett, E. (1988) *Reforming the Soviet Economy: Equality versus Efficiency*, Washington D.C., The Brookings Institution.

IMF/World Bank/OECD/EBRD (1991) *A Study of the Soviet Economy*, Paris, OECD, vols. 1-3.

Izyumov, A. and Kortunov, A. (1991) "The monster: a profile of the Soviet military-industrial complex", *Moscow News*, vol. 8, no. 8.

Khanin, G.I. (1990) "Krisis uglublyaetsya", *EKO*, No. 1.

Kincade, W.H. and Thomson, T.K. (1990) "Economic conversion in the USSR: Its role in perestroika," *Problems of Communism*, vol. 39, no. 1.

Kornai, J. (1980) *Economics of Shortage*, Amsterdam, North-Holland.

Kramer, M.N. (1987) "Soviet arms transfers to the Third World", *Problems of Communism*, vol. 36, no. 5 (1987).

Kurtzweg, L (1987) "Trends in Soviet gross national product" in U.S. Congress, Joint Economic Committee (1987) *Gorbachev's Economic Plans*, Washington D.C., USGPO.

McIntyre, J.F. (1987) "The USSR's hard currency trade and payments position" in U.S. Congress, Joint Economic Committee *Gorbachev's Economic Plans*, Washington D.C., USGPO.

Narodnoe Khozyaistvo SSSR v 1989 g. (1990), Moscow, Finansy i Statistika.

"Nine-month economic performance data", *Summary of World Broadcasts*, SU/1233 C2/1-15, 19 November 1991.

Nordhaus, W.D. (1991) "Soviet economic reform: The longest road", *Brookings Papers on Economic Activity*, no. 1.

"O gosudarstvennom plane ekonomicheskogo i sotsialnogo razvitiya SSSR na 1990 god," *Ekonomicheskaya Gazeta*, 1990, no. 47, pg. 14.

Pozharov, A.I. (1981) *Ekonomicheskie Osnovyy OboronnogoMogushchestva Sotsialisticheskogo Gosudarstva*, Moscow, Voennoe Izdatelstvo.

Ritter, W.S. Jr. (1991) "Soviet defense conversion: The Votkinsk machine-building plant", *Problems of Communism*, vol. XL, no. 5.

Rutskoi, A. (1991) "Problemy konversii predpriyatii i organizatsii oboronnogo kompleksa Rossii budget resheny", *Ekonomika i Zhizn*, No. 52 (December 1991).

Ryzhkov, N.I. (1989) "Sluzhit interesam naroda", *Ekonomicheskaya Gazeta*, No. 24 (July).

Sapir, J. (1990) *L'Economie Mobilisee*, Paris, Editions La Decouverte.

Sapir, J. (1991) *The Soviet Military System*, Oxford, Polity Press.

Smyslov, V.I. (1991) "Gosudarstvennaya programma konversii oboronnoi promyshlennosti," *Voprosy Ekonomiki*, no. 2.

Steinberg, D. (1990) "Trends in Soviet military expenditure," *Soviet Studies*, Vol 42, no. 4.

U.S. Central Intelligence Agency (1985) *Soviet Acquisition ofMilitarily Significant Western Technology: An Update*,Washington D.C., September 1985.

U.S. Central Intelligence Agency (1986a) *The Soviet Weapons Industry: An Overview*, Washington D.C., DI 86-10016, September 1986.

U.S. Central Intelligence Agency (1986b) *Handbook of Economic Statistics, 1986*, Washington D.C., CPAS 86-10002, 1986.

U.S. Central Intelligence Agency (1988) *Revisiting Soviet Economic Performance Under Glasnost: Implications for CIA Estimates*, Washington D.C., SOV 88-10068, September 1988.

U.S. Central Intelligence Agency/Defense Intelligence Agency (1987) *Gorbachev's Modernization Program: A Status Report*, Washington D.C., Paper presented to the U.S. Congress Joint Economic Committee.

U.S. Central Intelligence Agency/Defense Intelligence Agency (1989) *The Soviet Economy in 1988: Gorbachev Changes Course*, Washington D.C., Paper Presented to the U.S. Congress Joint Economic Committee.

U.S. Central Intelligence Agency/Defense Intelligence Agency (1990) *The Soviet Economy Stumbles Badly in 1989*, Washington D.C., Report presented to the U.S. Congress Joint Economic Committee, 20 April 1990.

U.S. Central Intelligence Agency/Defense Intelligence Agency (1991) *Beyond Perestroyka: The Soviet Economy in Crisis*, Washington D.C., Report presented to the U.S. Congress Joint Economic Committee, DDB-1900-164-91.

"Union ministry forecasts economic decline", *Summary of World Broadcasts*, SU/1215 B/1-2, 29 October 1991.

Voronin, L.A. (1989) "Narodnokhozyaistvennyy plan—realnost, zadachi, garantii", *Planovoe Khozyaistvo*, No. 12.

Yeltsin, B. (1991) "My perkhodim nakonets k novomu ekonomicheskomu kursu", *Ekonomika i Zhizn*, No. 45 (November 1991).

Yudin, I. (1989) "Defence industry on khozraschet", *Soviet Military Review*, no. 10, pp. 24-26.

Zaleski, E. (1980) *Stalinist Planning for Economic Growth, 1933-1952*, London, Macmillan.

11

The Effect of Modernizing Soviet Machine Building on Defense and the Macroeconomy: 1995–2010

Gregory C. Hildebrandt

General Secretary Gorbachev is not the first national leader whose economic policies have foundered because of inattention to the scarcity relationships among guns, butter, and tools. During the first years of President Gorbachev's tenure, significant efforts were made to intensify the economy by rapidly modernizing the nation's capital stock. This program was intended to jump-start the Soviet economy by rapidly laying the foundation for a modern industrialized economy.

As summarized in the 12th Five-Year Plan (FYP), which covers the period 1986–1990, there was to be rapid expansion of the high technology sectors of the economy with particular emphasis given to electronics, machine tools and computers. For example, the plan was for instrumentation equipment to grow annually by 11 percent; numerically controlled machine tools by 13 percent; and computer equipment by 18 percent.[1]

At the same time, the Soviets continued to assign the defense sector high priority. While there was some slowdown in the rate of growth of Soviet defense spending between 1974 and 1983, the CIA believes that around 1984–1985, the real growth of defense spending began to rise at about 3 percent per year and continued at approximately this rate of growth through 1988.

Additional evidence for this buildup occurred in 1989 when Premier Nickolay Ryshkov indicated that planned defense growth rate for 1986–1990 was greater than that planned for the national economy. And in 1990, President Gorbachev stated that defense spending was to rise by almost 8 percent per year during the 1986-90 time period.[2]

The modernization program and continued high levels of defense activities combined with several other factors to generate large budget deficits and, in turn, inflation. Even though production performance continued along its modest trend, a disconnect between both wages and the money holdings of individuals and retail prices resulted in shortages of consumption goods. The modernization program was effectively halted by 1988; in 1989, defense spending was cut. There is now a shift in emphasis toward the Soviet consumer and a plan developed to transform the economy into a "full-blooded market."

Continued inflation, however, has resulted in a series of fits and starts in this economic revolution designed to transform the Soviet Union into a market economy. The pace of the transition to a market economy is now a matter of much uncertainty and debate. There are concerns that the large price increases associated with rapid transition would have an adverse effect on unemployment, equity and social stability.[3]

Even if the Russians move to a market economy quickly, as is anticipated, technical progress is needed to obtain the high productivity associated with a modern industrialized economy. A market economy can be expected to coax out entrepreneurial reserves to increase productivity by both improving the Soviet production process and the value of output. If the transition to a market economy is unsuccessful, however, the Russians can be expected to depend once again on large doses of administered technical progress to increase productivity.

In addition to institutional arrangements, success in increasing productivity also depends on the composition of final demand. This is particularly true in this case where there is direct competition between weapons manufacturing and the production of producer and consumer durables within the machine-building sector.

Also, a very significant proportion of national scientific and engineering resources has been devoted to military research and development. The application of these high-technology resources to civilian activities could have a large effect on both process effectiveness and product quality. While the effect of such an application of resources might be expected to be larger if a market system is in place, there would still be some benefits to the civilian sector if the transfer of resources is administered in the traditional Soviet fashion.

In this chapter, we explore some of the issues facing the leadership in their efforts to increase productivity during the 1995–2010 time period. The basic approach is to view the 13th FYP from 1990–1995 as a transition period in which the defense share is reduced to 5 percent of GNP. We pay particular attention to the machine tool sector— an important part of Gorbachev's original modernization program. This sector is at the core of an industrialized economy and produces a significant part of the machinery delivered to the Soviet machine-building sector where the high-quality producer and consumer durables are produced. Soviet planners have always been particularly interested in machine tools. In fact, it may have been Alexander Gershenkron who described Stalinist planning as the transformation of machine tools into machine tools into machine tools.[4]

We also assume that during the 1990–1995 transition period, the annual growth of investment in machine tools is maintained at 5 percent. This is less than the original objectives of the 12th FYP, and permits the Russian leadership to continue to pay attention to the consumer as defense spending is cut. Total factor productivity is also assumed to grow at only a modest rate during the 13th FYP, reflecting the emphasis given to consumption rather than modernization.

For the sake of comparison, we also consider an alternative scenario in which the defense share at the completion of the 13th FYP is 15 percent of GNP. This is roughly consistent with the historical trends estimated by the U.S. government.[5]

Beginning in 1995, we assume that there is a return to a high-tempo modernization program that may either be market or command directed. Among the alternatives considered are those in which investment in machine tools grows rapidly at the same time as this sector experiences very rapid growth in total factor productivity.

As we have indicated, such enhancements in productivity may be derived, in part, from the transfer of scarce scientific talent from defense research and development activities. To the extent that significant progress has been made toward a market economy, one might expect these resources to be effectively directed toward those activities that rapidly raise productivity. In fact, because we employ a simple supply-side model in this analysis, total factor productivity growth is really the only reasonable method of distinguishing between economic performance in a market versus a centrally planned economy.

Under either high and low defense burden regimes, an important question facing the Russian leadership is the extent to which increases in investment in machine tools can increase economic performance, with and without enhancements in total factor productivity growth. The larger the requirement for total factor productivity growth, the greater may be the incentive to rapidly forge market institutions. We

shall see that without productivity growth the increases in investment really won't help matters very much.

Models of the Soviet Economy

Before describing the structure of the model of the Soviet economy
that contains a specified machine tool sector, it is helpful to begin
with a simplified aggregate model of the Soviet economy. Figure 11.1
contains an aggregate model of the type typically employed in long-
run growth forecasting.

In this model, GNP is produced with inputs of labor, capital and
total factor productivity. This GNP is distributed to consumption,
defense and investment. This latter final demand category builds up
the nation's civilian capital stock. These simple models typically
treat the labor force (and population), the growth of total factor
productivity, and depreciation as exogenous variables.

Several dashed lines describing possible linkages between defense
and the economy, which we (and others) have excluded in the
empirical analysis, are also included in Figure 11.1. One dashed line is

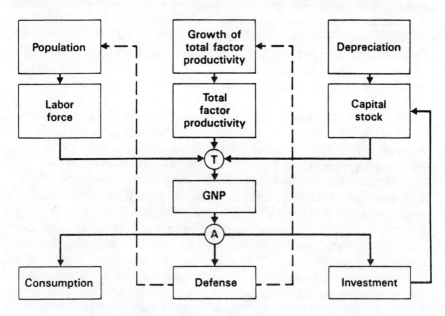

T = Technical relationship   A = Accounting relationship

FIGURE 11.1 Soviet aggregate economic model.

drawn between defense and the growth of total factor productivity. Defense spending can adversely affect the growth of total factor productivity by tying up a significant share of a nation's research and development (R&D) engineers. If these engineers were assigned to the civilian sector, the technologies of the civilian enterprises could become more productive. One would also expect there to be greater diffusion of these technologies in the civilian sectors than is the case for the specialized and secretive defense industries. As a result, the civilian activities of these engineers would represent a type of public good, and the cost of these engineers in either the defense or civilian sector would not fully capture their productivity to the civilian economy.

A second dashed line is drawn between defense and the population. This reflects the fact that military service might aid in the socialization of the population and increase the quality of the labor force. Once again, however, we note that the relationships represented with the dashed lines have been excluded from the empirical analysis.

One way to think about the operation of this aggregate model is in terms of a simple equation of growth accounting. The growth of GNP can be expressed as the sum of the growth of total factor productivity, the marginal product of capital times the share of GNP allocated to net investment, and labor's share of national income times the growth of the labor force. We have:[6]

$$g_{GNP} = g_{TFP} + MP_k \bullet S_{in} + S_l \bullet g_{Lab},$$

where

g_{GNP} = growth of GNP
g_{TFP} = growth of total factor productivity
MP_k = marginal productivity of capital
S_{in} = share of GNP allocated to net investment
S_l = labor's share of national income
g_{Lab} = growth of the labor force

Suppose, for illustration, that the share of GNP allocated to defense decreases by one percentage point and the resources are transferred to net investment. The change in the growth of GNP, therefore, would equal the marginal product of capital. If this marginal product equals, say, 0.1 in the Soviet Union, annual GNP growth will increase by a tenth of a percentage point. A five percentage point shift from net defense to net investment would increase annual GNP growth by half a percent. This illustrates the principle that even fairly large reallocations from defense will not increase economic performance very much unless they are accompanied by increases in productivity.

As indicated, this type of model is typically used to estimate long-term forecasts, and it can be used to identify the trade-off between defense growth and consumption growth. Such a trade-off relationship, estimated before Gorbachev's announced defense cuts, is presented in Figure 11.2.[7]

In progressing to a more complex model, it is helpful to understand how weapons production is depicted in detailed econometric-trend models. Figure 11.3 contains a simplified view of how machinery value added in these models is transformed via a historical relationship into machinery final demand, which is distributed to consumer durables, military machinery, and machinery investment. Notice that these models assume that military and civilian machinery can be exchanged for each other on a ruble-for-ruble basis.[8]

Figure 11.4 may clarify this point. Because the level of machinery final demand that is produced is distributed to either civilian and military machinery, the model assumes that the production possibility curve (PPC) associated with these end uses is linear with a

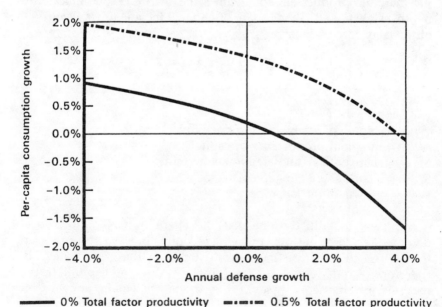

FIGURE 11.2 Soviet growth alternatives (1990–2010), 4 percent investment growth.

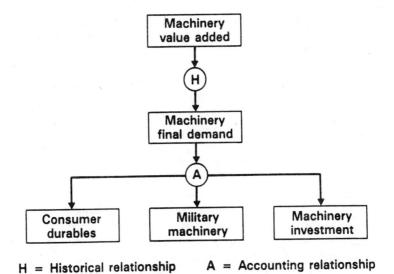

H = Historical relationship   A = Accounting relationship

FIGURE 11.3 The machinery balance in Soviet econometric-trend models.

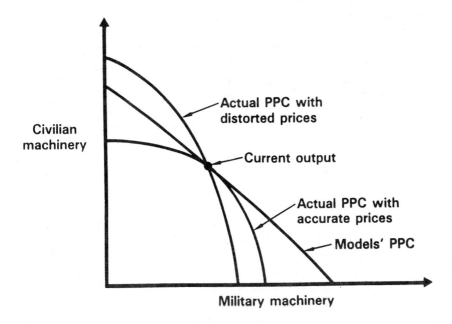

FIGURE 11.4 Econometric-trend models' machinery sector's production possibility curve (PPC).

slope equal to minus 1. As a result, if the ruble value of military machinery production declines by some amount, one obtains a like ruble increase in civilian machinery. In Fig. 11.4, this is illustrated with the "Models' PPC" line.

In contrast, suppose that the prices used to measure military and civilian machinery accurately reflect the ability to convert one good into the other at the current output level. Then, if the capital equipment, including the machine tools and other producer durables used to produce military and civilian machinery, is not transferable from one final use to the other, it would not be possible to exchange military machinery into civilian machinery without experiencing diminishing returns.

By shifting labor from military to civilian machinery production, and using the existing capital in civilian machinery production more intensively, it would be possible to obtain some extra output, but there would be a decrease in the increase in this civilian machinery output as equal increments of labor are transferred from military machinery production. The bowed-out curve, designated "Actual PPC with accurate prices," depicts this possibility.

There is also the view, however, that Soviet prices do not accurately reflect the rate of transformation in production. In fact, normal distortions are believed to be aggravated by the large subsidies used in weapons production, which tends to artificially lower the prices. If we combine these distortions with the fact that the capital used in production is not directly transferable, the curve, "Actual PPC with distorted prices," applies. Initially, as one moves from current output levels, a reduction in military machinery of a ruble results in more than a ruble of civilian machinery, but the extra amount obtained declines as more and more equal amounts of labor are transferred.[9]

Although, this latter curve may be the most realistic representation of the Soviet situation, the extent of price distortion in weapons production is not well understood. Also, for marginal changes, it would be the annual growth increment that would be reallocated. If there is adequate time to plan this reallocation, the new machine tools and other producer durables would be transferable from one end use to another without any marked tendency for diminishing returns to affect the trade-off possibilities.

Therefore, as long as either prices are not excessively distorted, or the reallocations are not larger than the machine-building final demand growth increment, the linear production possibility curve (Models' PPC) may provide a reasonable representation of the trade-off possibilities. In any event, data limitations dictate that this type of model be used in our analysis. As we find out more about the Soviet defense sector, it will be possible to determine the extent to which this is a reasonable assumption.

Machine Tools Within Macroeconomic Model

To capture the effect of machine tools on macroeconomic performance, we extend the aggregate model by explicitly defining an additional sector. This sector, which is actually the "investment in machine building" sector, produces the equipment and machinery investment that is delivered to the machine-building sector. Some of these producer durables are used within the machine tools sector itself, and some are delivered to other machinery sectors. It may not be unreasonable to assume that the core of these producer durables are machine tools, and that there is a fairly stable relationship between total investment goods and the machine tools delivered to this sector.

Figure 11.5 contains a model of the Soviet economy that we use to understand the effect of this sector on defense and the economy. "Machine tool value added" is transformed into final demand and distributed to the sector's capital stock or to the other machine-building sectors. The resulting final demand is distributed to consumer durables, military machinery, and other machinery investment. The latter investment category is delivered to the rest of the economy.

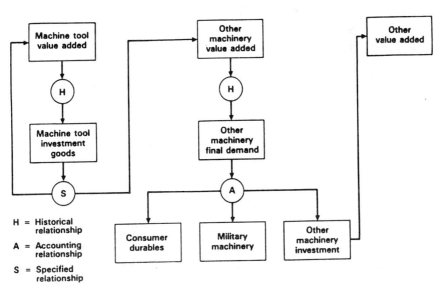

H = Historical relationship

A = Accounting relationship

S = Specified relationship

FIGURE 11.5 Disaggregated Soviet machinery balance with investment in machine tools explicit.

Not shown in Figure 11.5, but important to the analysis, is the relationship between investment in machinery and equipment and investment in structures. The Soviets are attempting to expand modernization investment at the expense of expansion investment. This latter investment category includes a higher ratio of structures to machinery and equipment than does modernization investment. We assume that the Soviets are able to increase the percentage that machinery and equipment investment is of the total.

While this model presents somewhat of a lockstep view of how an economy operates, and, indeed, it may have been the type of model envisaged by Stalin, it does permit us to isolate in a simple fashion the effect of restructuring on defense and the economy. We first use the model to examine the effect of changes in the growth of total factor productivity on GNP and per capita consumption under the assumption that the annual growth rate of investment in machine tools equals 15 percent, and the defense share of GNP equals 5 percent over the 1995–2010 time period. The results are reported in Figures 11.6 and 11.7. The growth of total factor productivity indicated in the figures is that in the machine-tool sector itself. It is assumed that this effect cascades

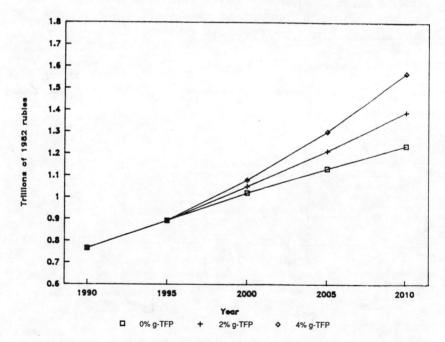

FIGURE 11.6   Soviet GNP with 15 percent annual growth rate of investment in machine tools and 5 percent defense share of GNP, 1990–2010.

through the economy, but diminishes each stage. Total factor productivity in the machine-building sector is half that of the machine-tool sector, and total factor productivity in the rest of the economy is half that again.[10]

Figure 11.6 shows that changes in total factor productivity growth has a marked effect on the GNP trend. Somewhat surprising, however, is the observation from Figure 11.7, that increases in total factor productivity growth reduce the per-capita consumption trend.

It might be useful to understand the process whereby this happens. Increases in the total factor productivity increase the output of this sector. There is, therefore, greater investment in other machinery building, and greater output of this sector, which is also experiencing enhanced productivity growth. The greater investment output produced by the other machine building is, in turn, delivered to other sectors of the economy outside of machine building. The output of these other sectors, therefore, also increases. But the investment in structures comes from these other sectors, and the rapid machinery and equipment investment that is generated with this productivity growth also increases structure investment.

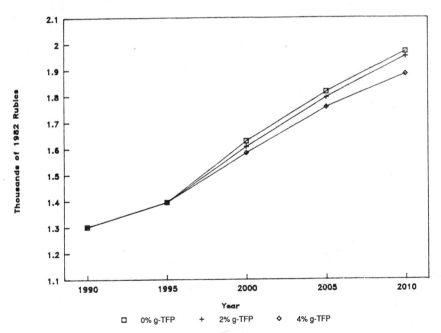

FIGURE 11.7 Soviet per capita consumption with 15 percent annual growth rate of investment in machine tools and 5 percent defense share of GNP, 1990–2010.

We are assuming that the annual growth of investment in machinery and equipment is 3 percentage points greater than the annual growth of investment in structures during the 1995–2010 period. Nevertheless, the net effect is that although the GNP increment is larger with higher total factor productivity growth, the investment increment is larger still, leading to smaller per capita consumption. This illustrates the importance to the Soviets of rapidly increasing the machinery and equipment share of total investment.

Figures 11.8 and 11.9 show the effect of increases in the defense share from 5 to 15 percent of GNP. Predictably, the effect on the GNP trend is fairly modest; the effect on the per capita consumption trend is somewhat larger.

The reason for the difference in effect is that even a fairly significant change in weapons production is still a fairly small percent of civilian investment; and civilian investment is itself only a small percent of the civilian capital stock. Large increases in weapons production do not, therefore, have a significant effect on the growth of the civilian capital stock. One the other hand, the part of defense that does not compete directly with investment is converted by the

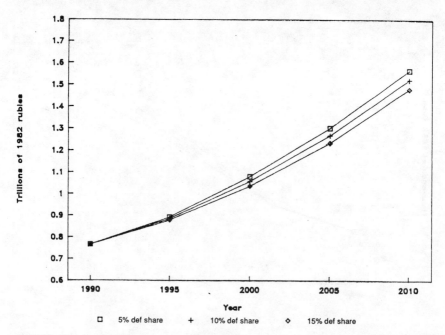

FIGURE 11.8 Soviet GNP with 15 percent annual growth rate of investment in machine tools and 4 percent total factor productivity growth, 1990–2010.

model into consumption on a ruble-for-ruble basis. That part, therefore, leads to a corresponding increase in consumption.

Finally, Figures 11.10 and 11.11 show the effect of changes in the growth of investment in machine tools on GNP and per capita consumption. While there is a small increase in GNP with a larger growth rate for this type of investment, it is not observable on the chart. The investment in machine tools is simply too small a part of the economy for changes in the growth of this investment category to have a significant effect on GNP. We do, however, pick up a noticeable reduction in per capita consumption as the extra investment produced both directly and indirectly by the increase in investment in machine tools is greater than the GNP increment (net of defense spending).

Figures 11.10 and 11.11 highlight the limitations of an extensive growth modernization program. Even when such a program is focused on a key sector of the economy, as was the case in the original modernization program, it cannot by itself be expected to have a significant effect on economic performance. To increase economic performance in a modernization program, increases in total factor productivity growth are required.

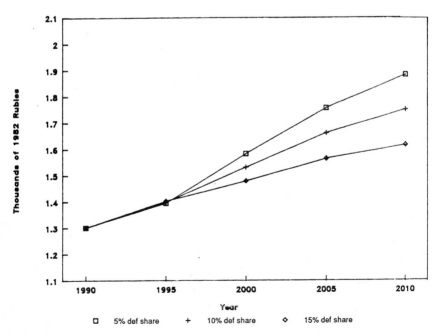

FIGURE 11.9 Soviet per capita consumption with 15 percent annual growth rate of investment in machine tools and 4 percent total factor productivity growth, 1990–2010.

Conclusions

We see from this analysis the critical importance of total factor productivity growth. The organizational changes and effective use of scientific talent that might induce such productivity enhancements can have a dramatic effect on GNP. However, even this increase might fail to aid the consumer if the Russians do not develop mechanisms to carefully manage their investment resources.

As we have seen, it also important to carefully husband the resources of the investment sector by emphasizing modernization rather than expansion investment. The Russians are, of course, aware of this and are attempting to increase the ratio of investment in machinery and equipment in total investment. However, even greater efforts may be required in this area than they are planning.

Changes in defense share have a rather significant effect on consumption; the effect on GNP is not quite so marked. However, we have not modeled the possible effect of defense spending on total factor productivity growth, so we may be understating the effect of changes in defense share on GNP.

Finally, we do not find evidence that an extensive growth strategy

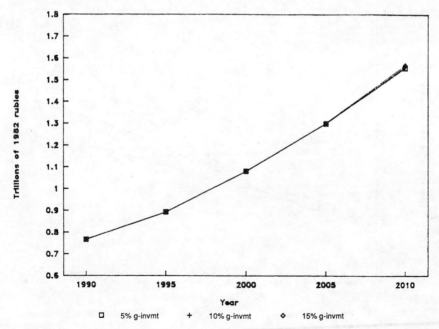

FIGURE 11.10 Soviet GNP with 4 percent total factor productivity growth and 5 percent defense share of GNP, 1990–2010.

in the well-defined machine tool sector will, by itself, have a significant effect on GNP. This may be an important reason why the original modernization program was flawed. To shift to a modern economy, organization forms are needed that both promote total factor productivity and carefully manage the nation's scarce capital resources.

Notes

1. The modernization plan is discussed in "Gorbachev's Modernization Program: A Status Report" in Allocation of Resources in the Soviet Union and China—1986, Part 12, Hearings before the Subcommittee on National Security Economics of the Joint Economic Committee of the United States, March 19 and August 3, 1987, p. 36.

2. A discussion of the increase in Soviet defense spending is contained in James Noren, "The Effects of Perestroika on the Defense Sector and Resource Allocation in the USSR," a paper presented at the RAND-Hoover Symposium on the Defense Sector in the Soviet Economy, 29–30 March 1990. Noren discusses the Ryshkov statement, which appears in "On the Program for Forthcoming Activities of the USSR Government," *zvestiya*, 8 June 1990, p. 3. The Gorbachev statement is reported in *Pravda*, April 29, 1990, p. 2.

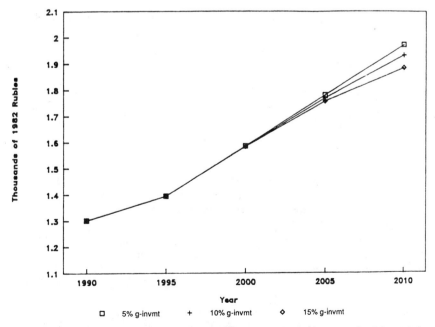

FIGURE 11.11 Soviet per capita consumption with 4 percent total factor productivity growth and 5 percent defense share of GNP, 1990–2010.

3. For a discussion of the economic aspects of the first several Gorbachev years, see James Noren, "The Soviet Economic Crisis: Another Perspective," *Soviet Economy*, January-March 1990, p. 3–55. The importance of inflation in disrupting Soviet reforms has been emphasized by Martin Feldstein during a presentation at the Pew Foundation Conference on Economics and National Security, Palm Beach, Florida, March 1990. Other factors affecting the deficit include a drop in the world price of oil, a loss of wage discipline, and restrictions on the production and sale of vodka. General Secretary Gorbachev has used the term "full-blooded market" on several occasions. One example was reported in the *Los Angeles Times* on 6 May 1990, p. 6. As discussed in "The Soviet Economy Stumbles Badly in 1989," a paper presented by the Central Intelligence Agency and the Defense Intelligence Agency to the Technology and National Security Subcommittee of the Joint Economic Committee, Congress of the United States, 20 April 1990, p. 7, Gosplan has estimated Soviet open inflation and repressed inflation of 5 and 5.5 percent, respectively, in 1989.

4. Chairman of the Council of Ministers Ryzhkov has announced that the USSR will reduce the share of income devoted to defense by between one-third and one-half between 1990 and 1995. When this statement was made, the Soviets had announced defense spending at about 9 percent of GNP. However, more recently, in a speech in Tula, as reported in *Izvestiya*, 29 April 1990. p. 2, President Gorbachev has announced that defense spending was as much as 13.5 percent of GNP.

5. See D. Derk Swain, "The Soviet Military Sector: How it is Defined and Measured," in Henry S. Rowen and Charles Wolf, Jr., eds., *The Impoverished Superpower: Perestroika and the Soviet Military Burden*, ICS Press, 1990, pp. 93–110, for a discussion of the CIA's estimate that the Soviet defense burden is 15–17 percent of GNP.

6. We assume a Cobb-Douglas production function in which the second term after the equal sign is more typically represented as $S_k \cdot g_{Cap}$, where S_k = capital's share of national income and g_{Cap} is the growth of the capital stock. But $MP_k = S_k \cdot$ (GNP/K) and $g_{Cap} = \text{In}/K$, so we obtain $S_k \cdot g_{Cap} = MP_k \cdot S_{nin}$).

7. In this simple model, consumption and defense can be exchanged for each other on a ruble-for-ruble basis. The curvature depicted in Figure 11.2 does not arise from diminishing returns but from the changes in the end use shares going to consumption and defense. Much of discussion associated with Figure 11.4 below also relates to this issue.

8. For simplicity, foreign trade in machinery and capital repair activities have been excluded from Figure 11.3. For a discussion of Soviet econometric-trend models, see Gregory G. Hildebrandt, ed., *RAND Conference on Models of the Soviet Economy, October 11-12, 1984*, The RAND Corporation, R-3322, October 1985.

9. The subsidies received by the Soviet defense sector are discussed in Dmitri Steinberg, "Defense Allocations Under Gorbachev: Analyzing New

Data for 1988–1990,"a paper presented to the IV World Congress for Soviet and East European Studies, Harrogate, England, July 21–26, 1990.

10. The actual model contains three sectors, "machine tools," other machine building, and civilian nonmachine building. For each sector we employ Cobb-Douglas production functions in which labor's share equals 0.65. Soviet economic data are obtained from *Allocation of Resources in the Soviet Union and China*, Part 14 and *U.S. CIA Handbook of Economic Statistics, 1987: A Reference Aid*, CPAS 87-10001 (Washington, D.C.: GPO, September 1987. The labor force data were obtained from the Department of the Census, and information on structures versus machinery investment are contained in *PlanEcon Report 2*, nos. 25 and 26 (June 27, 1986). We assume that the Soviets are able to emphasize modernization investment at the expense of expansion investment. Specifically, we assume that the annual growth of investment in machinery and equipment is 3 percentage points greater than the investment in structures during the 1995–2010 time period.

12

Economic Reform and Arms Reduction in Eastern Europe: Insights from Evolutionary Economics

Peter Murrell

Introduction

In Eastern Europe, successful arms reduction, depends on the success of economic reforms. Failure to reform would certainly lead to reversion to the old order, which includes a pivotal role for the military in society. (This link between the military's role and the failure of reforms seems to have suggested itself constantly in the events in the Soviet Union during 1991.) Without economic restructuring, the present moves to arms reduction will not bear fruit.

As a succession of geriatric regimes fell in 1989, it became obvious that the biggest problem was not the establishment of democracy, but rather the reconstruction of the economies of Eastern Europe.[1] Indeed, the problem has become more ominous in the light of two years' experience of reforms: the goal of reform is now simply to save the economies of Eastern Europe from disastrous performance over the next few years.

Now that all external political barriers to reform have fallen, Eastern Europe is dismantling the centrally planned economies that had been in place for forty years. Throughout these four decades, Western politicians and economists fostered the belief that the removal of the planned system would lead to a dramatic improvement in living standards. But now that discussion has descended from broad desires to practical measures, the problems of transition to the market seem daunting. The problems suggest that failure, in the form of falling standards of living for many years, is a real possibility. The combination of dashed expectations,[2] weakness of nascent democracy, and renewal of ethnic rivalries will make a potent brew for the rise of regimes that might threaten the stability of the European continent.[3] Such instability would be a direct threat to peace and security throughout the world. It would have serious implications for arms reduction not only in the East but also in the West.

During the economic transition, the ideas of economists will play a central role in determining policies.[4] This is already evidenced by the high profiles of Leszek Balcerowicz in Poland and Vaclav Klaus in Czechoslovakia. Given the immensity of the task, it is not surprising that reform ideas lean heavily on the central tenets of economic theories. Ideas for reform change dramatically, depending on the theory adopted. Moreover, predictions of the likelihood of success of particular reforms depend on the mode of analysis used. Rarely in history has prediction of the fate of nations, perhaps that fate itself, rested upon the veracity of abstruse economic theorizing.

In this chapter, I examine the nexus between peace and security and the economic ideas used to underpin reforms in Eastern Europe. The hypothesis is that the biggest threat to European peace and security over the next few years arises from the possibility of abject failure of economic reform.[5] Moreover, the success of reform depends on the types of policies adopted, which in turn depend on the economic theory that guides the process. In discussing the appropriateness of two different theories to guide reform, this chapter provides both a normative and a positive analysis of the link between reforms and peace and security issues. The normative element derives from the recommendations implicit in the consideration of alternative reform policies. The positive element emanates from the qualitative predictions of the likelihood of success or failure of particular reform policies.

This chapter addresses two further national security matters. First, it analyzes the particular policies that are relevant when reductions in arms production must occur. One of the thorniest questions arising from such reductions is whether arms-producing enterprises should be converted to civilian production. I approach this question in a manner consistent with the paper's analysis of reforms in general, analyzing answers that would be offered by two different economic theories.

Second, the paper attempts to improve forecasts of which reform policies will succeed. The potential threat posed by any country is proportional to its economic strength. Therefore, predictions about the effects of reforms are also predictions of the potential military threat posed by a reforming country. With irredentist claims increasing and calls for fraternal assistance still a recent memory, threats to peace and security could arise from variations in military strength across the region. Because military strength depends on economic performance, it is important to generate insight into the likely success rates of different types of reform programs.

In reflecting on the likely effectiveness of different reform programs, I consider two rival sets of economic doctrines that could support reforms—traditional neoclassical theory, which is the basis for many of the reform proposals now being advocated and implemented in Eastern Europe, and evolutionary, or Schumpeterian, economics. After briefly describing the fundamental features of the two theories, I summarize empirical findings that lead to the conclusion that the evolutionary approach, rather than the neoclassical one, explains the crucial failings of the Eastern European economies, the failings that reforms must correct. I show that the alternative paradigms have radically different ramifications and consider the implications for the economic performance of Eastern European economies over the transition period. The last sections directly examine the question of arms reduction and military conversion in a manner that draws upon the lessons of this chapter.

Alternative Perspectives:
Neoclassical Versus Evolutionary Economics

Neoclassical theory is familiar to most readers, so only a brief review is needed. In this paradigm, independent economic agents are viewed as making decisions on the basis of clearly known objectives and constraints, expressed as functions of tangible goods and monetary variables. Agents interact at arm's length through the price system, with prices completely describing the available alternatives. The price system transfers all information and mediates all exchanges. All transfers of information and exchanges occur when the economy is in equilibrium. For normative purposes, neoclassical analysis uses the criterion of Pareto efficiency. This criterion—whether there are opportunities to better the lot of one person without making another worse off—is powerful only in a limited domain, where the main object of interest is the equilibrium allocation of physical resources, rather than out-of-equilibrium informational processes.

At the simplest level, the evolutionary (or Schumpeterian) paradigm rests on two premises.[6] First, to understand the success of capitalist processes, one must primarily focus upon the mechanisms that produce growth and change, not equilibrium. Second, one must begin theorizing with a satisfactory description of the behavior of economic agents, taking full account of problems of decision making and organization in the face of uncertainty and limits on information-processing abilities. The description of economic processes must follow directly from this view of the nature of agents.

At the center of evolutionary theory is the notion that innovation has been the driving force behind the immense increases in wealth that have occurred since the industrial revolution. The theory attaches a broad meaning to the notion of innovation: progress has come not simply from new technologies, but also from organizational and institutional innovation. In other words, innovation should not only conjure up the invention of the blast furnace or the semiconductor, but also the development of the multidivisional corporation and fast-food franchising.

In emphasizing growth and change, the evolutionary perspective implicitly accords little importance to the property of allocative efficiency and competition within equilibrium, the focus of the neoclassical paradigm. As Schumpeter stated most forcefully, these features are of secondary importance compared to capitalism's mechanisms for change and innovation:

> [I]t is. . . . competition within a rigid pattern of invariant conditions, methods of production and forms of organization in particular, that practically monopolizes attention [in the traditional, neoclassical paradigm]. But in capitalist reality as distinguished from its textbook picture, it is not that kind of competition that counts but the competition from the new commodity, the new technology, the new source of supply, the new type of organization. . . . This kind of competition is much more effective than the other as a bombardment is in comparison with forcing a door, and so much more important that it becomes a matter of comparative indifference whether competition in the ordinary sense functions more or less promptly. (Schumpeter 1950, 84–85)

Implied in this quote—and the evolutionary approach—economic reform proposals centering on the pursuit of allocative efficiency will be of second order of importance.

In modeling processes of growth and change, the evolutionary approach begins by acknowledging the effects of pervasive uncertainty and the consequent demands on informational resources on the behavior of economic agents, particularly on organizations.[7] Thus, evolutionary economics views agents as facing not only financial and physical barriers but also limits on information-processing capabilities and the difficulty of exercising control in complex organizations. This has profound consequences for the construction of effective organizations.

A system organizing many individuals must have a means of

coordinating their actions and handling information flows among them. The exercise of routine operations is an efficient way of handling such coordination. By repetition of tasks varying only over a narrow range, an organization is able to economize on scarce information-processing resources. Hence, the efficiency of an organization is intimately tied to the exercise of a particular "routine," or narrow range of routines.

In this view, it is important to realize exactly where the organization's information, or technology, resides. Information should not be thought of as held by individuals, but rather as subsisting in the interactions between individuals. Information and skills, then, have value largely or wholly through interactions during the exercise of a particular organizational routine. The productivity of an organization (and of the individuals within the organization) therefore depends on the ability to continue operations with little variation from past behavior.

So far, emphasis has been placed on routines as the solution to the problem of coordination within organizations. Routines are also an aspect of the solution to problems of incentives and distribution of income. A routine might be thought of as an equilibrium of the complex, noncooperative game that is at the heart of efficient organizational design. And as is well known from game theory, such games usually have many equilibria of widely varying efficiency. Moreover, the process of reaching efficient solutions entails a long search. Hence, the perpetuation of a routine is in itself a protection against the creation of conflict that would arise from any attempt to find an alternative solution to the organizational game. During conflict, of course, the efficiency, and indeed the existence, of the organization would be under great threat.

Of course, organizations are not totally inflexible. They do change routines. But the search for alternatives is limited by the stock of organizational information, which is intimately bound to the exercise of an existing routine. Hence, the search for new routines is best characterized not as a wide-ranging choice from a universe of alternatives, but rather as a history-bound process of discovery within a neighborhood of existing operations. Moreover, when a search occurs, the existing routine is threatened, jeopardizing the stability of the organization by calling into question the division of organizational income.

Given reliance on routines and constraints on search, societies that attain efficiency in a changing world must have a mechanism to free themselves from the inertia inherent in the operations of an existing set of organizations. Under capitalism, the mechanism is provided by several features of market processes. First, markets automatically reallocate resources from inefficient organizations to efficient ones. Second, exit and bankruptcy remove inefficient organizations. Third, new organizations, some of which find an effective organizational structure, are constantly entering the market. Then, in a process that marks the evolutionary approach to economic change: "Patterns of differential survival and growth in a population can produce change in economic aggregates characterizing that population, even if the corresponding characteristics of firms remain constant" (Nelson and Winter 1982, 9). And, of course, surviving and growing firms reflect properties of the economic environment in which they have prospered.

I can now summarize the elements of the evolutionary paradigm that are most important for thinking about economic reform.

1. The use of routines and the fact that the search process reflects the historical experience of an organization cause much *persistence in organizational behavior.*
2. The evolutionary approach emphasizes the concept of the *economic environment*—the set of external influences, including the other organizations in society, that affect an enterprise's performance. In a stable environment for a long enough time, routines and behaviors will be conditioned by the context in which organizations have survived and prospered.
3. Hence, for a period after a change in environment, the behaviors observed will be a reflection of the past environment.
4. The evolutionary approach emphasizes the importance of selection processes, or *entry and exit,* in accomplishing change. Changes within organizations are deemphasized in favor of a focus on shifts in control over economic resources from inefficient (technologically obsolete) to efficient (technologically progressive) organizations or to new enterprises better suited to the new economic environment.
5. To aid in the efficacy of the selection process, a variety of types of organizations must be generated. This is especially true when a radical change in environment is considered. But it also must be emphasized that a variety of organizational forms is characteristic of modern capitalism (Nelson 1990).
6. The uncertainty and the limits on information processing that are emphasized in the evolutionary approach to organizations must also be acknowledged as constraints on the effectiveness of policymakers. Knowledge of the behavior of the economy under conditions unlike the past will be highly inaccurate.

The Use of the Neoclassical Paradigm in the Analysis of Reform Programs for the Eastern European Countries

Before proceeding to examine some deeper consequences of the two paradigms for economic reform, it is necessary to establish two points. First, I must show that the neoclassical paradigm has an important influence on economic reforms: that it is not simply a straw man. That is the subject of this section. Second, I must show the relative merits of the two paradigms in addressing the problems that reforms must solve. This will be done in the next section.

It is not surprising that neoclassical analysis is used as the basic building block in designing and understanding reform programs. The paradigm directs and shapes the very discourse of economic analysis, identifying which features are to be considered of central importance and, by implication, which are not. Consider, for example, the following characterization of reform by Hardt and Kaufman (1989, xviii):

> The process of reform requires some degree of decentralization of decisions about the allocation of resources and of economic management. The goal is an economy in which choices are made rationally, on the basis of objective criteria, and where resources are used efficiently. Knowledge of the costs of inputs is essential. Change from administered to market-determined prices is a precondition to a rational system. Self-management, self-financing, and accountability at the enterprise level is necessary, along with incentives for innovation and high performance. There should be substantial disengagement of the government and the Communist Party from micromanagement of the economy, reduction or elimination of subsidies, and adherence to Western standards of statistical reporting.

The assumption that an inefficient allocation of resources is the primary problem plaguing planned economies and that decentralization and market-determined prices are the most essential reforms are firmly rooted in both the neoclassical paradigm and the traditional approach to reform.

Even before the 1989 revolutions that dramatically opened Eastern Europe to Western ideas, the neoclassical influence upon reform discussion in the region was strong. For example, Csikos-Nagy (1972) drew heavily on neoclassical theory when characterizing Hungary's 1968 reform, using such concepts as rational allocation of resources and Pareto efficiency. Winiecki (1986), who was playing an important role in Polish reform debates, examined the problems plaguing Eastern European economies using analysis strikingly similar to that found in standard Western works. Kornai (1986, 1728) states that the common ideas behind reforms and reform attempts in Hungary, China, Czechoslovakia, Poland, and the Soviet Union were the need for the autonomy of firms (decentralization), the elimination of shortages, the focus on the profit incentive guided by appropriate price signals, and the use of the market.

In the progression of proposals for the reform of the Soviet economy, elements of the neoclassical paradigm are clear. For example, the Abalkin plan that existed for some months during 1989–1990 gave central importance to the price mechanism: "[T]he successful introduction of an economic reform is impossible if current retail prices and the procedures for their formation is retained" (*PlanEcon Report* 1989). Similarly, both the now-defunct 500-day program and Gorbachev's largely ignored program introduced in October 1990 emphasized the freeing of prices and the creation of a competitive market environment, with due acknowledgment of the invisible hand.[8] These plans bespeak an indebtedness to the standard Western economic model.

The Polish reform was perhaps the most radical to be introduced in Eastern Europe. The program's initial concentration on removing subsidies, freeing prices, decentralizing decisions, and using foreign competition as a disciplining device is strictly within the neoclassical paradigm. More importantly, the reform plan implicitly assumes that, after the introduction of the orthodox stabilization measures, existing producers would be driven by competition to maximize profits. The surprise at the depth of the recession resulting from the stabilization program indicates the extent to which poststabilization behavior needs to be explained in terms other than rational maximization. Of course, the evolutionary perspective provides a transparent explanation of the behavior.

Empirical Evidence on the Relevance of the Evolutionary and Neoclassical Paradigms as Guides to Reform

In order to judge which of the two paradigms should govern the design of reform programs, it is helpful to ask which of the two theories best diagnoses the illnesses of the economies that are being reformed. Much evidence on this point can be offered; I will concentrate on my own empirical work.[9] Both my work and other findings lead to the conclusion that the evolutionary paradigm has more explanatory power than the neoclassical paradigm in diagnosing the ills of centrally planned economies. And it is these ills that have caused the headlong rush to reform.

Central Planning and the Slowdown in Rates of Growth

Neoclassical theory argues that allocative efficiency is the most important feature of a well-functioning economy and that poor resource allocation is the most salient characteristic of a planned economy. There are at least two ways to test this proposition. One is to measure and compare the different levels of allocative efficiency attained by various economies. Such studies have been attempted, and they certainly do not show that planned economies are significantly less allocatively efficient than market economies.[10]

A second way to test whether allocative efficiency is the central characteristic distinguishing socialist from capitalist economies is to observe whether socialist economies consistently perform more poorly than market economies, relative to their respective potential levels of performance. In a recent paper, Murrell and Olson (1991) found that from 1950 to 1965 there is little evidence in growth rates that distinguishes the performance of centrally planned from market economies.[11] On average, the centrally planned economies operated as much below potential as did the market economies. (Table 12.1 presents a brief summary of the Murrell-Olson results.) It is difficult to conclude from this evidence that centrally planned economic systems were any less dynamic than market systems during 1950–1965.

The results change dramatically from 1965 to 1980. While the performance of the market economies, relative to potential, did not change at all, the overall performance of the centrally planned economies declined markedly. The average growth rate of the planned economies was 2.48 percent per annum less than its potential in this latter period, as opposed to only 1.62 percent in the earlier period.

Rather than performing consistently worse than market economies,

TABLE 12.1   Comparison of Growth Performance of Planned and Market Economies

	Actual Growth Rate, 1950–1965	Estimated Shortfall from Potential Growth Rate, 1950–1965	Actual Growth Rate, 1965–1980	Estimated Shortfall from Potential Growth Rate, 1965–1980
Market economy average	3.75	1.74	3.36	1.76
Planned economy average	4.43	1.62	3.24	2.48

Source: Murrell and Olson (1991).

as the neoclassical approach predicts, centrally planned economies tend to perform more poorly than market economies only after a period of time. This is exactly what one would predict from evolutionary theory, which downplays the significance of allocative efficiency and instead emphasizes the contrast between the stability of institutions in centrally planned economies and the dynamic creation and destruction resulting from relatively free entry and exit in market economies.

Two Explanations of Foreign Trade Levels

The two paradigms explain foreign trade levels by different systemic features. Neoclassical economists conclude that the complexities of bureaucratic decision making and the state's monopoly on foreign trade lead to low levels of trade in centrally planned economies. Evolutionary analysis focuses on two facts: that independent economic agents operating at arm's length find it difficult to exchange some types of goods (Dunning 1981; Helpman and Krugman 1985; Markusen 1986; and Ethier 1986); and that the transfer of technology—which encourages trade—is best accomplished within organizations (Markusen 1983). As a consequence of these two facts, the presence or absence of markets within a country might be of secondary importance in determining the level of foreign trade. Rather, the unhindered development of different organizational forms, such as multinational enterprises, is the most important determinant of foreign trade levels. Thus, to compare the neoclassical and evolutionary perspectives, it is important to decide whether the absence of internal markets or the absence of multinational enterprises is most responsible for low levels of foreign trade in planned economies.

Murrell (1991b) finds that the absence of multinational enterprises in Eastern European economies accounts for observed differences in trade levels from those in market economies. That paper explores the effect of adding a variable representing the level of involvement of multinational enterprises in a country to an existing study that examines systemic influences on the level of foreign trade of centrally planned economies (Browning 1985).[12] The variable on multinational activity completely dominated the "system" variable denoting the presence of central planning. The multinational variable was significant at standard levels in all estimated regression equations, whereas the system variable was not significant.[13] This result alone shows that the destruction of planning and the creation of markets is not sufficient to drive a viable reform package.

Rationality as Evidenced in Foreign Trade

Many economists argue that planning leads to an irrational economic structure. In Murrell (1990), I used the Heckscher-Ohlin model (the standard neoclassical model of foreign trade) and endowment data from the market economies to define what constitutes a rational structure of foreign trade.[14] Then, I estimated how far the trade behavior of various economies deviates from this structure, in order to examine the degree of irrationality of centrally planned trade.

Table 12.2 summarizes the results of the study. The data used to make the calculations have undergone rather complicated transformations, making it difficult to interpret the absolute values of the statistics. However, it is sufficient for present purposes to view the numbers as ordinal indicators of foreign trade rationality, with lower numbers evidencing greater rationality. Comparisons clearly show that models from neoclassical theory provide little evidence that the foreign trade of the planned economies is irrational.[15]

Product Versus Process Technological Change

Neoclassical theory attributes the technological deficiencies of planned economies to incentive problems and bureaucracy. Unless managers are motivated by profit maximization, they will not have

TABLE 12.2 Measures of Rationality of Foreign Trade (conformity of trade patterns to those consistent with the Heckscher-Ohlin Model)

Countries	Rationality of Foreign Trade
OECD + developing countries	1.338
OECD countries	0.946
23 developing countries	1.731
7 poorest OECD countries	0.778
Bulgaria	0.303
Czechoslovakia	0.022
East Germany	0.012
Hungary	0.361
Poland	1.566
Romania	0.159
6 Eastern European countries listed above	0.404
USSR	0.336
Yugoslavia	1.340

Notes: Lower figures indicate greater "rationality," as evidenced in foreign trade flows. The figures for groups of countries are averages. Estimates are for 1975.

Source: Adapted from Murrell (1990).

appropriate incentive to pursue the creation and adoption of new technologies. Bureaucracy impedes technological advance by slowing resource reallocation and by separating R&D from the production process. This analysis implies that planned economies should exhibit similarly poor performance in creating and adopting both new product technologies and new process technologies.

The evolutionary approach predicts that centrally planned economies will do better at introducing new process technologies than new product technologies, for many reasons. First, new products often arise from outside a sector, whereas new processes often emerge within existing firms (Utterback 1979, 48, 50). Thus, absence of entry—a characteristic of planned economies—should limit new product technologies. Second, because the costs and benefits of new processes are easier to calculate than those of new products (Beardsley and Mansfield 1987, 130), conservative planners are more easily persuaded of the benefits of new processes. Third, new process technologies are more easily spread without internal organization (Brada 1981, 211). Because Eastern European enterprises rarely create subsidiary plants, spread of ideas by internal organization is absent in Eastern Europe, thus hindering the spread of new products more than new processes. Fourth, the importance of internal organization in disseminating new product technologies means that importers of the technology must rely on multinational enterprises, which are largely absent from the economies of Eastern Europe.[16]

Murrell (1990, 69–70, 113–115) strongly supports the predictions of the evolutionary perspective. The evidence indicates that the centrally planned economies have a large comparative advantage over market economies in sectors with high rates of process innovations and a comparative disadvantage in sectors with large amounts of product innovations. A summary of these results is presented in Tables 12.3 and 12.4. The figures show that the poorer OECD countries outperformed the six Eastern European countries in producing new products in all but one of the measures generated.[17] Furthermore, the planned economies outperformed their comparable market economies in producing new process technologies in more than half of the measures generated.

Reforms From an Evolutionary Perspective

We must now examine the way in which reforms are viewed from the evolutionary perspective. This examination has two objectives. First, it identifies the central problems that any reforms must address. In doing so, it pinpoints how reforms can fail, providing information

TABLE 12.3 Measures of Comparative Advantage of Planned and Market Economies in Sectors with High Rates of Process Innovations

	1975	1976	1977	1978	1979	1980	1981	1982	1983
Export measure (higher figures indicate superior performance)									
Low-income OECD countries	0.95	0.96	0.95	0.89	0.85	1.00	0.98	0.97	0.95
6 Eastern European countries	1.46	1.16	1.27	1.25	1.16	1.42	1.58	1.71	1.64
Import measure (lower figures indicate superior performance)									
Low-income OECD countries	1.09	1.18	1.21	1.24	1.24	1.18	1.19	1.19	1.16
6 Eastern European countries	1.41	1.38	1.43	1.47	1.45	1.56	1.51	1.64	1.50
Export-import measure (higher figures indicate superior performance)									
Low-income OECD countries	0.86	0.81	0.79	0.72	0.69	0.84	0.83	0.81	0.81
6 Eastern European countries	1.04	0.84	0.89	0.85	0.80	0.91	1.04	1.05	1.09

Note: The low-income OECD countries are market economies whose incomes lie in the same range as those of Eastern Europe: Austria, Greece, Ireland, Italy, Portugal, Spain, and Turkey. The six Eastern European countries are Bulgaria, Czechoslovakia, East Germany, Hungary, Poland, and Romania.

Source: Murrell (1990).

TABLE 12.4 Measures of Comparative Advantage of Planned and Market Economies in Sectors with High Rates of Product Innovations

	1975	1976	1977	1978	1979	1980	1981	1982	1983
Export measure (higher figures indicate superior performance)									
Low-income OECD countries	0.95	0.94	0.96	0.91	0.94	1.05	1.02	1.01	1.00
6 Eastern European countries	0.67	0.69	0.71	0.65	0.67	0.63	0.66	0.63	0.56
Import measure (lower figures indicate superior performance)									
Low-income OECD countries	1.07	1.03	1.03	1.02	1.01	1.01	1.02	1.00	0.98
6 Eastern European countries	1.23	1.25	1.31	1.34	1.21	1.06	1.00	1.08	1.04
Export-import measure (higher figures indicate superior performance)									
Low-income OECD countries	0.89	0.91	0.93	0.89	0.93	1.03	1.00	1.02	1.02
6 Eastern European countries	0.54	0.55	0.54	0.49	0.55	0.59	0.67	0.58	0.53

Note: The low-income OECD countries are market economies whose incomes lie in the same range as those of Eastern Europe: Austria, Greece, Ireland, Italy, Portugal, Spain, and Turkey. The six Eastern European countries are Bulgaria, Czechoslovakia, East Germany, Hungary, Poland, and Romania.

Source: Murrell (1990).

crucial to making predictions about the macroeconomic consequences of any particular set of policies. Second, the examination suggests how reforms should proceed. This makes it easier to identify programs that are likely to succeed and, therefore, which countries will have significantly stronger economies over the next few years.

The Central Dilemmas of Reform

Present reform plans emphasize the importance of correcting or rationalizing defective allocative mechanisms by introducing elements of markets (e.g., macrobalance, decentralization, free prices, convertibility, and so forth). Because the proposals stem from a strong belief in the primacy of allocative efficiency, the lack of which is felt to be the fundamental failing of Eastern European economies, the plans call for changes to be introduced across all sectors in the economy. An evolutionary diagnosis of Eastern European problems, on the other hand, indicates that such changes will cause immediate adverse consequences.

The organizational routines in a society are a product of the environment in which they have been selected and to which they have adapted. In Eastern Europe, the past environment was the centralized, bureaucratic system of administrative allocation and control. Given that the system performed tolerably and was stable for a number of decades in a number of countries, it is reasonable to suppose that organizational routines were selected according to the needs of the environment and were largely suited to that environment. These routines are likely to be unfit for any new environment, however. Therefore, a radical reform of the economic system—the environment—will undermine economic performance. The decline in performance is all the more certain if the change in environment produces adversity that removes the possibility of simply continuing past behavior. Organizational efficiency tends to diminish rapidly in the face of adversity, when existing routines are no longer viable and when cooperative agreements must be broken and replaced with less attractive ones (Nelson and Winter 1982, 121–124).

Problems might also arise if the environment is changed without regard for the fact that enterprises might continue their past behavior. If enterprises find enough slack under the new conditions, there is reason to expect that the characteristics of past behavior will persist into the future.[18] Such persistence will be especially pernicious in one particular case: generation of excess demand within the state production sector. Kornai (1980) has argued cogently that excess demand is intrinsic to economies with large state productive sectors. In the short run, while reforms are being implemented, existing organizational behavior, which has generated excess demand so consistently in the past, will still be an important determinant of economic outcomes. Therefore, until large-scale destruction and creation of economic institutions have taken place, it is likely that the Eastern European economies will have a much stronger tendency to generate excess demand than economies that have had dominant private sectors in their recent past. Of course, if macroeconomic adversity is serious enough, excess demand might be temporarily squeezed out of the economy. But if the evolutionary approach's insistence on the persistence of past behavior is correct, it will take an extremely large, and costly, amount of adversity to retain macroeconomic stability. Indeed, such a scenario might accurately characterize the Poland of 1990.

Using the principles of evolutionary theory, I will briefly delineate the four main problems that are likely to be encountered on the road to reform. Any reform program that does not solve these problems will risk failure, macroeconomic instability, and possibly a large decline in standards of living.

1. Radical economic reform will lower the productive efficiency of the state sector, while in the early stages of reform the private sector will not be large enough to take up the slack. At the same time, the efficacy of selection processes in the private sector requires a fairly stable environment, similar to the one at the end of the reform process. A viable reform must provide continuity with the past for the state sector and continuity with the future for the private sector.

2. Experience shows that only draconian market-type macroeconomic measures will control excess demand in the state sector. However, encouragement of the selective process requires a nonrestrictive macroeconomic policy to provide a fertile environment for new private-sector firms. Reforms must combine macroeconomic stringency in the state sector with nonrestrictive macroeconomic policies in the private sector.

3. In the absence of draconian fiscal, monetary, and exchange rate policies, the old-style bureaucratic intervention will be needed to contain the excess demand pressures emanating from the state sector. Thus, reforms must find a way of combining bureaucratic intervention in the state sector with free markets in the private sector.

4. Immediate exposure of the state sector to foreign trade is extremely risky, for two reasons. First, the introduction of world prices and trading conditions might cause a large decline in state-sector productivity. Second, openness without macroeconomic austerity will lead to the accumulation of foreign debt, given the tendency toward

excess demand in the state sector. However, because openness to foreign trade is the long-term goal, selection processes in the private sector must occur in an environment that includes foreign competition. The reforms must combine continuing insulation of the state sector with openness of the private sector.

A Reform Package Based on Evolutionary Principles

As the foregoing makes clear, the central question facing economic reformers who are guided by the evolutionary approach is how to handle the state and private sectors in seemingly contradictory ways.[19] Any reform that does not manage to do so will, if not fail, at least cause undue economic trauma and expose the whole transition process, both political and economic, to the possibility of reversal, with consequent risks for the peace and stability of the European continent as a whole. Yet, for completeness, it is necessary to show that there is a viable reform policy that steers clear of the problems that I have identified. If such a policy were not defined, one could reasonably object that the present argument only shows that reforms will inevitably be very costly.

The only possibility is a dual economy. Since there will inevitably be a long period in which the old state enterprises will continue to produce a large proportion of the country's output, the state sector should be run along traditional lines. In fact, the early months or years of transition might even require recentralization. At the same time, the private sector of the economy should be allowed to function freely in order to create internationally competitive enterprises.[20]

It is possible to give only the broadest overview of the principles of operation of a dual economy. Nevertheless, identification of a few general principles suggests what types of reforms would be viable according to the evolutionary perspective. First, the new private economy and the old state sector should be separated in roughly the same manner as the rest of the world and bureaucratic centrally planned economies have been separated in times past. The state sector should retain its nonconvertible currency for some time. The new private sector should operate with a new, convertible currency.

Second, the state sector should operate as it has in the past, with the traditional bureaucratic mechanisms. Radical price reform need not be undertaken and might, in fact, be harmful.[21]

Third, state enterprises must adhere to strict budget balancing, through the traditional means of central targets, monitoring, and intervention. Accumulation of hard-currency debt (including the new convertible currency) by the state sector should not be allowed.

Fourth, the immediate objective of the dual economy should be the shrinking of the state sector. However, this should not be attempted with the heavy hand of intervention. Once private-sector activity is allowed and a stable economic environment for private enterprise is established, the state sector will shrink by natural attrition as the labor force, attracted by better opportunities, gradually moves from the state to the private sector.

Fifth, growth of the private sector must be encouraged. There should be no restrictive macroeconomic policy in this sector and no bars on foreign competition. In addition, the following measures should be undertaken:

1. Multinational corporations should be allowed to function as freely as they do in other modern, developed economies.
2. Joint-stock firms formed by any groups of individuals, foreign or domestic, should be allowed.
3. The government should encourage "privatization by selection." Private firms (including foreign ones) or groups of employees should be allowed to bid for existing state enterprises.
4. Special circumstances might demand swift and complete privatization of some sectors of the economy. In agriculture, for example, the immediate benefits of private enterprise would probably be large—a practical policy of privatization by handing out parcels of land seems eminently feasible—and widespread support from the workers is likely.

Arms Reduction and Economic Conversion

Given the large role of the military in the affairs of the former Warsaw Pact nations, any program of economic reform must be able to address the issue of arms reduction. The evolutionary perspective has two important points to add to the debate on conversion of military-related production facilities. These points do not follow from the neoclassical paradigm and are perhaps inconsistent with it. They bear on the costliness of organizational change and the spillovers that can occur when economic change in one sector produces adversity in another.

The Difficulties of Converting Existing Facilities

Building new organizations is a costly and difficult process. However, starting over might be less costly than transforming old organizations, where behavior and language have adapted to existing conditions, the organization has been aligned with the structure of the physical plant, and commitments that would be expensive to revoke have been made to existing members. Because of the difficulties of changing the elements of organizational structure, the reconstruction of existing organizations involves costs that are not present in the construction of new organizations. Hence, there can be no a priori assumption that converting arms-producing facilities is better than simply closing them.

The difficulties would be especially large if reorganization required fundamental changes in a facility's sectoral specialization, production technology, or market orientation. In fact, the conversion of arms-producing facilities would require changes in all three. A change in sectoral specialization follows from the limited civilian use for goods traditionally produced for the military. The change in production technology arises from the fact that attention to costs will be required much more after economic reform than it ever was for the cosseted military sector. Lastly, enterprises will no longer be able to rely on their old markets and will find that the new ones have very different tastes from those of their former military masters.

In conclusion, it could be unproductive to commit a large expenditure of resources to reconversion grants and subsidies for enterprises in transition from military to civilian production. Resources might be much more productive in funding start-up enterprises in a new private sector.

The Spillover Effects of Rapid Change

For the arms-producing sector, the decline in efficiency that occurs with adversity will be inevitable, since retrenchment is an unavoidable concomitant of arms reduction. No sensible policy would be able to avert the decline in efficiency. However, policymakers must consider the effects on the enterprises, primarily in the civilian sector, that have relied either directly or indirectly on the military for some sales in the past. If military-related markets are suddenly lost, then these enterprises might suffer a large overall decline in efficiency due to the effects of adversity on their ability to maintain existing organizational agreements. Hence, there is every chance of large spillover effects on the civilian sectors from a precipitate reduction in military purchases, with the possibility of chain reaction to enterprises that have never been connected with the military in any way.

This observation leads directly to the question of decisions on the speed of reduction of the arms-producing sector. Given a nonlinear relation between organizational performance and degree of adversity, and given that declines in performance in one sector will produce adversity in others, it seems appropriate to reduce military purchases gradually. Because gradual reduction would avoid the possibility of a chain reaction of declines, it might result in a larger sum of discounted national income over the relevant time period than would a program of immediate reduction.[22] The appropriate speed of reduction (i.e., closing arms-producing plants) is thus determined primarily by the ability of the civilian economy to absorb the accompanying loss of sales.

It might seem paradoxical to continue operating enterprises that are producing essentially worthless goods. But the paradox vanishes in light of the inherent externalities in the creation, design, and destruction of large organizations. These externalities arise both from the nonmarket elements of coordination intrinsic in organizations and from the public-goods nature of organizational performance. Cooperation, although essential for efficiency, is extremely hard to establish and it is fragile. If the austerity produced by large changes in economic arrangements (such as the closing of military markets) ruins existing cooperative arrangements, the productivity of workers in civilian enterprises will decline because each worker's productivity is intimately tied to the continuing cooperation that they have with their fellow workers.

Conversion or Gradual Closing of Arms-Producing Enterprises?

The policy for arms reduction can be seen to be consistent with the general reform program outlined in the last section. That program's principles were that the greatest benefits of reform would come from the creation of new enterprises, that a radical change in existing arrangements could cause large declines in efficiency, that there would be negative spillovers from changes in the state sector to the new private sector, and that there would be a need to use old institutions to isolate the worst consequences of these externalities. Each of these principles is mirrored in the policy for arms reduction adumbrated above. Hence, closing the armaments-producing sector is preferable to converting it.[23] Gradual closing is necessary in order to protect the civilian sector of the economy from large periods of austerity. During the period of decline, arms will be produced that might be superfluous compared to political demands.

Conclusion

A secure Europe depends on the progress of economic reforms in Eastern Europe. Hence, the ability to predict the performance of the Eastern European economies is vital to understanding the future security problems of Europe. But now prediction is most difficult because of the radical changes that are occurring. When an economy is undergoing fundamental reconstruction, it is unlikely that the usual quantitative economic models could produce reliable forecasts of the outcome of reforms. An alternative to traditional macroeconometric models is to rely on broad qualitative generalizations. In this chapter, I have produced generalized predictions by focusing on the economic theories that underlie reforms. I have argued that reform programs focusing on decentralization and the freeing of prices in order to obtain allocative efficiency might produce very poor results. In contrast, reforms that are more sensitive to persistence in the behavior of state enterprises and the need to focus policy changes on the creation of a new private sector are more likely to be successful.

This chapter has concentrated on an abstract idea—the ability of two competing paradigms to examine the processes of economic reforms. One might wonder whether my themes are relevant to the pressing practical problems of power and security. But there is no doubting the potential for political instability in Eastern Europe and with it the threat to European security. Economic success or failure will be critical in determining the levels of instability, and success or failure will hinge on the economic principles underlying reforms. Perhaps economic ideas and economists are exerting a more profound influence over events than at any time in history. Hence, it is vital for peace and security to consider the intellectual basis of present economic policy in Eastern Europe.

Notes

This chapter describes and integrates research conducted by the author under the auspices of the Economics and National Security Program of the Pew Charitable Trusts. I thank that program for its valuable support, as well as the Center for Institutional Reform and the Informal Sector (IRIS) at the University of Maryland. The valuable research assistance of David Fike, Barbara Hopkins, and Kamil Yilmaz is gratefully acknowledged. Jerry Adams gave generous help in the writing of the chapter. I am also grateful to Chris Clague, Jacques Cremer, Richard Nelson, and Mancur Olson, whose results are reported here, for advice on research.

1. For brevity of expression, I include the Soviet Union among the Eastern European countries.

2. For evidence of how economic changes can alter expectations very quickly, see *Warsaw Voice*, November 25, 1990, which reported that the number of Polish teenagers expecting to buy a house within 15 years declined from 35 percent in 1989 to 25 percent in 1990.

3. Lest this seem overly dramatic, one should remember the regimes that ruled Berlin, Budapest, and Bucharest in the 1930s—the last extended period when these cities were masters of their own political destinies.

4. Economists played a large part in the formulation of the platforms of the political parties in the recent Hungarian elections. Moreover, the design and implementation of the radical Polish policy seems to be driven largely by economic ideas rather than political forces.

5. Many analyses connect the rise of fascist regimes in Europe earlier this century with the failure of the European macroeconomy.

6. Elements of the evolutionary perspective derive from a number of sources. The original insights were most clearly stated by Schumpeter. Nelson and Winter (1982) provide a modern exposition. The present discussion closely follows their treatment, emphasizing elements most critical to reforms.

7. The justification for the view of organizational behavior taken in the evolutionary paradigm is provided in detail in Nelson and Winter (1982).

8. For the 500-day program, see "Transition to the Market", written by a working group formed by a joint decision of Gorbachev and Yeltsin and produced in Moscow in August, 1990. For Gorbachev's program see the *FBIS* report of October 18, 1990, and the document "Guidelines for Stabilization of the Economy and Transition to the Market Economy," transmitted by Gorbachev to the Supreme Soviet, October 15, 1990.

9. In particular, I concentrate on work carried out under the auspices of the Economics and National Security Program of the Pew Charitable Trusts. Further empirical evidence can be found in Murrell (1990). Empirical evidence produced by other scholars is summarized in Murrell (1991a). In the past twenty years, numerous theoretical findings have cast doubt on many of the traditional conclusions of the neoclassical paradigm. Hence, theoretical economists have gradually retreated from the postulate that unfettered markets are always the most efficient form of economic organization.

10. Thornton (1971), Whalley (1976), and Desai and Martin (1983) have conducted studies attempting to derive measures of allocative inefficiency. Initially, their results were interpreted as a serious criticism of central planning. However, subsequent studies by Toda (1976) and Whitesell (1987) have questioned the significance of the results. Toda presents evidence that measures of allocative inefficiency in planned economies are statistically insignificant. Whitesell argues that such measures are relevant only if one compares losses in planned economies to losses in market economies, since neither system operates at the first-best optimum. He presents results from such a comparison, concluding that decentralizing reforms are not likely to lead to significant economic gains.

11. The growth performance is adjusted to account for differences in "potential growth." A country at a lower level of income should be expected to have a higher average growth rate than a country at a higher level (closer to *potential*). For a more complete description of this adjustment measure, see Murrell and Olson (1991).

12. The data sources, the exact derivation of each variable, and the

methodological procedure followed can be found in Browning's original article (1985) and in Murrell (1991b).

13. In addition, in one estimation the economic system coefficients have a positive sign (albeit nonsignificant), indicating that a planned system actually raises the level of trade, ceteris paribus.

14. Details of how I construct this rationality measure are too complicated to be fully explained here. Briefly, the Heckscher-Ohlin model can be interpreted as summarizing the behavior of economies acting in accordance with the dictates of allocative efficiency. Thus, the trade of inefficient countries can be viewed as being affected by variables that should be irrelevant if efficiency were the sole objective (in addition to the usual variables, the factor endowments). In geometric terms, the trade patterns of inefficient countries vary across more dimensions than those of efficient countries because of the effect of the additional variables. Moreover, the efficiency-reducing variables increase in size as the level of allocative efficiency in a country declines. This suggests that one can measure the rationality of a country's trade by finding the geometric distance of its trade pattern from the space of efficient trade patterns. The greater this distance is, the less rational a country's trade pattern, with rationality defined as conformity to the standard neoclassical trade model.

15. This finding is consistent with that of other researchers. See, for example, Rosefielde (1973, 1981). The conclusion, of course, is not that foreign trade is rational, but rather that a model based on the neoclassical paradigm does little to pinpoint whatever irrationality there is.

16. Mansfield et al. (1982, 61) found that, in one sample of R&D projects, 72 percent of new product ideas were transferred overseas through affiliates, whereas only 17 percent of new processes were transferred in a similar fashion.

17. The technical details of the generation of these measures are too cumbersome for presentation here. Those interested should consult Murrell (1990).

18. This statement is based on both the theory and practice of organizational behavior. See, for example, Nelson and Winter (1982).

19. A neoclassicist would argue that the central question of reform concerns how to introduce rational economic incentives that ensure allocative efficiency. The most important element of the answer to this question implies treating all sectors of the economy equally.

20. In other words, the new private sector should be as free of intervention as private enterprises in modern developed economies.

21. As a result, prices in the old and new sectors might differ. Hence, there is a need for trade between the two sectors to be regulated and controlled by a state bureaucracy.

22. Implicit in this argument is the assumption that the state cannot compensate all enterprises for their losses in sales due to reductions in arms purchases. This is a reasonable assumption given that many such losses are the indirect consequences of changes occurring elsewhere in the economy.

23. This does not preclude sales of arms-producing enterprises (at possibly low prices) to the private sector, so long as these sales are not facilitated by "conversion grants," that is, subsidies.

References

Beardsley, G. and E. Mansfield (1987). "A Note on the Accuracy of Industrial Forecasts of the Profitability of New Products and Processes." *Journal of Business* 5(1):127-35.

Brada, Josef C. (1981). "Technology Transfer by Means of Industrial Cooperation: A Theoretical Appraisal." In *Polish-U.S. Industrial Cooperation in the 1980's*, edited by P. Marer and E. Tabaczynski. Bloomington, Ind.: Indiana University Press.

Browning, Martin (1985). "The Trend Level of Imports by CMEA Countries." *Journal of Comparative Economics* 9(4):363-70.

Csikos-Nagy, Bela (1972). "Macrostructural and Microstructural Performance of the Economy." *Soviet Studies* 23(3):474-83.

Desai, P. and R. Martin (1983). "Efficiency Loss from Resource Misallocation in Soviet Industry." *Quarterly Journal of Economics* 98(3):441-45.

Dunning, John (1981). *International Production and the Multinational Enterprise*, London; Boston: Allen & Unwin.

Ethier, Wilfred J. (1986). "The Multinational Firm." *Quarterly Journal of Economics* 101(4):805-833.

Hardt, J.P. and R. Kaufman (1989). "Introduction." In *Study Papers submitted to the Joint Economic Committee of the United States* 1, *Gorbachev's Economic Plans*, Joint Economic Committee, U.S. Congress, November, 1987.

Helpman, Elhanan and Paul R. Krugman (1985). *Market Structure and Foreign Trade: Increasing Returns, Imperfect Competition, and the International Economy*, Cambridge, Mass.: MIT Press.

Kornai, Janos (1980). *Economics of Shortage*, New York: North-Holland Pub. Co.

Kornai, Janos (1986). "The Hungarian Reform Process." *Journal of Economic Literature* 24(4):1687-1737.

Mansfield, E., A. Romeo, M. Schwartz, D. Teece, S. Wagner, and P. Brach (1982). *Technology Transfer, Productivity, and Economic Policy*, New York: Norton.

Markusen, James R. (1983). "Factor Movements and Commodity Trade as Complements." *Journal of International Economics* 14(3/4):341-56.

Markusen, James R. (1986). "Explaining the Volume of Trade: An Eclectic Approach." *American Economic Review* 76(5):1002-11.

Murrell, Peter (1990). *The Nature of Socialist Economies: Lessons from Eastern European Foreign Trade*, Princeton, N.J.: Princeton University Press.

Murrell, Peter (1991a). "Can Neoclassical Economics Underpin the Economic Reform of the Centrally-Planned Economies?" *Journal of Economic Perspectives* 5(4):59-76.

Murrell, Peter (1991b). "The Effect of (the Absence of) Multinationals' Foreign Direct Investment on the Level of Eastern European Trade." *Economics of Planning* 24: 151-160.

Murrell, P. and M. Olson (1991). "The Devolution of Centrally Planned Economies." *Journal of Comparative Economics.* 15(2):239-265.

Nelson, Richard (1990). "Capitalism as an Engine of Progress." *Research Policy* 19(3):193-214.

Nelson, R. and S. Winter (1982). *An Evolutionary Theory of Economic Change*, Cambridge, Mass.: Harvard University Press.

PlanEcon Report (1989). (December 1) PlanEcon, Inc., Washington, D.C.

Rosefielde, Steven (1973). *Soviet International Trade in Heckscher-Ohlin Perspective: an Input-Output Study*, Lexington, Mass.: Lexington Books.

Rosefielde, Steven (1981). "Comparative Advantage and the Evolving Pattern of Soviet International Commodity Specialization 1950-1973." In *Economic Welfare and the Economics of Soviet Socialism: Essays in Honor of Abram Bergson*, edited by S. Rosefielde. New York: Cambridge University Press.

Schumpeter, Joseph A. (1950). *Capitalism, Socialism, and Democracy*, New York: Harper.

Thornton, Judith (1971). "Differential Capital Changes and Resource Allocation in Soviet Industry." *Journal of Political Economy* 79(3):545-561.

Toda, Y. (1976). "Estimation of a Cost Function when the Cost is not Minimum: The Case of Soviet Manufacturing Industries, 1958-1971." *The Review of Economics and Statistics* 58(3):259-68.

Utterback, J. M. (1979). "The Dynamics of Product and Process Innovation." In *Technological Innovation for a Dynamic Economy*, edited by C. T. Hill, and J. M. Utterback. New York: Pergamon Press.

Whalley, J. (1976). "Thorton's Estimates of Efficiency Losses in Soviet Industry: Some Fixed Point-Method Recalculations." *Journal of Political Economy* 84(1):153-9.

Whitesell, Robert S. (1987). "Comparing Allocative Inefficiency in Four Countries: U.S., USSR, Hungary and West Germany." Paper presented at the 3rd Annual workshop on Soviet and East European Economics, Georgetown University, July 1987.

Winiecki, Jan (1986). "Are Soviet-Type Economies Entering an Era of Long-Term Decline?" *Soviet Studies* 38(3):325-48.

About the Book and Editor

Changing world political perspectives are making possible arms reduction in many parts of the world. One might hope that the resources from military spending, the so-called peace dividend, could be quickly transformed into improved civilian living standards. But economic theory and empirical studies suggest that transformation may not be so simple. We do not fully recognize the diversity of the channels through which arms reduction and its correlated policy measures have their affect, the differences between economies, and the difficulties of measuring various possibilities of arms reduction and transformation and of evaluating their impacts on output and welfare.

In the United States and other industrial countries, analysis with macroeconomic, interindustry, and computable general equilibrium models suggests that much depends on the macroeconomic policies that accompany arms reduction and points to substantial dislocations between civilian and defense industries.

With respect to the developing countries, there has been a long-standing controversy as to whether defense spending advances or hinders economic growth.

In the former Soviet bloc economies, in some of which defense spending accounted for a much larger share of GDP than had been estimated earlier, arms reduction is linked to the need to restructure from a planned economy to the operation of free markets. This is complicated by the fact that in some of these countries the defense establishment represented the most advanced industrial sectors.

This book considers the impact of arms reduction and conversion in the different parts of the world. Contributors view the macroeconomics of arms reduction broadly, considering macroeconomic dimensions quantitiatively but also recognizing the impact of alternative policy strategies and economic organizations.

F. Gerard Adams is professor of economics at the University of Pennsylvania.